I0675476

Resurrecting Pepys

Samuel's Heirs and the Pepys Cockerell Legacy (1625–2025)

Allen Firth studied mathematics at Southampton University and statistics at University College London, leading to a management career in financial services, before switching in later life to further post-graduate studies at Oxford University and Oxford Brookes University, gaining a doctorate in managing conservation of the historic environment. He worked as a Conservation Officer for Stratford-on-Avon District Council for 16 years before retiring.

His previous books have been 'The Book of Bourton-on-the-Hill, Batsford and Sezincote' (2005), and 'Jane Austen's Regency Dashwoods – Sense and Sensibility, India & the Cotswolds' (2019).

Resurrecting Pepys

Samuel's Heirs and the Pepys Cockerell Legacy (1625–2025)

Allen Firth

Grosvenor House
Publishing Limited

All rights reserved
Copyright © Allen Firth, 2025

The right of Allen Firth to be identified as the author of this
work has been asserted in accordance with Section 78
of the Copyright, Designs and Patents Act 1988

The book cover is copyright to Allen Firth

This book is published by
Grosvenor House Publishing Ltd
Link House
140 The Broadway, Tolworth, Surrey, KT6 7HT.
www.grosvenorhousepublishing.co.uk

This book is sold subject to the conditions that it shall not, by way of
trade or otherwise, be lent, resold, hired out or otherwise circulated
without the author's or publisher's prior consent in any form of
binding or cover other than that in which it is published and
without a similar condition including this condition being
imposed on the subsequent purchaser.

A CIP record for this book
is available from the British Library

Paperback ISBN 978-1-83615-441-9
Hardback ISBN 978-1-83615-442-6

Contents

Preface & Acknowledgements

In 1795, having returned from a long military campaign in India as Lord Cornwallis's Quartermaster General, Colonel John Cockerell purchased the Sezincote Estate in the North Cotswolds, found for him by his brother, the architect Samuel Pepys Cockerell. Cockerell family connections to the 17th century diarist Samuel Pepys have long been recorded, but the incorporation of 'Samuel Pepys' in this architect's name, and the significance of the Pepys Cockerell family's role as the famous diarist's successive heirs is now more fully explored. Assiduous guardians of Samuel Pepys's personal correspondence, covering the period 1662 to 1703, their role was of particular importance for his legacy. Their collection of Pepys's private letters, held by the family for over two centuries, was only made public in the early 20th century. As well as providing insights into Pepys's life, the letters also enabled corroboration of, or sometimes challenges to, the accuracy of many of his Diary entries.

Researching future generations of the Pepys Cockerell family has revealed a surprisingly wide range of high-profile relatives with their own impressive national influences and impacts. The narrative here, largely featuring sketches of individual lives, also reflects the wide-ranging experiences and social histories of influential upper middle-class families in the three centuries after Samuel Pepys's death in 1703. Much of the story mirrors Britain's increasing global involvement, with India particularly prominent.

The Samuel Pepys name was not only reintroduced by his heirs some fifty years after his death, but then continually recycled by subsequent family generations. Their relationship to the famous 17th century naval administrator and diarist no doubt afforded them great pride, acting as a spur to their own significant achievements. Pepys's immediate heir had been his nephew John Jackson whose daughter Frances Jackson married John Cockerell in 1740. John and Frances inherited the Pepys legacies and initiated the resurrection of both the Samuel and Pepys names when christening their second son Samuel Pepys Cockerell. 'Pepys

Cockerell' thereafter became effectively a double-barrelled family surname for numerous descendants through to the 20th century. The extent and persistence of perpetuating the Pepys connection is perhaps best exemplified by the fact that even in the late 19th century William Acland Cockerell (1844-1919) and his wife Ada gave two of their children the forenames Samuel Pepys and Paulina Pepys, exactly matching the naming of the famous diarist and his sister some 250 years earlier.

Alongside this continual reuse of Pepys names, the Cockerell name itself increasingly gained its own public recognition and profile through this period. Charles Robert Cockerell, for example, was the 19th century's leading British classicist architect, and Anna Theresa Cockerell became Countess of Shrewsbury in 1855. The combined Pepys Cockerell name therefore had double impact through the eighteenth, nineteenth and twentieth centuries, the Cockerell family achievements running in parallel with retention of the Pepys name among many of the family. Their responsibility as successive heirs for protecting and curating the Pepys Cockerell Collection, incorporating many of Samuel Pepys's legacy documents, was an anchoring factor right through until the Collection's fragmented passage out of family ownership from the 1920s onwards. For the next hundred years many remaining legacy artefacts continued to be passed down one of the Pepys Cockerell family branches, only ending with the auction of items from Elizabeth Pepys Cockerell's estate in the early 21st century.

Research has largely been documentary, but a significant strand has focused on portraits of some of the key family members, and what they tell us about their status and the visual impressions they wished to project. Before photography was available, portraiture, both professional and amateur, was the main way of capturing and displaying likenesses, albeit with unverifiable degrees of accuracy and flattery. While access to professional portraiture remained financially out of reach for most of the population, it is not surprising that the affluent Pepys, Cockerell, and Pepys Cockerell families indulged in commissioning many such portraits, usually by highly rated contemporary artists in what is often termed the 'golden age' of British portraiture in the 18th and early 19th centuries.

While the evidence for this extensive commissioning of family portraits is partly provided by references in letters and texts, we are fortunate in having access to images of several of these paintings. Interspersed in the narratives below, these portraits, and knowledge of their artists, add an important context and dimension to the outline biographies of individual family members. With the last of the main Pepys Cockerell branch of the family, Elizabeth, passing away in the early 21st century this account, outlining their legacy, is timely and coincides with the 200th anniversary of the first publication of Pepys's Diary. A further personal motivation was a purchase from Elizabeth Pepys Cockerell's estate of a family double portrait originally shown, and highly praised, at the Royal Academy Exhibition of 1809. It features the wife and daughter of the prominent architect Samuel Pepys Cockerell (1754 –1827), his name being the first, but by no means the last, resurrection of the combined 'Samuel Pepys' name. He was followed by Samuel Pepys Cockerell (1794-1869), Samuel Pepys Cockerell (1844-1921), and Samuel Pepys Cockerell (1880-1915).

A variety of sources has been used. Of the several biographies of Samuel Pepys, those by Claire Tomalin and Stephen Coote have been extremely valuable in portraying Pepys's motivations and character, which seemingly influenced his relatives, not only in honouring his memory and legacy but also inspiring their own achievements. The Dictionary of National Biography has also been an invaluable source for many of the other individuals featured. Papers forming part of the so-called Pepys Cockerell Collection, notably Pepys's private correspondence, have enabled understanding of his many personal characteristics and rich circle of friends and admirers. Extensive personal use has been made of ancestry.com, and the work of other researchers using this resource is gratefully acknowledged. Extracts from a small number of literary sources have been incorporated and acknowledged in the text.

Assistance from staff at the Bodleian Library, National Portrait Gallery, Courtauld Institute, and the RIBA Library has been invaluable and is gratefully acknowledged.

Introduction

In late 1753, fifty years after Samuel Pepys's death, his great niece Frances was once again pregnant. Having married the eminently eligible bachelor John Cockerell in 1740, Frances had already given birth to two daughters, Anne and Paulina, born in 1749 and 1751, and their first son John in 1752. The name Anne was that of Frances's mother, and Paulina that of her grandmother, Samuel Pepys's sister, reflecting their Pepys family descent. Choosing John as their first son's name had been easy, simply mirroring his father's, as was common practice, and almost an obligation. But what if this current pregnancy produced another boy? We know that Frances was proud of her Pepys family link, and in later years would regale younger family members with Samuel Pepys anecdotes passed on by her father, John Jackson, the nephew that the great man had entrusted as his immediate heir. As well as these family stories being naturally passed down, the fact that Pepys had gone to great lengths to protect his legacy inevitably put extra pressure on John Jackson and his descendants to keep the Pepys reputation alive.

Frances's pregnancy did indeed produce a boy, their fourth child. What better way for Frances and John to play their part in perpetuating the Samuel Pepys connection than by choosing Samuel and Pepys as her second son's two forenames … and that's exactly what she and her husband did. The boy was baptised Samuel Pepys Cockerell. The Dictionary of National Biography [Volume 4, p655] records that it was through his mother Frances that Samuel Pepys Cockerell (1754-1827) '*became the representative, and inherited many interesting relics, of the great diarist*'. The later Cockerells and Pepys Cockerells were committed to sustaining this Samuel Pepys link, not least because they were his successive heirs, having responsibility for much of his formal legacy, memorabilia, and intangible family memories. This responsibility was honoured well into the 20th century, only then gradually falling away as the collection of documents and other heirlooms passed out of the family's ownership.

Returning to the 18th century, if John Cockerell and Frances Jackson had concerns that the pressure of expectation exerted by the name Samuel Pepys might be an unfair imposition on their second son, they needn't have worried. Samuel Pepys Cockerell, far from tarnishing the reputation of his famous relative, became architect to the East India Company, and surveyor to St Paul's Cathedral, as part of a long and distinguished architectural career. His pride in the association with his famous relative was only natural, probably encouraged by his mother Frances in particular, conscious of the influence of her grandmother Paulina Pepys and her great uncle Samuel Pepys, whose fame was still very much alive. Notably, this fame in the 18th century was based on his outstanding commercial and public service achievements, principally at the Admiralty (or Navy Board), and had nothing to do with his coded Diary, only deciphered and published much later.

Whether or not he always felt honoured with this associative choice of names, Samuel Pepys Cockerell was certainly not shy about using them. When his brothers John and Charles were writing to each other in India in the 1780s and 1790s, they referred to him solely as 'Pepys', rather than his first name Samuel. Also, when he was one of the first people to welcome the child prodigy artist Thomas Lawrence to London, Lawrence refers to him as Mr Pepys. In promulgating 'Pepys' as his dominant identity he was effectively creating a brand within the rich cultural Georgian circles he revelled in, just as recent figures in the arts simplify their identities to single iconic names, such as Prince, Stormzy, Madonna, and Banksy.

He and his wife Anne Whetham would in turn give one of their sons the same Samuel Pepys forenames, this full Samuel Pepys Cockerell name being repeated twice more in future generations, the last of these descendants only dying in the 20th century. Alongside this, use of Pepys as a middle name for other children was common in most of the future generations. This deliberate and transparent link with Samuel Pepys, their famous 17th century relative, was further bolstered by the fact that a substantial number of Samuel's artefacts and documents were passed down through this Pepys Cockerell family line, at least one in each generation acting as his successive heirs.

A large set of his private correspondence, documents, and other artefacts including paintings became known as the Pepys Cockerell Collection.

Those who perpetuated the combined Pepys Cockerell name may have done so through feeling some obligation. Nevertheless, through their various successes they contributed individually and collectively to their own substantial legacy, recorded here. Several of the descendants emerging from this initial mid-eighteenth century 'Samuel Pepys' resurrection succeeded to a host of high-profile public roles. This would have delighted Samuel, given his sense of identity and self-regard. These descendants included an Archbishop of Canterbury, a Countess of Shrewsbury, a Governor of the Bank of England, two Surveyors to St. Paul's Cathedral, a succession of baronets, and numerous renowned artists and architects. There would also be many senior military figures, notably several with influential naval connections, resonating with Pepys's crucial role in radically modernising and restructuring the seventeenth century Admiralty, an important catalyst for Britain's emerging naval dominance in the 18th and 19th centuries.

The narrative follows a largely chronological pattern and, as we travel in time through the many generations of descendants, some strong recurring themes are evident. These are now outlined.

Passages to India

In 1600, three decades before Samuel Pepys's birth, Elizabeth I, nearing the end of her life, granted a charter to the East India Company giving it certain trading and other commercial privileges. Competition for trade with the Far East was emerging as a key element of expansionary ambitions for post-medieval European countries. The Portuguese, Dutch and English were establishing trading bases in the East, building on existing links and routes, mainly associated with indigenous spices. Naval capacity and technical advances were integral to their competing aspirations.

These far-flung trading initiatives and inevitable frictions between countries, at a time of emerging national identities, were inextricably linked with tensions on their own doorsteps in Europe.

The largely naval nature of the Anglo-Dutch Wars in the mid-17th century perfectly illustrates the contemporary jostling for supremacy at sea, not only for defence but to secure safe trade routes. This highlights the importance of Samuel Pepys's ground-breaking actions in this period to improve the efficient operations of the navy across a wide spectrum of activities encompassing shipyards, weaponry, administration, manpower, and training.

As will be seen when tracing the lives of his later relatives, India provided fertile ground for career advancement, wealth, and marriages. Their individual connections with India mirrored the military, commercial, administrative, and political aspects of Britain's involvement with the sub-continent. While this was by no means unique to Samuel's relatives, nor even rare, in their case it did much to shape the lives of an extraordinary number of the family through several generations. Indeed, many of those featured were born in India.

The Navy

This was at the heart of Pepys's life and career. It is only much later that his Diary took centre stage, thereby largely eclipsing his influence on the development of the British Navy. There are strong indications that Samuel Pepys's 17th century initiatives to improve the Navy also inspired several of his relatives in pursuing naval careers. And although the deliberately named Samuel Pepys Cockerell (1754-1827) was not directly involved with the Navy he was, at the time of the Napoleonic Wars, a member of the Society for the Improvement of Naval Architecture, with the same broad agenda as Pepys had adopted and followed a century and a half earlier.

A further century later, once again with the pending threat of war, another relative, Arthur Pollen (1866-1937), carried out detailed scientific investigations into naval gunnery, range-finding, and accuracy. Inexcusably, his work was largely ignored and sidelined, compromising the British Navy in the period leading up to the First World War. If his recommendations and technology had been implemented, the Battle of Jutland in 1915, the only serious (but indecisive) naval engagement between the British and German fleets during the war, would arguably have had a significantly different outcome. Arthur did, however, receive some belated recognition and financial compensation, and his work was also subsequently adapted and used by the navies of several other countries. His outspoken naval critiques in the decades immediately leading up to the First World War, together with later commentary on more general naval matters, were influential in naval strategy and tactics in the first half of the 20th century. Given his own criticism of existing 17th century naval administration and operation, Samuel Pepys would have been enthusiastically supportive and proud of this five times great nephew.

Forging New Celebrity Identities

Given his relatively modest background, Samuel Pepys achieved far more than could have been expected, even allowing for him having potentially influential relatives. While helped significantly by the social and political connections his wider family provided, these would have been of little use without his own considerable abilities, self-awareness, and determination. He also had to battle with a chronic health condition for much of his life, eventually risking an excruciating and dangerous operation to deal with it.

Most of his relatives had the potential benefit of similar family connections, but again these were of limited use without inherent abilities and character. It will become clear that there was no shortage of these essential factors among his later relatives, and the achievements of several of them brought recognition and various degrees of celebrity. However, alongside these many family achievements, there were inevitably examples of family misfortune and tragic loss both personal and financial. One family couple, for example, fell victim to the infamous South Sea Bubble scandal in the early 18th century, described in the text. More significantly, there were several violent and mysterious family deaths, as well as victims in the carnage of the First World War.

Commercial Focus

In his work with the Admiralty Samuel Pepys always had a commercial and economic focus with a particularly keen interest in practical and technical aspects. His organisational skills and recognition of the importance of recording accurate details reflect this. These elements of his inherent abilities and character are also evident in the care and diligence he showed in compiling his Diary entries, duly recording his activities, experiences, and thoughts with a frankness which exposed his personal flaws as well as his career advancement and substantial achievements.

And here we have one of the contradictions in Samuel's character. On the one hand, mainly in his private life, he was somewhat chaotic and wilful, for example with a libertarian approach to relations with the opposite sex. On the other hand, he liked to keep accurate records and was, at least in his public life, scrupulously careful to portray the characteristics and behaviours expected by those he was dealing with as he rose in social and political status. This latter trait didn't translate into an overly deferential attitude to authority or peer pressure. In pursuit of more efficient and effective commercial naval operations he was more than willing to challenge his senior colleagues, and occasionally his superiors, with what he regarded as incompetence or corruption. Not entirely immune to feathering his own nest, this was on a relatively far more minor scale than the abuses he identified, and he no doubt self-justified his actions as being an associated perk of the role he had tailored for himself through hard work and commitment.

Samuel's commercial, administration, and management skills, together with a predisposition to exploit these to the full, were in turn evident in the following centuries among many of his relatives. Again, most notably, it is a central character, Samuel Pepys Cockerell (1754-1827), whose business acumen made him the one to whom other family members deferred on financial, property, and investment matters. Having been given the forenames Samuel Pepys at birth, and having unashamedly cultivated his 'Pepys' identity, there was considerable pressure to emulate Samuel Pepys's success, particularly in business affairs. As the fourth in the line of Samuel Pepys's successive heirs he had, in any event, direct responsibility to protect his illustrious predecessor's legacy and bequests, both physical and intangible.

Political Focus

Samuel Pepys served as an MP, including for Castle Rising in Norfolk, and had many opportunities for political influence. He could hardly have lived in a more politically charged time and place than 17th century England, complicated by dramatic shifts in governance and religion, culminating in revolution and civil war. Samuel's life may have started and ended under reasonably stable monarchies, but the period in between was one of upheaval and turmoil, and the realities of political life under the pre- and post-Civil War monarchies were radically different. Samuel had to be constantly aware of the ebb and flow of the political tides. He was generally successful in avoiding the worst dangers although not entirely as he ended up in prison more than once, albeit only for short periods.

While his 18th and 19th century relatives never had to weather such severe political storms or associated personal dangers, choices nevertheless had to be made, including the extent to which entering the political arena was attractive or beneficial. As will be outlined, several relatives did make the positive decision to play active political roles, others were drawn into it, and many simply avoided it, one very decisively. The contrasting attitudes of Samuel Pepys Cockerell's brothers John and Charles illustrates the point. Sir Charles Cockerell (1755-1837) regarded his elections as an MP especially important in consolidating his social standing and influence, rewarding his supporters with bespoke medals to recognise their contributions. At the other end of the spectrum the eldest brother, Colonel John Cockerell (1752-1798), on his return from military service in India, positively rebuffed his brother's suggestion and encouragement that he should seek election as an MP, seeing politics as a murky environment not at all to his taste.

Religious Focus

Samuel Pepys, in common with most of the population, was a frequent churchgoer and he professed a strong religious belief. After his wife's death, her bust was erected at their London church. However, as with politics, there were deep religious divisions within society, primarily between Catholic and Protestant ideologies, but with numerous variations of these, and all intertwined with political factors. Most of the Pepys family in the 17th century held to the Protestant religion and puritan ethics, but Samuel was wise enough not to emphasise the nature of his own faith or political views too strongly, particularly as he had to deal closely with Charles II and James II, neither of whose contrasting positions aligned directly with his own.

Samuel had to steer a safe passage through these stormy religious and political waters and not just metaphorically; Samuel accompanied Charles II on his voyage back to England from exile in the Netherlands, after popular support for the 1649-1660 Commonwealth, shaped by Oliver Cromwell, had crumbled. Charles II, with the understandable exception of seeking retribution against those most directly responsible for his father's execution, adopted a largely pragmatic approach to both politics and religion, and this restored a degree of societal stability. James II, in contrast, unwisely insisted on strongly and openly favouring Catholicism, and exacerbated this with his far less flexible political approach. These stances met predictable and widespread resistance, leading to a second, albeit less violent, 17th century civil upheaval – the so-called Glorious Revolution of 1688 – resulting in the Protestant William of Orange supplanting James, who went into exile.

During this long volatile and eventful period, we gain insight into the years 1660 to 1669 by reading Pepys's Diary. For a much broader appreciation of his adult life in its lengthier historic context, we are indebted to Samuel's heirs, particularly the Pepys Cockerells, for safeguarding his substantial collection of private correspondence, dating from 1662 through to his death in 1703, only published much later in the 1920s.

As we move through future generations, there are many Pepys relatives who followed a religious calling. Among these was Edmund Addington Goodenough, Dean of Wells Cathedral, but the most prominent was William Howley, Archbishop of Canterbury, who presided over the period of transition from the Georgian to Victorian eras. It would be William and the Lord Chamberlain who had the duty of formally informing the young Victoria in 1837 that she was now Queen.

Cultural Focus

Samuel Pepys took an interest in a wide range of cultural fields, including music, literature, theatre, and art. He learnt to play several musical instruments and arranged music and dance lessons for his wife Elizabeth. He sat for his portrait, collected many sketches and prints, attended the London playhouses, and was always keen to indulge in new experiences which explored the full range of the senses. While he doesn't appear to have had a particular passion for architecture, any more than his other many and varied interests, he had clear ideas and confidence about adapting and converting his own properties.

His later relatives also enthusiastically entered this wide cultural arena, making major contributions both as practitioners, most notably as architects, and also as patrons, commissioning portraits from both young and established professional artists. His 18th and 19th century descendants had personal connections with the artist Sir Thomas Lawrence, the tragedienne actress Sarah Siddons, the author William Makepeace Thackeray, and the landscape architect Humphrey Repton, all featured in the text.

Literary Focus – the Diary, the Pepys Library & his Private Correspondence

Any commentary here must inevitably acknowledge Pepys's Diary, but his passion for literature is better represented by his substantial collection of books, pamphlets, documents, and other written material, eventually forming the Pepys Library. His collection was on a massive scale by the standards of the time, also being unusually diverse and eclectic, reflecting his wide-ranging fascinations and enthusiasms. He was obsessive about this collection and determined to protect it for the future. In this aim he succeeded, with the Pepys Library at Cambridge having a special place in the nation's literary history.

In addition, Samuel Pepys's private correspondence, often involving exchanges with prominent 17th century characters, is of considerable historical importance. The majority of this correspondence, together with other material, was retained by his heirs and passed down through future generations of the family.

Much of it, part of the so-called Pepys Cockerell Collection, and held by these successive heirs, was only eventually published in the late 1920s with the permission of Pepys's latest heir and guardian, John Pepys Cockerell (1867-1930). The context, accuracy, and understanding of Pepys's Diary entries are enhanced by reviewing his private letters of matching dates.

Family Letters and What They Tell Us

While none of Samuel Pepys's relatives had more than modest literary impact, letters survive in sufficient volume to provide insights into their privileged world. There are many long-distance letters between three Cockerell brothers spanning the late 18th and early 19th centuries, when two of the three were engaged with the East India Company in the subcontinent, while the third was architect to the Company, based in London. Letters between this third brother and his son, who was sent on a European Grand Tour in the early 19th century, add richness to family relationships as well as mirroring letters between Samuel Pepys and his heir John Jackson, sent on a similar Grand Tour over two hundred years earlier.

As well as Pepys's own private correspondence, the family letters available to us are those in archive records, notably at the Bodleian Library and the Royal Institute of British Architects Library. The value of these various letters in terms of giving a rounded idea of family relationships and priorities is limited by the fact that the large majority are written by males, and the female voice is rarely heard. Nevertheless, the letters express concern for the welfare of both male and female family members and friends, especially at times of difficulty. Certainly, where the texts of individual Wills (both male and female) are available, sons and daughters are generally treated equally when specific monetary legacies are involved. Nevertheless, primogeniture usually still applied to the families' main estate holdings, with eldest sons automatically inheriting. The sequence of heirs of Samuel Pepys's legacy passed predominantly down the male line.

The evidence in available family Wills is valuable in revealing far more than merely the nature and values of bequests; it provides additional insights into family circumstances and histories, as will be outlined in the main text. Through successive generations the evidence suggests a tight-knit mutually supportive family and, even as branches of the family naturally diverged, close links were retained, including marriages between relatives.

In Sickness and in Health

Samuel Pepys and his wife Elizabeth both suffered from chronic health conditions each of which, and their associated treatments, may have contributed to the couple remaining childless. Samuel chose to undergo and endure an excruciating and life-threatening operation to get rid of bladder stones, and family letters contain several references to health and sickness.

We also have details of a few autopsies or post-mortems, notably those of Samuel Pepys himself (in 1703) and his great-great-nephew Colonel John Cockerell (in 1798), who had been Lord Cornwallis's Quartermaster General in India.

Also recorded are a few deaths in bizarre, violent, or very unusual circumstances, reflecting the risky and adventurous careers of several family members. Leading a quiet, low-profile life – as most of them could have afforded and chosen to do – doesn't appear to have been a common family trait.

Military Exploits

Although Samuel Pepys was never in active military service, his high-profile administrative post at the Admiralty and associated involvement with the practical aspects of the Navy meant that he was well versed in contemporary military affairs, including the politics of war. As well as living through a period of frequent wars with external enemies and rivals, he also experienced a violent internal civil war with its additional emotional and social dimensions contributing to this volatile period of English history.

Alongside Colonel John Cockerell, mentioned above, the family produced several other senior military figures and officers. They featured across wide geographical and chronological theatres of war, including India in the 18th century, South Africa and the Crimea in the 19th, and Flanders and the Middle East in the 20th.

Resurrected Names

One recurring theme through the generations of relatives is the repetition of forenames. The name Pepys itself was frequently incorporated as a second or middle forename, but others were also repeatedly resurrected from earlier family use, including Samuel, Paulina, Frances, Anne, John, Charles, and Elizabeth. The family, to varying degrees among different branches, clearly wished to keep the links with Samuel Pepys and his 17th century family alive and honoured.

The above text outlines some of the key themes in the book's narrative, the structure of which leans heavily on following successive generations over a 400-year period. If the treatment of individual lives forms the beating heart of the text, family trees and branches are its skeleton.

Family Trees & Branches

From its roots in the early 17th century, Samuel Pepys's family tree of descendants and relatives quickly grows and becomes unwieldy within a few generations, with the number of branches rapidly increasing, and sub-branches adding to this growth and complexity. To manage the generational narrative attempted here, covering four centuries, selective pruning has been essential.

Beyond the first two generations after Pepys's death, decisions on focus are enforced. Of the several family tree branches and sub-branches which could be featured, it is the 'Pepys Cockerell' line, descended from John Cockerell and Frances Jackson, Pepys's great niece, which thereafter dominates and self-selects by providing successive Samuel Pepys's heirs, and guardians of his legacy. Not surprisingly, given their key role and responsibility, it was this family branch which most determinedly honoured the Pepys name and memory. As well as fulfilling their guardianship role, the Pepys Cockerell descendants themselves delivered impressive achievements, and in turn passed on and safeguarded much of their own family history and heirlooms, including portraits of various family members. One such painting, a double portrait of Samuel Pepys Cockerell's wife and eldest daughter, was both a catalyst for this book and the generator of some art-detective work, as narrated separately in Chapter Ten.

Despite tracing many of the Pepys relatives here, even more tactical pruning in later generations means that a far greater number remain in the shadows, leaving room for further research. However, an ending of sorts is reached by following the trail of the main Pepys Cockerell line through to its natural expiry with the death of Elizabeth Pepys Cockerell in the 21st century, the last family owner of the Pepys Cockerell double portrait mentioned above. Elizabeth also inherited other portraits of Cockerell family members, including one born during Samuel Pepys's lifetime, a generation before the Pepys and Cockerell families became entwined. After Elizabeth's death in 2016, various Cockerell Pepys ephemera were sold at auction, there being no obvious living relatives to whom they could be bequeathed.

While many Pepys Cockerell items have now been dispersed and no longer form a coherent collection, much of the family's historic narrative remains accessible from various records. The family history, with its significant national achievements, is full of variety, fortitude, adventure, and cultural contributions, but also several tragic and violent episodes. With its key individuals' lives in each generation rarely dull or mundane, the approach is largely chronological, and this shapes the structure of the text. Each of the successive generations is positioned in parallel with its corresponding historical context, highlighting key social and cultural changes over the lengthy four century period. His descendants' family histories are befitting of Samuel Pepys's own substantial legacy, and this account attempts to honour their stature and impact.

CHAPTER ONE

Generation Zero – Origins & Jacobean Angst

The early seventeenth century provides the initial context for exploring the Pepys family tree. In relating the stories of the key family members chronologically over four centuries from 1625 to 2025, Samuel's parents John Pepys (1601-1680) and Margaret Kite (1609-1667) are nominally 'generation zero'. All the other family members and generations covered are descended from John and Margaret.

John Pepys (1601-1680) & Margaret Kite (1609-1667)

Samuel Pepys's parents are the obvious starting point for the narrative. The historic context for this generation is complex, and the intent here is simply to give an informal snapshot of factors most affecting and influencing John, Margaret, and their children, given their social and economic background. Of their eleven children, seven died before reaching adulthood, a reflection of their modest domestic circumstances and the prevalent contemporary impact of disease together with other untreatable health conditions. Alongside many other factors, deficiencies in diet, sanitation, and health expertise rendered this sad family experience all too common at the time. The comparison with four generations later is stark. When, in the Georgian period, Samuel Pepys Cockerell (1754-1827) and his wife Anne also had eleven children, all would reach adulthood. The contrast is largely attributable to this later family's wealthier domestic and social context, but also to scientific and medical advances over the intervening century and a half, counteracting many of the negative aspects applying in the early 17th century.

In that earlier harsh environment, Samuel (born in 1633) and Paulina (1640) were the 5th and 10th of John and Margaret's 11 children and they survived until 1703 and 1689 respectively.

PEPYS COCKERELL EARLY FAMILY TREE - GENERATIONS ZERO TO FOUR

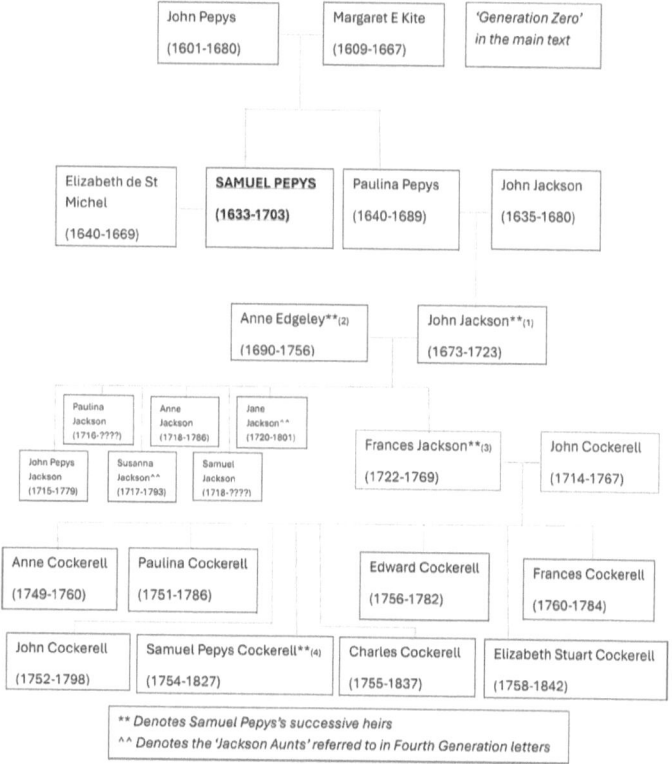

Early Pepys and Cockerell family tree

We focus on Samuel and Paulina's adult lives in coverage of the next generation, but even in their childhood and formative years they would both have had some sense of the turbulent historic context into which they were born and brought up.

The early and mid-17th century featured acute religious and political tension. As noted in the Introduction, one of the main conflicts was between Catholic and Protestant beliefs and philosophies, a major factor in sparking the Civil War in the 1640s. These tensions became intertwined with the way the church and the state were structured and governed. Despite the Reformation a century earlier, Henry VIII's break with Rome, and assertion of the independence of the Church of England with the monarch as the defender of this reformed institution, old values nevertheless survived among much of the population. At the same time, the country's governance structure, with the monarch as head of state and having ultimate power on national and constitutional matters, was coming under challenge, with Parliament increasingly flexing its muscles. Charles I would have preferred to rule without Parliament and often did just that, periodically disbanding the assemblies …. until he needed them again to raise taxes.

Charles's wife Henrietta Maria was a staunch Catholic, and Charles, while professing to fully uphold the Church of England Protestant religion, was increasingly veering to a 'high church' version, which involved the sort of rituals more associated with Catholicism. Much of John Milton's contemporary literature reflects strands of public opinion on these sensitive matters, even though he had to address these obliquely or subtly to avoid sanction or even arrest. Overlaying all these undercurrents were financial and political self-interests, producing more elements of conflict both between individuals and between classes, with powerful alliances vying for advancement.

In summary, the tensions in society had complex dimensions, and not everyone could avoid taking sides either on religious matters or on the relative power of monarch and parliament in controlling the state. Most would keep their views on these matters private, which was easy enough for the ordinary citizen, but for those already in, or aspiring to, influential positions, treading carefully was essential. As the possibility of Civil War loomed in the late 1630s, the stakes were dramatically raised, and it became increasingly clear that supporting the eventual losers in these conflicts could be career-ending or even fatal.

Matters were brought into laser sharp focus by Charles, who doubled down on the principle of the divine right of monarchs, with minimal concessions to constraints on his powers, thereby inflaming both religious and secular tensions. Debate about the role of Henrietta Maria in stiffening his resolve has long been an historic and academic battleground. In any event, as well as probably sincerely believing his own primacy on these matters, and holding ground for his own sake, the king also no doubt felt a responsibility not to compromise his royal successors by conceding elements of power and control to Parliament. His uncompromising stubbornness inflamed and frustrated his critics, simply increasing pressure for change at a time when there was a growing and powerful gentry class with financial and political clout.

While there was strong alignment between Protestant and Parliamentary leanings, with similar strong associations between Catholic and Royalist sympathies, there was no simple pattern of views. There were Catholics who held Parliamentary values and those who supported Royalist values but were Puritans and very firmly on the Protestant side of the religious divide. The Pepys family into which Samuel was born mostly held Protestant views, but this did not prevent several of them also being fervent Royalists, a good example of the complex religious and secular positions of individuals and families. Even within families, loyalties were frequently strained, with several examples of brothers being on opposing sides when the Civil War broke out. The Pepys family members were wise enough to avoid acting on their views too strongly, openly, or provocatively. Although Samuel would not be old enough to have to make choices during the Civil War, which began when he was just nine, he would later need to hedge his bets as he strove to fulfil his lofty ambitions while navigating a complicated set of circumstances and pressures.

Samuel Pepys's mother, Margaret Kite, was the daughter of a Whitechapel butcher but, other than that, we know little about her family background. She married John Pepys in 1626 and died in 1667. John Pepys, Samuel's father, was a tailor and although respectable he was not personally wealthy or possessing any outstanding talents. He did however have influential relatives, and it is through them that his son Samuel Pepys was assisted in pursuing his ambitions. Indeed, it appears to have been Samuel's exposure to these more illustrious relatives, their lifestyles and sophistication that greatly inspired and shaped his aspirations. Samuel recognised in himself some inherent abilities but knew that in themselves these could only be expected to take him so far. Powerful and influential sponsorship would be a crucial and essential ingredient in achieving any serious high office.

CHAPTER TWO

First Generation – Civil War, Interregnum, & Restoration

Samuel Pepys

Elizabeth Pepys*

[* The legend at the foot of Elizabeth's print reads "*From the original in the possession of S P Cockerell Esq*". He is the pivotal figure Samuel Pepys Cockerell (1754-1827), introduced earlier. In curating many original Pepys artefacts, he played a vital role in bolstering Samuel's legacy.]

Samuel Pepys (1633-1703)

The entry for Samuel Pepys in the Dictionary of National Biography below is surprisingly short compared with those for figures of similar national prominence. It is revealing that the single word description of his main claim to inclusion is '*diarist*'.

His contemporaries would have been bemused by this, his fame at that time resting on his influential role at the Admiralty. At his death, the Diary was still secret and almost entirely encoded in a form of shorthand, although Pepys had incorporated many names of people and places in their normal format, presumably because they were not readily dealt with by his form of shorthand. More than a century would pass before his code was deciphered.

However, by the time of the 20th century Dictionary of National Biography entry the Diary had at last been decoded and

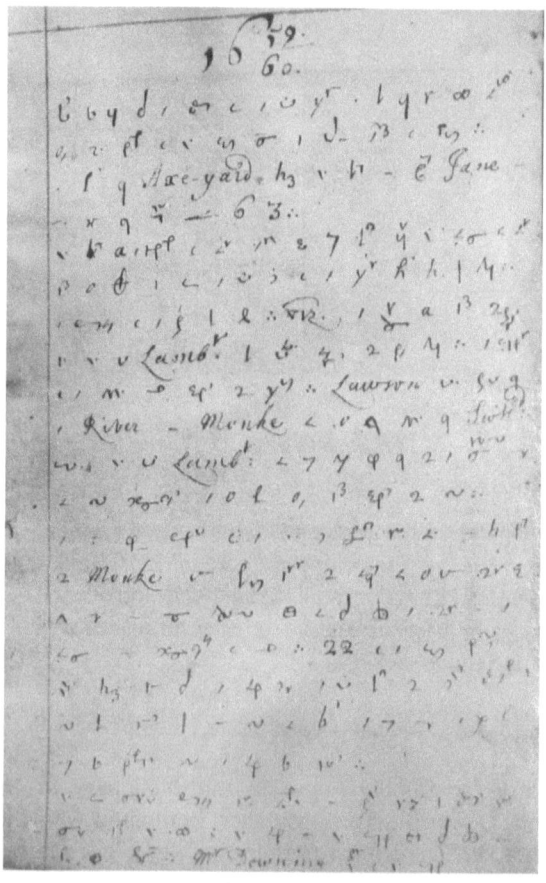

Typical page of Pepys's Diary, coded in a form of shorthand

published in the 1820s, after which Pepys's profile as a diarist increasingly overshadowed his substantive career achievements.

PEPYS, SAMUEL (1633-1703), diarist; son of John Pepys, a London tailor, was educated at St. Paul's School, London, and Trinity Hall and Magdalene College, Cambridge; M.A., 1660; entered the family of his father's first cousin, Sir Edward Montagu (afterwards first Earl of Sandwich) [q. v.], 1656; 'clerk of the king's ships' and a clerk of the privy seal, 1660; surveyor-general of the victualling office, 1665, in which capacity he showed himself an energetic official and a zealous reformer of abuses; committed to the Tower of London on charge of complicity with the popish plot, and deprived of his offices, 1679, but released, 1680; secretary of the admiralty, 1686; deprived of the secretaryship of the admiralty at the revolution, after which he lived in retirement, chiefly at Clapham. Fifty volumes of his manuscripts are in the Bodleian Library, Oxford. His 'Diary' remained in cipher in Magdalene College, Cambridge, until 1825, when it was deciphered by John Smith and edited by Lord Braybrooke. An enlarged edition by Mynors Bright [q. v.] appeared in 1875-9, and the whole, except a few passages which cannot be printed, was published in eight volumes (1893, &c.) by Mr. Henry B. Wheatley. [xliv. 360]

It is unquestionably his Diary with which Samuel Pepys is now most associated. However, a daily record kept in the 17th century by someone without Pepys's profile, together with his exposure to influential people and events, would not have had the breadth and variety of personal experiences which make his Diary so valuable both historically and of general interest. This was only made possible by his stellar career and associated social climbing; it is the combination of a successful career and an idiosyncratic personal lifestyle which provides such colour and fascination. He consorted both with society's 'low-life' and 'high-life', and part of the Diary's richness lies in its very personal, detailed, and sometimes explicit experiences, not least in illuminating a wide spectrum of society, enabling a vivid picture of life in 17th century London.

No attempt is made here at charting Samuel's life; excellent biographies already exist. Instead, the focus is mainly on his personal characteristics and those achievements which potentially influenced later heirs and descendants seeking to honour, but also leverage, the Pepys name and legacy. The bare bones of his life and times can briefly be summarised. Born in 1633, his 70 years spanned a tumultuous period politically, religiously, militarily, and socially, punctuated by a series of historically iconic events. Many of these events were ones he witnessed or recorded first-hand, including the English Civil War period, the execution of Charles I [1649], the Interregnum and Commonwealth era under Oliver Cromwell, the Restoration of Charles II [1660], in which he played a perhaps surprising role, the London Plague [1665], the Great Fire of London [1666], the Glorious Revolution [1688], the reigns of Charles I, Charles II, James II, William and Mary, and the Coronation of Queen Anne [1702], the last of the Stuart monarchs. Most notably, his lifetime coincided with the dramatic transition from a divine monarchy to the hybrid constitution still largely intact today.

The period 1600-1700 is often referred to by historians as the Century of Revolution, and not just because of the mid-century Civil War and the later so-called Glorious Revolution. The transformed constitution emerging from the dramatic overturning of the status quo proved very robust and effective, putting Britain in a strong position to expand its trading interests across the globe, underpinned by its burgeoning naval power. For this latter, Samuel Pepys must take a significant degree of credit for his role as Chief Secretary to the Admiralty under both Charles II and James II. Obsessed with order in most of his professional activities, in stark contrast with his personal life, he was perfectly suited to transform a chaotic and inefficient navy into one which could provide resources for supporting private naval trading initiatives in addition to the core business of the Admiralty in military defence. The two functions had always overlapped, Elizabeth I notably taking this a step further in failing to condemn what was effectively state-sponsored piracy as part of foreign policy.

In Pepys's time, and early in his naval reforms, dual commercial and military ambitions would be tested in the Anglo Dutch wars of 1665-1667 and 1672-1674, and not always successfully. Responses to setbacks in these predominantly naval actions only served to strengthen and highlight the necessary progress which Pepys had identified and initiated. The maladministration and corruption in the dockyards which Pepys had targeted crept back during the mid-18th century but was addressed by William Pitt the Younger's government in the 1780s, resulting in Britain becoming the most powerful global naval force at the turn of the 19th century. This status was further cemented at Trafalgar in 1805 and largely remained so through to the First World War and a few years beyond.

Samuel Pepys's personal life had its own challenges and turbulence. His close family were of modest standing and wealth, and he had to make some bold decisions to fulfil his own ambitions. Never short of self-confidence, his many achievements were substantially enabled and assisted through a few members of the wider Pepys family having illustrious and influential connections. It was these networks that ensured a good education and time spent away from London at the country residences of wealthy relatives, including a grand establishment at Ashstead, Surrey, which Samuel would later describe as '*my old place of pleasure*'. In the early 1640s, Samuel was sent out of London to live in the Fens with his father's relatives who were deeply committed to Puritanism. Among these relatives was *'Sir Sydney Montagu (who died in 1644) … the youngest brother of the Earl of Manchester and Lord Montagu of Broughton. He was thus a member of one of the richest and most distinguished families in the kingdom, and his house at Hinchinbrooke was an ample tribute to his status. He had entertained Charles I there on a number of occasions, for if Sir Sydney was a Puritan of the most severe type and much given to theological speculation, he was also an ardent Royalist.'* The influence of Edward, one of these Montagus, was particularly helpful to Samuel because '.. *Pepys was growing up in a world where the old securities, the old certainties, were under serious threat.*' [Coote, pps 6-9]

Samuel certainly exploited these opportunities and family links, but ultimately his achievements rested mainly on his own considerable efforts and abilities. His ambitions and determination were matched by a keen sense of needing to acquire the specific skills he lacked. After initial education in Huntingdon, he was educated for a time at St Pauls School, *'the largest of London's fee-paying schools ….. while he would fill his leisure hours with the widest range of intellectual pursuits from the writing of history to an interest in the new science'* [Coote, p10]. St Paul's was typical of a 17th century grammar school still focused on classical subjects rather than anything commercial or scientific. Although grateful for the quality of teaching, Samuel was determined not to be constrained by this limited curriculum. For example, once he had embarked on a career as a promising civil servant in the Navy Office, the young Samuel arranged to supplement his education by engaging Mr Cooper, mate of the navy ship *Royal Charles*, to give him some arithmetic lessons. He reports, *'after an hour's being with him at arithmetique, my first attempt being to learn the mutiplicacion table, then we parted till tomorrow'*. Continual self-improvement and adaptability were features of his character and his success. This applied not just to theoretical matters but to practical and political skills, which he developed piecemeal through experience. Samuel also had a charismatic presence which enabled him to deal productively with people from all walks of life and backgrounds, from carpenters to royalty, and in environments ranging from what we would now call lads' culture to the most sophisticated learned and artistic circles.

Pepys seems to have been motivated predominantly by achievement of status, respectability, recognition, and legacy, rather than by money. While he realised that a certain level of wealth was needed to achieve respectability, mainly evidenced through his focus on securing a dwelling and its furnishing which would be fit for hosting important guests, he was not obsessed with wealth for its own sake. Nevertheless, having been through periods in his life when he had struggled financially, building a solid financial buffer was only natural. The few times when he recorded his increasing wealth in the diary it was often simply with a degree of pleasant surprise and self-congratulation, contrasting it with his relative early poverty. This is particularly reflected in a passage from the Diary in which he recognises that keeping up appearances would be important as his profile in society progressed, and he therefore committed a significant proportion of his income to clothes. Preparing his monthly account for October 1663 he noted a 41l [£41] drop in his savings, a very considerable sum at the time, commenting that …

> ' …it hath chiefly arisen from my layings-out in clothes for myself and wife viz., for her, about 12l; and for myself, 55l or thereabouts – having made myself a velvet cloak, two new cloth-suits, black, plain both – a new shag-gown, trimmed with gold buttons and twist; with a new hat, and silk top[s] for my legs, and many other things, being resolved henceforward to go like myself. And also two periwigs, one whereof costs me 3l and the other 40s ….. But I hope I shall with more comfort labour to get more, and with better success than when, for want of clothes, I was forced to sneak like a beggar.'

Pepys was determined to live in style once he had securely escaped from poverty. As well as focus on himself and his clothes he also paid to have alterations and improvements made to his home. Frequently redecorating internally, one diary entry records that he had, '*set my plasterer to work about whitening and colouring my musique roome*'. Coote, p68, notes that '*the covering of bare, limewashed plaster with material hung from eyelets in the walls was de rigueur for an upwardly mobile couple in Restoration London, and Pepys eventually chose green serge hangings and elected to have gilded leather for the upholstery of his dining room chairs. The whole process was pleasing to his delight in possession, even if it was inconvenient and expensive*'.

Keeping up appearances included entertaining guests at home. On 24th January 1661 Samuel and Elizabeth were hosting a dinner party at their Seething Lane house for several members of the Navy Board, and part of his Diary entry reads …

> '*So my poor wife rose by 5 a-clock in the morning, before day, and went to market and bought fowle and many other things for dinner – with which I was highly pleased. And the chine of beef was done also before 6 a-clock …. Things being put in order and the cooke come, I went to the office, where we sat till noon; and then broke up and*

I home – whither come …. my guests. I had for them, after oysters – at first course, a hash of rabbits and lamb, and a rare chine of beef – next, a great dish of roasted fowl, cost me about 30s, and a tart; and then fruit and cheese. My dinner was noble and enough … I believe this day's feast will cost me near 5l.'

As noted, Samuel's character had many contradictory aspects. For example, he liked order in many elements of his life, not least in the rigorous organisation of his Library and the Diary, but at the same time his day-to-day personal conduct reflected a desire to live without constraints and to act spontaneously, following his unpredictable impulses. He moved in quite exalted circles at times but, in parallel, frequented some notoriously dubious London locations and indulged in pursuing female companions from all levels of society. This reflects two sides of the same coin. Public respectability was, for him, highly valued and protected; respectability in his private life almost the opposite, with a somewhat cavalier, and certainly far from puritan, attitude marking his personal behaviour both inside and outside the family home.

He liked the freedom to act as he pleased; the constraints and increasing responsibilities that day-to-day life imposed, particularly as his career and position in society flourished, were irksome to him. For example, he complained about, *'the inconvenience that doth attend the increase of a man's fortune by being forced to keep more servants, which brings trouble'*. However, he often brought those troubles with servants, and especially female ones, on himself.

Two of his main challenges included poor health and troublesome female relationships. As already noted, Pepys suffered chronic pain for a large part of his early years, caused by a growing bladder stone, eventually removed in a dangerous and extremely tortuous operation. And while his marriage was characterised by great love it was also tempestuous, with Elizabeth leaving the family home for several months at one point. There was also disappointment in the marriage failing to produce any children. Despite Samuel's many dalliances, neither is there any evidence of any extra-marital offspring. If it was his fertility that was the main factor, it is possible that his bladder stone operation somehow contributed to this, but we will never know.

Samuel's Diary, and particularly its direct style and the frank and uncensored nature of its content reveal, among so much else, a self-obsessed side to his character. He was inclined to see and express life's experiences, whether serious or mundane, solely from his own perspective. A sense of this is given in his diary entry for 6th January, 1663.

> *And after dinner to the Dukes house and there saw Twelfth Night acted well, though it be but a silly play and not relating at all to the name or day. Thence Mr Battersby (the apothecary), his wife and I and mine by coach together, and setting him down at his house, he paying his share, my wife and I home and find all well. Only, myself somewhat vexed at my wife's neglect in leaving of her scarfe, waistcoat, and night-dressings in the coach today that brought us from Westminster, though I confess she did give them to me to look after – yet it was her fault not to see that I did take them out of the coach.*

However, it is only fair to acknowledge that Pepys was generally brutally honest about his own shortcomings and rarely tried to justify his faults with disingenuous or biased diary entries. Assuming he always intended, or at least suspected, that the Diary would one day be exposed to scrutiny, he certainly didn't set about creating a glowing account. In recording events both personal and external, together with his own feelings and reactions to them, it is as if he was observing himself as a psychological case study, one which he deemed important and fully deserving of detailed insights. This directly reflects his sense of his own considerable worth. It is unsurprising that Claire Tomalin's biography of Pepys has as its subtitle, '*The Unequalled Self*'.

In trying to analyse Pepys's character, among the many attempts made by various commentators, I find myself most closely aligned with that set out in the Introduction to '*The Diary of Samuel Pepys*' (G. Gregory Smith, 1906). In investigating his character, one extended extract [pps xxix-xxx] notes :-

'We are deluded by the actuality of the Diary, by its crowd of facts and by its frankness, into the belief that nothing has escaped us. ... Yet we do know something of Pepys's spirit, and that not less clearly from some critical asides of his than from the direct narrative of his fussing and playing. He tells us that, having incurred some expense over a framed print, he thought the sum 'more than is fit to lay out on pleasure,' yet, 'it being ingenious,' he 'did not think much of it.' And again, and often, he speaks of the zest of life which possesses him. 'So to sleep, he says, 'every day bringing me a fresh sense of the pleasure of my present life; and at another time, 'And I did, as I love to do, enjoy myself.' Intense curiosity and the sheer joy of living, these are the main elements of his character. The Diary may be said to be a commentary on these; and they explain the Diary. He is delighted with anything new 'for information sake,' with experiments of all kinds, in ship-building, in physiology, in new musical instruments, in strange dishes, unfamiliar taverns, fresh street acquaintances, in optical toys, in head-gear and coats, – in all with infinite relish, be it the inspection of a dockyard or the taking out of the wheels and springs of a watch. Every page evinces this uncontrollable curiosity, and also the range and keenness of his love of pleasure. No man has lived so fully, or bent his mind and body so to the mood of the moment. He finds pleasure in his vows of restraint , even in rehearsing the most vexing contretemps. The whole-heartedness of this interest in everything around him has tempted us sometimes to find analogies in the ways of children. The irrepressible habit of inquiry, the bubbling delight in raree-shows, cake-feasts, and new clothes, the simple cunning, the soothing of conscience by the veriest quibbles and appeals to the letter when the desire is still unsubdued, the unreasonableness, and at the same time the honest admiration of those who excelled in any accomplishment – all these boyish traits come to mind as we read the Diary. Yet how strange it is that despite this impression, and the direct evidence of the book that the writer was not much more than a boy in years when he *began his record, we so often think of him as a man of maturity. Indeed, the offhand popular opinion persists in making him an old fellow. It is possible that neither impression is quite correct, and that the true explanation is to be found in the adaptability of his character. His talent is of the passive kind; it assimilates, reciprocates. We catch him in different attitudes; he catches himself, and with no note of surprise, in every kind of inconsistency, intellectual and moral. The enigma of his mixed life of cowardice and manliness, of genuine affection and infidelity, of public honesty and corruption, cannot be solved unless we allow that he lacked the more aggressive qualities of character, even the untamed assertion of the child, and that he was merely receptive of each and every influence which he encountered. If there be any connexion between these varied experiences, anything which binds them together and helps us to explain them, one with another, it is his vanity. To his egotism we are indebted for this sustained record of his daily mood. By it he was prompted to the frankness which has amazed posterity. He would have been not less amazed had he found himself convicted of a critical purpose in thus jotting down what he saw and felt, or sometimes thought he saw and felt; certainly still more amazed had he learned that he planned this cipher-tale for us, and for his greater fame.'*

The only part of the above passage I question is the last few phrases; while he clearly wrote the Diary primarily for his own satisfaction, in the moment, and not primarily for later readers, I believe he thought of it absolutely as part of his legacy, likely to outlast him and reflect the essence of him 'warts and all' in preference to a sanitised autobiography. If he had been worried about its later 'discovery' tarnishing or blighting his reputation he could have easily destroyed it. He didn't. The decision to write it in code may arguably have been with the intention of it being inaccessible to his contemporaries and those immediately following, to avoid embarrassment, but with the belief that someone would eventually decipher it. Regardless of the extent to which this was, even if only subconsciously, anticipated by

Pepys (a notion largely dismissed by Gregory Smith in the above passage), the Diary's initial hidden nature and later revelation in my view reflects some such intent by Pepys. I recognise this remains a hotly disputed element of the overall Pepys story.

His youthful and occasionally naive excitement, enthusiasm, and boundless curiosity should not be mistaken for childishness in the way he conducted his public life. Any such behaviour would have been quickly exposed and necessarily prevented delivery of his lofty ambitions. There is overwhelming evidence that he was an intelligent, serious, and effective operator in the adult and harsh 17th century world into which he was born. Whatever the extent to which this was merely superb acting rather than reflecting his true character, it nevertheless succeeded. He developed close friendships with several high profile and extremely capable individuals, allegiances based on mutual respect, and he attracted and reciprocated generous and genuine affection. In the Introduction section of '*Private Correspondence and Miscellaneous Papers of Samuel Pepys 1679-1703 in the Possession of J. Pepys Cockerell*', Tanner (1926, p xiv) comments that, '*outside the circle of his more intimate friends, Pepys corresponded upon a great variety of subjects with distinguished men. Of these the most eminent was Isaac Newton, of whom he enquired concerning the doctrine of chances*'. The correspondence between the two goes into some detail about probability theory and examples of its application in practice.

Samuel's career progression was rapid, and particularly impressive given his health issues and modest immediate family background. He rose within the naval administration ranks to become the most proactive and influential member of the Navy Board, to the extent that Charles II directly sought his opinions. He was recognised and respected not just for his insights into the failings of the way the navy was organised, notably the inefficient procurement procedures, but also because of his hands-on understanding of the dockyards, the ship building process, and those managing their construction. This again evidences his ability to communicate with, and gain the respect of, people at all levels of society. This wasn't done in a cynical way with only social status as the motivation; he genuinely embraced and respected the experiences of others with skills, knowledge, and different attitudes from which he drew inspiration, whether it was in the fields of politics, commerce, handicrafts, or music to name but a few of his passionate enthusiasms.

He in turn inspired those around him to widen their own interests, to learn new skills and develop latent abilities. Despite risking and indeed experiencing jealousy, he encouraged and supported his wife with her dancing and music, employing teachers to give her variety in her daily routine which was often dominated by onerous domestic duties and pressures.

These personal domestic concerns were part of the Pepys family daily experience alongside the religious and political tensions, upheavals, and conflicts, both physical and moral, which formed the backdrop to his life, and often emerged centre-stage for him personally. His political intuition and foresight helped minimise risks and he generally sidestepped episodes of danger. He frequently avoided censure by disingenuously holding opposing positions as the moment demanded, being a master of contradictions in line with the character analysis outlined above. Nevertheless, he didn't manage to escape entirely unscathed and was twice imprisoned. However, in each case the evidence for indictment was, like his own position, ambiguous, and he quickly regained his freedom on both occasions. Many people found themselves under suspicion during these volatile political times and he was no exception, his rapid rise to influential positions being inevitably accompanied by rivalries and jealousies.

He reached retirement with a sense of some relief and with an impressive set of achievements duly documented, underlining his record-keeping obsession. The sense of relief may have reflected his fear of being found out in his personal conduct, which was often at odds with his ambitions for a respectable status in society. Again, the conflicting sides of his character play a part. Described as *'wordly wise, punctilious in convention, morbidly fearful of making a faux pas and of having his innocent actions misconstrued, who, when he thought he should not be in a playhouse, sat in a corner in dread of recognition',* but *'on other occasions not so innocent had less thought of repentance than of ravelling the clues to his escapades'* [Gregory Smith, p xxviii].

He remained focused on his many intellectual interests in his retirement years. However, as the tumultuous seventeenth century ended and a new century dawned, Samuel Pepys's health, although fluctuating, was inexorably declining. The following extracts from contemporary letters give glimpses of his last few years, predominantly spent at Clapham, of which more later.

In the first two years of the new century, his poor health seemed to be improving, as letters from two high-profile friends indicate.

1st July 1700 [Letter from the Earl of Clarendon to Samuel Pepys.]
"Yours of the 24th past was doubly welcome in bringing me the good news of the improvement of your health …. I hope your being thus long at Clapham … will make you relish the pleasure of a garden, which will be no burthen to your other perfections."

10th December 1701 [Letter from John Evelyn to Samuel Pepys.]
"There could nothing come to me a more grateful present than that you lately sent me : the re-establishment of your health .."

However, this upturn was short-lived, and the following letter-extract hints that Pepys may not have done enough to prevent or slow the subsequent rapid deterioration. Any self-neglect on his part may relate to his increasing focus and rush to organise and secure his legacy.

1st March 1703 [Letter from Mrs Ballard to Samuel Pepys.]
"I am very much concerned at your honour's continued illness … Madam Skynner [Pepys's mistress] … told me that the paine in your honour's back still remaine, and with great concerne … thought your honour did not take that care of your health as your present condition requires."

As well as securing his legacy, Samuel was keen to ensure that his close family relatives would be looked after once he was gone.

In one of his last letters he petitions the navy for favourable financial treatment of his brother-in-law and other family members, at the same time accepting, in its opening sentence below, his loss of any real influence.

> *April 1703*   [Samuel Pepys to Sir George Rooke, Commander-in-Chief of the Fleet.]
> *"I have too long outlived my relation to the Navy to pretend to any remains of interest in, or even being remembred by many who have now (with yourselfe) the honour of being at the head of it."*

Despite this loss of influence, the letter goes on anyway to ask for just such special consideration.

The final letter cited here makes it clear that Pepys is close to death.

> *20th April 1703*   [Letter from Pepys's nephew and heir, John Jackson, to Pepys's close friend and ex-navy colleague, William Hewer (who we meet again shortly), urging William to impress on Pepys the urgency of putting his few remaining worldly affairs in order.]
> *"After the frankness wherewith my Uncle asked and the Doctors gave him their opinions yesterday concerning the doubtfullnesse of his condition, in order to the adjusting some little remains of his temporal affairs, I presume, Sir, you will find him desirous of applying himself thereto without delay."*

Pepys died the following month. With the precision in factual matters that Pepys had both lived by and insisted on, the exact time of his death was duly recorded by his nephew John Jackson as being at 3.47am on 26th May 1703, according to Pepys's own gold watch.

Approaching the end of his eventful life, retired, widowed, and childless, Samuel's main priority was to tie up the loose ends of his complex life and, most importantly, to secure his personal legacy. He was particularly concerned that there should be appropriate care and guardianship of his impressive and significant Library, the result of a lifetime's assiduous collection of a great volume of books, pamphlets, miscellaneous papers, and documents. Within this collection was his Diary, then still secret and written in a form of coded shorthand.

In his last few years, and without any natural heirs, Pepys formed a strong relationship with his nephew John Jackson, the second son of his sister Paulina. He had become increasingly impressed with John, contrasting with his rather dismissive and condescending attitude towards Paulina, her husband, and their first son. Keen to put proper arrangements in place, Samuel decided that John Jackson would be his heir and carry the responsibility for the guardianship of his treasured legacy.

If John was to be effective in this great responsibility he would need to deal with several people of considerable status, education, and culture. Pepys decided that one important part of John's preparation should be a Grand Tour, visiting important cultural sites on the continent, with Italy the most favoured destination. Pepys's enthusiasm for collecting is reflected in him commissioning John to purchase any particularly interesting artworks and artefacts he found while abroad. Many letters passed to and fro in 1700 and 1701 between Samuel and his nephew while John was on his travels. One extract gives a flavour.

Letter from Mr John Jackson in Leghorn [Livorno] to Mr Pepys, July 1700

HONOURED SIR, – This is the 7th day of our being here; having mett with such continual importunitys and regalos [choice feasts] from the luxurious merchants, that 'twas impossible to get away sooner.

.. I have since made some few further purchases and left them in the hands of Mr Arundel .. to be presently putt on board the Benjamin, Captain Tiler commander, who hopes to sail in very few days. [There then follows a lengthy list of these 'few further purchases'.]

I am just now going on board our feluca; hope to reach Lerici to morrow morning and Genoua at night, where I expect to meet with your next commands. In mean time, with humblest duty to yourselfe, and services to Sir J. Houblon's family, Captain Hatton, Dr Smith, etc. ; Mr Hewer, Mrs Edgeley, Mrs Crawley's, and your whole Clapham-society ; and amongst them particularly to Mrs Skynner, remain Honoured Sir, Your most obedient Nephew,

J. JACKSON

[The letters above are from a large collection of Pepys private correspondence which passed down the sequence of Pepys's heirs through to John Pepys Cockerell (1866-1930), who allowed publication, edited by J. R. Tanner, in 1926 and 1929. John Pepys Cockerell features later in the text, as do the Hewers, Edgeleys, and the '*whole Clapham-society*'. Mrs Skynner was Pepys's mistress after his wife had died. The Clapham location plays a large part in the Pepys/Jackson/Cockerell story, as outlined shortly.]

As well as securing protection of his physical legacy, with John Jackson as his trusted heir, what Samuel Pepys could not have known was that his name itself, initially dying with him in 1703, would be brought back to life. However, as already noted, barely fifty years after Pepys's death John Jackson's daughter Frances Jackson, having married into the Cockerell family in January 1740, would resurrect the Samuel Pepys name by christening her second son Samuel Pepys Cockerell in 1754. Samuel Pepys, with an assertive sense of his place in the world, would have been immensely proud of this resurrection of his names, their use continuing over multiple generations.

Fame and celebrity survival is usually founded on some enduring impact of the individual's substantial achievements and legacy, often sustained through continual recurrence, most notably in the arts, for example through performances of Shakespeare's plays or Bach's music. Imagery, particularly when publicly accessible, is another mechanism for sustaining celebrity survival, such as the works of Constable, Turner, Henry Moore, and Tracey Emin in a British art context. Likewise, outstanding literary output, by major authors such as Jane Austen and Charles Dickens, is permanently recorded, read by successive generations, adapted for a wide range of media, and frequently reinterpreted.

Samuel Pepys's celebrity status is more complex, with particularly stark changes to his profile over time. His fame today rests almost entirely on the Diary, and even though only a tiny proportion of the population have read much or indeed any of it, the word association of 'Pepys' with 'Diary' is well-entrenched. In contrast, his impact on the structure and administration of the British Navy, which was the foundation of fame in his lifetime and the decades afterwards, is now largely unrecognised and forgotten.

The adoption of the Pepys element of the Pepys Cockerell name by several of his descendants was arguably motivated by more than merely name recognition and familiarity. Samuel's merit and achievements set a benchmark legacy for these heirs and descendants, and something to emulate, or at least avoid tarnishing. By claiming their share of the 'Pepys' brand, and its accompanying pressure and expectations, the Samuel Pepys connection gave the wider Pepys Cockerell family pride and confidence about their place in the world and in parallel a spur to their own ambitions. Undoubtedly aiming for more than simply being known simply as a Pepys descendant, many of their stories evidence notable successes in establishing their own strong identities and achievements.

Although it was through the high-profile and commercially successful architect Samuel Pepys Cockerell (1754-1827) that the Pepys label was explicitly perpetuated and duly passed on to one of his sons, it was one of his other sons, Charles Robert Cockerell (1788-1863), who perhaps best exemplifies the family's achievements and continuing public profile. In a letter sent from Milan on November 6th, 1816, to his father, Charles comments, *'I exult in being one of so remarkable a family'.*

Having researched Charles's career and several of his letters, strongly indicating his humility, this is not, as it could easily be misinterpreted, intended to be a boastful statement. Indeed, its context within the letter records his acknowledgement of his own good fortune and extreme gratitude for his father's guidance and achievements, as well as other contributions by his relatives to enhance the Cockerell and Pepys Cockerell families' considerable standing. Charles had already established his own positive reputation and degree of celebrity through his artistic, architectural, and archaeological travels in the Mediterranean since his departure from England in April 1810. Reports of his adventures and discoveries were circulating in London throughout his absence. His early letters home had been carried by his friend Lord Byron on the ship transporting the Elgin Marbles to London, which stimulated interest in all things connected with classical antiquity.

Charles's life story, related later, is just one of many impressive chapters in the amalgamated Pepys and Cockerell story. Such reputations, emerging in the late 18th and early 19th centuries, were to be further enhanced by several other Cockerell and Pepys Cockerell family members through into the 20th century.

Several obvious questions arise. Did the Pepys Cockerell and Cockerell family descendants exhibit any of the diarist Samuel Pepys's characteristics? How was any celebrity status handled, utilised, and manipulated by these individuals? Did they inherit more than just the Pepys name or connections? Is there any evidence of common family characteristics or predispositions? Were the polarised strengths and weaknesses of Samuel Pepys's somewhat chaotic and multi-faceted character in any way reflected in these descendants? Several of the family's eventful lives and substantial achievements are sketched here, and readers will form their own judgments on these questions.

Concluding this brief account of his life, with his health having been noticeably failing, most significantly from around 1700, and having spent his last few years arranging his affairs and doing his best to secure his legacy, Samuel Pepys died in the early hours of 26th May 1703.

> *May the 26th, 1703.*
> *Memorandum : That the exact time of my Uncle Pepys's departure was 47 minutes past 3 in the morning, by his gold watch.*   *J. J.*

('Private Correspondence and Miscellaneous Papers of Samuel Pepys 1679-1703 in the Possession of J. Pepys Cockerell' Volume ii pps 311-2. Published by G. Bell and Sons Ltd., London, 1926)

Later that day, an examination and partial dissection of his body was carried out; the details are recorded as follows.

AN ACCOUNT OF WHAT WAS REMARKABLE UPON OPENING THE BODY OF THE HONOURABLE SAMUELL PEPYS, ESQRE.

[May 26, 1703.]

The body was very much emaciated.

Upon opening the thorax (where the cartilages of the sternum were ossified) we found the lungs full of black spots, and all over of a very livid colour. There was a very strong adhaesion of them to the pleura on the left side just above the diaphragm, and upon incision they voided a spumous though not purulent matter.

There was little observable in the heart, only that there was scarce any blood in either of the ventricles.

Upon viewing the abdomen, it was remarked that the omentum, as well as the membrana adiposa, had a great tincture of yellow, as proceeding from a disposition to the jaundice.

The liver was not well colourd, some marble veins were spread through it, and the gall bladder had no choler in it.

The guts were discolourd, very flacid, and empty, but in some places were distended with wind, and perticularly those parts of them which lay neare the left kidney were inflamed, with no small tendency to a mortification.

The spleen was less than is usual, but not any way disorderd.

The right kidney was of a larger size than ordinary, very sound and well colourd.

The left, which had scarce the form of a kidney, adhaered so firmly to the hypochondrion and psoas muscle (which, with the membranes and some part of the parenchyma, were very much indurated) that it could not be separated without without the knife. Upon opening it, great quantity of a most foetid purulent matter gushed out, a large stone weighing an ounce and a half was found in the pelvis, and several others, viz., vi, weighing about three ounces, were so firmly fastend to the kidney that most of the glandulous susbstance seemd to be petrified.

The stones were all of very irregular figures, with long sharp pointed angles, one of which had almost piercd the parenchyma just against the hypochondrion. All the parts that were contiguous to the left kidney were extremely inflamed, and that part being mortified to a degree of sphacelus had spread a very great mephitis through the whole abdomen.

The inside of the bladder was very much inflamed and indurated, the neck gangraened, and the wound which was formerly made in the perinaeum upon his being cut for the stone was opened and the lips were mortified.

HANS SLOANE
JOHN SHADWELL
CHARLES BERNARD

Elizabeth Pepys (Samuel's wife, born 'de St. Michel') (1640-1669)

Elizabeth may have been as interesting a psychological case study as Samuel, all the evidence suggesting self-confidence and a strong character. Not afraid to argue with Samuel, she even abandoned the marital home for a while to assert her own independent spirit. However, compared with Samuel she has left far less trace, and little documentary record. An attempt to fill this vacuum was provided, very much tongue in cheek, by publication of a 20th century spoof purporting to be Elizabeth's own diary, 'The Diary of Elizabeth Pepys', edited by Dale Spender.

Elizabeth's grandfather was Sir Francis Kingsmill whose daughter Dorothea Kingsmill married Alexandre de St Michel, hence Elizabeth's maiden name. Intriguingly, after a multi-generational gap, the Kingsmill surname, not a common one, reappears here in a much later chapter.

Elizabeth's family were French Huguenots of some social standing. Like Samuel, she had several health issues, some of which may have contributed to there being no children from the marriage. She sadly died in her late twenties. Despite his many incidents of infidelity, Samuel's grief at her death appeared genuine and heartfelt. She is memorialised with a bust on the church they frequented, St. Olave's, in the City of London.

Memorial to Elizabeth Pepys at St. Olave's Church

Paulina Pepys (1640-1689)

In comparison with her famous brother, Samuel's sister Paulina left few personal records. However, her contribution in marrying and having children, which Samuel had failed to do, is pivotal because one of her sons, John Jackson, would become Samuel's immediate heir. It is through John and his wife Anne Edgeley that future generations provide all our key characters including the line of Pepys's successive heirs. A major part of John Jackson's responsibilities as Pepys's immediate heir was the guardianship of Samuel's extensive Library, Diary, miscellaneous associated documents, and various works of art. Much of this responsibility together with physical ownership of Samuel's material legacies, such as large volumes of private letters, paintings, and ephemera, would pass down through several generations of the Pepys Cockerell branch of the family.

Paulina's personal achievements or qualities may have been limited, and she left little personal legacy, but it is significant that future generations of the family often chose the name Paulina for their female offspring, honouring her role as matriarch of this family branch.

John Jackson (1635-1680)

(Paulina's husband and father of Pepys's heir John Jackson)

Apart from his dates of birth and death, we have few details of Paulina Pepys's husband John, and only Samuel Pepys's limited commentary on his character. Samuel was decidedly unimpressed with this brother-in-law. The reality was that the Pepys family had found it hard to find a suitable husband for Paulina. She was relocated by the family from London to Brampton, on the fringes of the Fens, the homeland of the wider Pepys family, with hopes that local connections may help.

Samuel had worried about her prospects. Claire Tomalin reports him commenting, *'God knows …. what will become of her, for I have not anything yet to spare her, and she grows now old and must be disposed of one way or another'*. Leaving aside the callous nature of his comments, Samuel's reference to her age was made when she was just 23, underlining contemporary perceptions about a woman's prime time for securing a marriage. Tomalin continues,

'In the end she may have found her own husband, since he was a Huntingdonshire lad, John Jackson, "a plain young man, handsome enough for her; one of no education or discourse, but of few words … I shall have no pleasure nor content in him, as if he had been a man of breeding", wrote Pepys when he met him. Neither he nor Elizabeth attended the wedding, which took place at Brampton on 27 February 1668. Pepys merely noted the news of it a few days later

and wrote to congratulate his father, not Jackson or Pall [Paulina] herself. The Jacksons settled down to farm at Ellington, not far from Brampton, and old Mr Pepys went to live with them; and when Pepys visited he observed that she had grown comelier, "but a mighty pert woman she is, and I think proud, he keeping her mighty handsome, and they say mighty fond". The three mightys showed he was not going to warm to his sister even as a bride enjoying her brief season of dignity and joy. It did not occur to him for a moment that pert Pall and her ill-bred husband were going to produce a son who would win his love, accept his guidance, act out his dreams, serve his projects and contribute largely to his own family happiness.' [Tomalin, p132]

Despite his limitations, and Samuel's low opinion of him, John Jackson was a faithful husband to Paulina, and their sons had a secure upbringing. They dutifully named their first son Samuel in honour of his uncle, but it was their second son John who features most prominently among the next generation. As noted, in due course Pepys was to formally appoint John, his nephew, as his heir and guardian of the legacies he was so determined to future-proof.

CHAPTER THREE

Second Generation – Foundation of the Pepys Legacy

This generation, spanning the late 17th and early 18th centuries, overlapped the later years of Samuel Pepys's life. Compared with the previous generation these individuals benefited from a more stable political, religious, social, and economic environment, with less direct and obvious conflict. However, even after the so-called Glorious Revolution of 1688, and the establishment of the new monarchy of Protestant King William and his wife Mary, the ripples from earlier decades of trouble were still significant, and challenges to the new order very real. The Battle of the Boyne in Ireland in 1690 is an obvious example, itself a highly symbolic clash of ideologies, primarily religious, which reverberate to this day.

Nevertheless, it was a period in which the relative political and religious stability at home enabled an acceleration of English aspirations for expansion of global trade and commerce. This was accompanied by claims on overseas territories needed to support the logistical requirements of this expansion, including safe ports and substantial bases able to sustain troops and cater for reprovisioning of supplies on trade routes. Competition between European powers, already lively during the 17th century, became ever more ruthless and dynamic. As new opportunities were identified across the globe, often associated with novel trading commodities, any slackening in the pace of exploiting these risked losing ground in the economic and commercial power struggle.

The European powers also wrangled and fought in Europe itself. Britain's position was strengthened by military successes on the continent during the War of the Spanish Succession, perhaps most famously at Blenheim in 1704 (the year after Pepys's death), with British forces under the Duke of Marlborough, together with Dutch and Austrian forces, defeating a Franco-Bavarian army. The Act of Union of 1707 was also significant, uniting Scotland with England and Wales under the name Great Britain. Previously perceived as a fringe player, this period established Britain as a serious European power, as well as securing for it several strategic global territories from which the British Empire would later rapidly develop.

At home, the emergence of the gentry and professional classes vying for status and wealth with the long-established land-owning families similarly intensified. Opportunities for personal and family advancement expanded significantly, leading to greater social mobility and distribution of wealth, particularly for those with the right connections. Pepys's heirs and relatives were to enthusiastically grasp these opportunities.

John Jackson (1673-1723) – Samuel Pepys's Heir

[The 1825 print below is noted as taken from the original portrait of around 1700. Just as for the print of Elizabeth Pepys above,

the legend at the bottom of the print (not shown here) notes that in 1825 the original portrait was *in the possession of S. P. Cockerell Esq.*]

For most of his life Samuel Pepys, who was always very aware of his own inherent abilities and aspirations, appears to have had a poor opinion of his sister Paulina and her limited horizons. And, as already alluded to, as well as having little regard for her

John Jackson Esq.
Samuel Pepys's nephew and direct heir

husband John Jackson (1635-1680) who he considered unsophisticated, Pepys also formed a negative view of their first son Samuel, effectively disinheriting him because he so strongly disapproved of his choice of marriage partner. However,

Pepys's view of his sister Paulina improved over time, and this was substantially attributable to his increasing respect and admiration for her other son who, like his father, was named John Jackson. This respect and admiration ultimately resulted in Pepys entrusting his legacy, which reflected his own sense of self-importance, to this potentially reliable and promising nephew. He was also probably determined that control of his legacy should remain within the family. Descriptions of this nephew indicate that he may not have been especially intelligent, worldly, or imaginative but he was certainly conscientious and dutiful. Pepys backed up this trust in his nephew by investing in his general education and business awareness, so that he would be able to deal with the challenges of managing Pepys's legacy. Of particular importance was the ability for his heir to engage and negotiate with the appropriate influential people on broadly equal terms.

As noted previously, part of John's education and development involved a European Grand Tour, an opportunity not available to Pepys himself. A century later, in a direct parallel with this investment in the next generation, John Jackson's grandson Samuel Pepys Cockerell (1754-1827) sent his son Charles Robert Cockerell (1788-1863) on a similar Grand Tour, with important national artistic, architectural, and archaeological consequences, and this is explored in more detail later. It exemplifies a recurring feature of the Pepys and Pepys Cockerell family stories, namely that financial and educational investment in the younger family members was central to enabling them to make their own marks, sometimes at a national level, just as Samuel Pepys had done. Indeed, although not experiencing a grand tour, Samuel had himself benefited from a sound education in his youth, through the encouragement and finance of his elder family connections.

Faith and investment in his nephew John Jackson were well placed, and Pepys's future reputation and fame were enhanced by John's assiduous execution of the provisions of his uncle's Will right up until his own death twenty years later in 1723, which triggered perhaps the most important of these provisions. This was the establishment of the Pepys Library (formally instituted in 1724) to permanently house Samuel's extensive collection of books and documents. Pepys' collection of some 3,000 books is housed in the Pepys Building at Magdalene College, Cambridge in bespoke book-presses, made for Pepys in one of the naval dockyards.

Frontage of the Pepys Library (above) &
the Commissioned Bookcases
History of the Pepys Building | Magdalene College (cam.ac.uk)

Pepys was a scholar of Magdalene College, and by codicils added to his will directed that his library – the collection of a lifetime – should pass into its possession and be housed in this building after the death of his nephew and heir, John Jackson (1723). The 3000 volumes (mostly bound especially for him) are to stand here, without addition or subtraction, 'for the benefit of posterity'. They are kept as he left them – arranged 'according to heighth' in the book-presses which he had made for him in a naval dockyard. His catalogue, shelf-list and library desk are still present.

A private library, wrote Pepys, should comprehend 'in fewest books and least room the greatest diversity of subjects, stiles and languages its owner's reading will bear'. The contents of his own library in fact reflect a remarkably wide range of interests. Literature, history, science, music and the fine arts are strongly represented. One of the treasures of the library is the series of diaries Pepys kept from 1660-1669.

Samuel had set out some general principles for compiling a private library, and evidencing his preference for order and categorisation, he notes that,

What I propose as principally to be attended to is,

1. *As to the Generall Scope and Purpose of it:*
   The comprehending in fewest Books and least Room the greatest diversity of SUBJECTS, STILES, and LANGUAGES its Owner's Reading will bear; with Reguard had to theyr AUTHORS, EDITIONS, and PROPORTIONS on each Subject, answerable to theyr Weight, and the particular Genius of their said Owner.
2. *In the Book-binder's Worke. Decency and Uniformity; with some Marke of theyr Propiety.*
3. *In theyr Registry. Clear, Comprehensivenesse, and Order, and that Three-fold, viz., Numericall, Alphabeticall, Classical.*

('Private Correspondence' ii pps 247-8)

Regarding his own Library, which after his death he intended to be publicly accessible, Samuel Pepys had left very specific instructions in a Scheme noted in the Codicil to his will, and this was the perfect guide for John Jackson to follow when carrying out his demanding role as Samuel's heir and executor. It is set out here as further evidence of Pepys's obsession with order and of his justifiable pride in the Library's quality and scope. He was determined that it should be an everlasting memorial to one of his passions, namely collecting (with educated discernment) a wide spectrum of books, documents, prints and other literary ephemera.

Details of the Scheme are set out in a document drawn up in 1703 shortly before his death :-

The Scheme referred to in my foregoing Codicil, relating to the Completion and Settlement of my Library, viz:

For the Completion of my said Library, I will and require, That the following Particulars be carefully, punctuality, and with all possible diligence and dispatch, performed and executed by my Nephew John Jackson, after my Decease, viz:

1st – That a General Review bee taken of my said Library, compared with its Catalogue; and all out-lying Books immediately lookt-up and putt into their Places.

2ndly – That my Collections of Stamps, or any others which shall then be depending, be finish, bound, placed, and properly entrd in my Catalogue and Alphabet.

3rdly – That all Setts of Books contained in my said Library under the Name of GROWING TRACTS, be compleated to the time of my Death; and room provided for the further Volumes of my Lord Clarendon's History, now under the Presse.

4thly – That Gronovius's Sett of Greek Antiquitys, lately publisht, be forthwith bought and added thereto; and any other considerable Desiderata supplied, at the discretion of my said Nephew, with the advice of his learned Friends.

5thly – That this being done, my said Library be closed, and from thenceforward no Additions made thereto.

6thly – That the whole Number and bulk of my Books being so ascertained, one or more New Presses be provided for the convenient containing them, so as to be neither too much crowded nor stand too loose.

7th – That my Arms, or Crest, or Cypher be stampt in Gold on the Outside of the Covers of every Book admitting thereof.

8 – That their Placing, as to Heigth, bee strictly reviewed, and where found requiring it, more nicely adjusted.

9 – That as soon as their order shall bee thus fixt, the whole be new numbred from the lowest to the highest.

10 – That the said new Numbers be stampt on a piece of Red Leather fixt at the head of the Back of every Book, where now the gilt Paper is.

11 – That all the Additaments with their new Numbers be then properly inserted in the Bodys of the Catalogue

>   *and Alphabet; and these elegantly and finally*
>   *transcribed, to remain unalterable, and for ever*
>   *accompany the said Library.*
>
> 12 – *Lastly, That as far as any room shall bee left for*
>   *further Improvements or Embellishments to my said*
>   *Books, by Ruling, Elegant Writing, or Indexing; the*
>   *same bee done at the Discretion and Convenience of*
>   *my said Nephew.*

['Private Correspondence' ii pps 319-320]

John Jackson was unmarried when Pepys died in 1703 and remained so for several years afterwards. It is unclear whether the onerous responsibilities Pepys had given him prevented or hindered him marrying in his young adulthood. In any event, when he did marry in his late thirties it was a prestigious partnership. As Samuel Pepys's heir, John clearly had a highly respectable pedigree, as had his bride Anne Edgeley, whose father was an archdeacon and held the office of Prebendary of St. Paul's Holborn between 1703 and 1721. As outlined below, Anne Edgeley herself had strong connections with Samuel Pepys, and these close links no doubt played a part in John and Anne meeting and deciding to marry.

John inherited most of Samuel Pepys's assets, albeit largely in the role of guardian. He was also an executor of the Will of Samuel's mistress Mary Skinner and, when she died, most of what Samuel Pepys had left her was in turn bequeathed to John. One bequest was that the '*heart shaped diamond ring*' which Mary wore in tribute to her life with Samuel Pepys should be given to John's wife Anne, '*Mrs Jackson*'.

Anne Jackson (nee Edgeley, c1690-1756)

Anne, the daughter of Archdeacon Samuel Edgeley, married Pepys's heir John Jackson in 1711. Anne was already connected to Samuel Pepys through his old Admiralty colleague and friend Will Hewer, one of her close relatives. A marriage to Pepys's heir was therefore a natural and convenient one for Anne.

Will Hewer, like Samuel Pepys himself, was childless at his death in 1715 and left his immense estate, including property and lands in Clapham, Westminster and Norfolk, to his nephew and godson, Hewer Edgeley, Anne's brother. Eight years later Anne

William Hewer by Sir Godfrey Kneller

became joint owner and guardian of Pepys's estate when her husband John Jackson, Pepys's heir, died. Therefore, the Edgeley family, through marriage and inheritance, ultimately acquired the estates of both Samuel Pepys and his naval colleague Will Hewer.

Anne's brother Hewer Edgeley took over the old Will Hewer home, Gauden House, in Clapham. This house was built decades earlier by Dennis Gauden, the Surveyor General of Victualling to the Navy, and visited by Samuel Pepys in 1663

while it was being completed. Some four decades later Samuel would live here in Clapham for most of the period from 1700 until his death in 1703. Back in July 1663, Pepys, then aged 30, records that,

> *I resolved to go to Clapham, to Mr. Gauden's, who had sent his coach to their place for me … When I came to Mr. Gauden's one first thing was to show me his house, which is almost built, wherein he and his family live. I find it very regular and finely contrived, and the gardens and offices about it as convenient and as full of good variety as ever I saw in my life. It is true he hath been censured for laying out so much money; but he tells me that he built it for his brother … Besides, with the good husbandry in making his bricks and other things I do not think it costs him so much money as people think and discourse.*

It is likely that Gauden House, Clapham Place is the same Clapham house which Anne Jackson (nee Edgeley) later specifically references in her own Will and which she pledges to her son John

Pepys Jackson (1715-1759) in recompense for enormous losses that she and her husband had suffered in the infamous South Sea Bubble financial calamity, of which more later.

At this time Clapham was still outside London's developed urban expansion westward, and a much better living environment, as the following extract from the Clapham Society website notes.

Pepys and Hewer both fell out of favour after the Glorious Revolution and, with increasing ill health, Pepys retreated to Hewer's house for several weeks in the summer of 1697, a much longer period in 1700, and then permanently in the summer of 1701, with all his books moved there the next year. While Pepys was very much an urban animal, Clapham had good air, and its height above sea level of one hundred feet, coupled with its distance from the City, provided considerable improvement for those used to the stench and noise of London. John Evelyn commented: 'I do most heartily congratulate the improvement of your health, since your change of air,' and later 'while I mourn your absence here, you are at Clapham, enjoying better health, a purer air, nobler retreats.' Pepys himself, having remarked on the improvement in his health, 'perfected by the air of this place', went on to write: 'if I must be left to philosophise by myself, nobody, I fancy, will blame me for choosing to do it in a serene air, without noise, rather than where there is nothing of the first, and nothing else but the last.'

Hewer had made the house much more pleasant to live in, decorating it with fashionable ornaments and furniture, and improved the gardens. Evelyn wrote: 'I went to visit Mr Pepys at Clapham where he has a very noble and wonderful well furnish'd house, especially with Indian and Chinese curiosities. The offices and gardens well accommodated for pleasure and retirement.' The fact that Evelyn himself had planned the improvements probably accounts for Evelyn's reference in a letter to Pepys to 'your Paradisian Clapham'. William Nicolson, about to be consecrated as Bishop of Carlisle, visited Pepys in 1702, and described the [Gauden House] *library,*

> *Models of the Royal Sovereign and other Men of War, made*
> *by the most famous Master-Builders; very curious and exact,*
> *in glass Cases. Mr Pepys's Library in 9 cases, finely gilded and*
> *sash-glass'd; so deep as to carry two Rows ... of Books on*
> *each footing. A pair of Globes hung up, by pullies. The Books*
> *so well ordered that his Footman (after looking the*
> *Catalogue) could lay his finger on any of them blindfold.*
> *Miscellanies of paintings, cuts, pamphlets, etc in large and*
> *lesser Volumes.*
>
> *Pepys played a full part in the community until his death in*
> *1703 and left a legacy of £5 to the poor of Clapham and a*
> *series of mourning rings to Clapham residents. He left his*
> *estate to John Jackson, the son of his sister Paulina.*

[https://claphamsociety.com/articles/pepys-to-clapham/]
Extracted 17/01/2024.

The reference above to '*a very noble and wonderful well furnish'd house, especially with Indian and Chinese curiosities*', reflects the emerging fashion for oriental artefacts. The role of India in British history would expand enormously during the 18th and 19th centuries, and several Pepys relatives would be heavily involved in this expansion, as outlined later.

Focusing back on Anne Jackson, in 1715 she and John named their first son John Pepys Jackson, a first partial incorporation of the Samuel Pepys name. The last of their seven children, Frances, was born in 1722, but in 1723 Anne was widowed in her thirties when her husband John Jackson died, Anne thereby inheriting most of the Pepys estate and associated responsibilities. In 1740, her daughter Frances married John Cockerell, and the latter part of Anne's life was largely spent with Frances at Bishops Hull, Somerset, the Cockerell's family home. The births of her Cockerell grandchildren Anne (b. 1749), Paulina (b. 1751), John (b.1752), Samuel Pepys (b.1754), and Charles (b.1755) must have given her great joy. Given her own Samuel Pepys connections and direct responsibility for his estate, resurrection of the Samuel Pepys name chosen for her second grandson no doubt gave Anne a sense of things having come full circle.

The Clapham Links Between the Second and Third Generations

Before concluding Anne's story, and moving on to the third generation, an item in the Victoria & Albert Museum, dating from this period, has direct links with our narrative. This rare item is a doll named 'Lord Clapham', and another represents his wife. It is not clear whether these dolls represent specific individuals, but the official V&A description below cites the Cockerells and dovetails perfectly with Anne's story, notably the marriage of her daughter Frances into the Cockerell family, for whom Clapham also had very particular significance.

Lord Clapham
Doll 1690-1700 (made)

Object Type
This doll, known as Lord Clapham, is thought to have belonged to the Cockerell family, descendants of the diarist Samuel Pepys (1633-1703). The daughter of Pepys's nephew John Jackson (the son of his sister Paulina) married a Cockerell, who had a family home in Clapham, south London.

Designs & Designing

Lord Clapham offers a fine example of both formal and informal dress for a gentleman in the 1690s. His formal outfit includes a coat, waistcoat and breeches, while his informal dress is represented by the nightgown. Accessories such as the stockings, stock (a form of stiff, close-fitting neckcloth) and gloves are very valuable since very few items of this early period survive in museum collections. Equally important is the demonstration of how these clothes were worn together.

Ownership & Use

Dolls were widely produced in the 17th century, although very few survive, due to the wear and tear they usually undergo. The high quality of Lord Clapham and his clothes indicates that he would have been expensive. There is little evidence of use, which suggests that he was admired by adults rather than played with by children.

Lord Clapham | Unknown | V&A Explore The Collections (vam.ac.uk)

Having lived long enough to enjoy her daughter marrying into the Cockerell family and having her own children, Anne died at the Cockerell's country home in Somerset in 1756. Among those living with her there had been her daughter, son-in-law, and her grandchildren. Their stories are taken up as we follow the next generation, including inherited responsibility for the Pepys legacy. This responsibility had two main elements, care of physical artefacts and documents and, equally importantly, keeping alive family memories of Pepys orally and in letters. It is clear from all the evidence we have that family pride in the Pepys connections remained extremely strong, and legacy responsibilities were continually honoured, even as the Pepys era in living memory inevitably faded and eventually expired.

Reflecting her complex and illustrious family connections, several details contained in Anne's Last Will & Testament relate to family relationships, inheritances, and legacies, including some very specific items relating to Samuel Pepys. Her Will refers to her mother, also named Anne, and several living relatives. Among these are her brother Hewer Edgley Hewer, who had no children, her daughters Ann (wife of Brabazon Hallowes), Frances (wife of John Cockerell), Jane, Susanna, her son John Pepys Jackson, and several granddaughters. The surname Hallowes is incorporated in the name William Hallowes Belli, featured in a later branch of the family.

In her Will Anne requests burial in Clapham, Surrey, where she had been born, grew up, and lived with her husband John Jackson before his death. The words she uses are, '*my body I commit to the grave to be buried as privately as possible in the Vault under the vestry room of the parish church of Clapham in Surry and desire my coffin may be placed as near Mr. Jackson's as it can*'.

While she makes generous bequests to her many close relatives, the amounts were constrained by the fact that she and her husband John Jackson were unfortunately among the many people who had suffered catastrophically in 1720 from investing in South Sea Stock. The value of Investments in the South Sea Company had been rising strongly, and seemingly inexorably, with many being enticed into buying the stock or increasing their existing holdings. However, the stock's value collapsed suddenly, with little warning – the bursting of the so-called South Sea Bubble. The passage in her Will reads,

> '*whereas the Trustees therein named biding the joint Consent and at the Special Instance and Request of my late husband and myself cause to be invested the said sum of six thousand and six hundred pounds in South Sea Stock in the year of our Lord one thousand seven hundred and twenty whereby in that general calamity it was most of it lost*'.

This enormous financial loss equates to approximately £1m today. She clearly feels a great responsibility and is concerned that her Trustees should be protected from any claims against them, because immediately following the above text, her Will continues with,

> '*Now I being willing and desirous as much as in me lies to indemnify and save harmless the said Trustees from any*

trouble claim or demand that my son John Pepys Jackson may have against them on account of the said loss do will order direct and appoint that the sum of three thousand and six hundred pounds be paid and secured by my Executrixes out of that Moiety of the fourth part of the late William Hewer's Estate which will devolve on me after the death of my late brother's widow and that it be settled on my son John Pepys Jackson to and for the uses and purposes of my Marriage Settlement which with the ffreehold Messuage at Clapham in the County of Surry part of the aforesaid six thousand six hundred pounds will make the whole good to him.'

Finally, Anne's Will confirms that, when it was drawn up, she was living at Bishop's Hull, Somerset, the Cockerell family home. Samuel Pepys Cockerell, her grandson, was born in 1754, two years before Anne died. With her childhood memories of Samuel Pepys himself – she was 13 when he died – she had probably been influential in the choice of her grandson's two highly significant forenames.

CHAPTER FOUR

Third Generation –
The Pepys Cockerell Connection

Most members of the third generation grew up in the early Georgian period. The reigns of George I and George II, covering the period 1714-1760, featured a far more stable religious, political, and economic environment than that of their parents and grandparents. Particularly among their class, they were economically fortunate in benefiting from great opportunities for consolidation and accumulation of wealth, often through mutually advantageous marriages. They were also able to benefit from advances in knowledge and associated emerging technologies in the early decades of what is frequently termed The Age of Enlightenment. Discoveries and improvements in the scientific field, including medical and health understanding, helped to make daily life easier and more pleasurable. Again, it must be stressed that the upper classes of society benefited disproportionately, at least until aspects such as sanitation and basic education filtered down to most of the population over future generations.

As already signalled in previous chapters, this is the generation in which the Cockerell family fully enters the picture, through the marriage of John Cockerell and Frances Jackson, Pepys's great niece. We start with the Jackson family members in this generation, the sons and daughters of John Jackson and Anne (nee Edgeley), taking them in the order of their births. Frances is the youngest and is given greatest attention in the text below. Her husband John Cockerell is then profiled, with the focus thereafter on the Cockerell and Pepys Cockerell families, whose members provided continuity in directly inheriting responsibility for Samuel Pepys's estate and legacy, including the ownership of a large collection of Pepys's private correspondence.

John Pepys Jackson (1715-1779)

John Pepys Jackson was the first son of the marriage between John Jackson (Samuel Pepys' immediate heir) and Anne (nee Edgeley). Giving him a first name of John, matching his father's, was common practice, but it is noticeable that the middle name they chose was Pepys, signalling an intent to retain this family connection to their renowned predecessor.

No records of John marrying or having children have been established, and the only other record we have about his life is from a 1756 document in the National Archives (D187/24/1), which at that time refers to him as '*John Pepys Jackson of Bishops Hull, Somerset esq eldest son of Anne Jackson of the same place widow deceased*'. This is significant because it evidences that when his mother Anne, in her old age, had moved to Bishops Hull to live with John Cockerell and Frances, her eldest son John had apparently moved with her. If he had had an independent career this is rather odd. What we also know is that his mother was especially determined to leave him well provided for both in her Will and in an Articles of Agreement document of 30 May 1755 in which she covenanted that John '*should have land with brick house on it at Clapham after her death and £3,600 after the death of Elizabeth Edgley Hewer*', as also referenced in the above National Archives document. It seems likely that the '*land with brick house on it*' is a reference to Gauden House at Clapham, referred to earlier.

It may be that all this security for John is considered necessary because of the substantial loss of John's natural inheritance resulting from his parents' disastrous South Sea Bubble investment loss, described earlier. However, perhaps he was also more generally vulnerable, financially or otherwise, so needed particular care. This would tally with him moving to Bishops Hull rather than forging his own independent life. It is perhaps also significant that he is not one of the executors of his mother's Will, with his sisters Anne and Frances being the ones chosen to fulfil that important role.

As the first son he would have been the natural and obvious next inheritor of the role of heir and guardian of Samuel Pepys's legacy including the private correspondence and other physical memorabilia, but again there is no evidence for this having happened. After their mother Anne Jackson's death in 1756 it appears that the role passes to her daughter Frances, and perhaps this is because John has not married, is unlikely to have children, and may also have some sort of dependency making him inappropriate to fulfil this crucial function. What we do know for certain is that after Frances, the role as Samuel Pepys's next heir and guardian of his legacy passes to Frances's second son, and this is covered in detail below.

Paulina Jackson (1716- ????)

It has proved impossible to establish anything meaningful about Paulina, with no primary source material found. The lack of records may indicate death in infancy.

Susanna Jackson (1717-1793)

Susanna's only identified record is her Will in which she leaves all her furniture, linen, wearing apparel, watches, trinkets and other things to her younger sister Jane. She rewards her servants with certain annuities and one-off bequests and leaves ten guineas to each of five nieces and nephews, namely Lady Barker, Elizabeth Belli, John Cockerell, Samuel Pepys Cockerell, and Charles Cockerell. In later letters between these three Cockerell brothers there are several references to their Jackson aunts, namely Susanna and her sister Jane, and these indicate a genuine fondness. The main part of Susanna's estate is left in equal shares to the five nieces and nephews named above.

Susanna appoints as her executors her sister Jane and her nephew Samuel Pepys Cockerell. The latter was named as executor in several family Wills, so he was clearly seen as reliable and trustworthy, and when the Will was proved after Susanna's death, Samuel is the main swearer of oath. He has already appeared several times above and is also key to much of the narrative in the following chapters.

Anne Jackson (1718-1786)

As with Paulina above, little has been established. We know that her brother Samuel (see below) was baptised in the first few days of 1719, with his birth probably late in 1718. Anne and Samuel may have been twins, but Anne could have been born separately extremely early in 1718, with Samuel's birth say 11 months later at the tail end of that year. On 3rd January 1742, Anne married Brabazon Hallowes, a surname which re-appears as a middle name in a later generation. She and her husband are one of the three parties named in the Articles of Agreement document referenced above under the entry for her brother John Pepys Jackson. This National Archives document (D187/24/1) is held at the Derbyshire Record Office, clearly linked with the fact that Anne and her husband Brabazon lived at Glapwell, Derbyshire. Anne died in 1786 at Glapwell, a location referred to in many family letters and which we know Colonel John Cockerell, of the next generation, visited on a tour of Britain after his return from India in the 1790s.

Samuel Jackson (1718- ?)

Samuel was baptised on 9th January 1719 in Clapham, but that is the only record readily available. Having attached the name Pepys to their first son, John and Anne Jackson gave his younger brother the first name Samuel, again reflecting the Samuel Pepys connections. His sister Frances was to take this name-hijacking one step further, as covered below.

Jane Jackson (1720-1801)

The only meaningful insight we have is provided by her Will, in which Jane appoints as executors her nephews Samuel Pepys Cockerell and Charles Cockerell. She leaves £500 of government stock to her niece Lady Barker "as a mark of my regard for her". Mirroring her sister Susanna's Will she leaves legacies for her servants. Physical assets in the form of furniture, wearing apparel, plate, watches, jewels and trinkets are left to be disposed of by her executors either in line with any separate written instructions she may by then have left, or at their discretion.

The remaining stock or money in the funds in trust she leaves to her four nephews and niece, namely John Cockerell, Samuel Pepys Cockerell, Charles Cockerell, and Elizabeth Stuart Belli, in four equal shares. Sadly, the eldest of these intended beneficiaries, Colonel John Cockerell, died only two months after

Jane's Will had been drafted on 4th May 1798, so that when she died three years later in 1801 his portion was shared between the other three. When the Will was proved after her death, Samuel Pepys Cockerell was again the one to swear the necessary oath to execute Jane's last wishes.

In summary, the main intended beneficiaries of these various Jackson Wills were the four Cockerell siblings John, Samuel Pepys, Charles, and Elizabeth. They are also the four for whom considerable detailed information and personal correspondence is available, enabling some insight into their diverse characters and life stories. They are the most prominent individuals among the Fourth Generation featured in the next chapter.

Frances Cockerell (nee Jackson) (1722-1769)

Like her sisters Susanna and Jane, the youngest sibling Frances was one of Paulina Pepys's granddaughters and a great niece of Samuel Pepys. The Jackson and Cockerell families both had property interests in Clapham and were possibly friends or neighbours, probably explaining how the first formal link between the two families came about. Frances married John Cockerell on 16th January 1740 at the Chapel Royal, Westminster, exactly a fortnight before her 18th birthday. The venue of the marriage underlines the family statuses of the bride and groom, as does the fact that fine portraits by leading artists of the day were commissioned for each of them. The portrait of Frances is attributed to Thomas Gainsborough.

Her marriage involved Frances moving across the country from her recorded country address at Harmston in Lincolnshire to the Cockerells' home at Bishops Hull in Somerset. While these were the respective country addresses of the two families, most gentry families held both country and town (i.e. London) residences and the capital offered ample opportunities for those of their social standing to meet marriage partners, as probably happened with John and Frances. Although now living much of the year in Somerset after her marriage, Frances would have continued to enjoy socialising in London. Indeed, as well as having had family connections with Clapham, her address when she died in 1769 was in Chelsea.

Frances Cockerell (nee Jackson) attributed to
Thomas Gainsborough

Although she was eventually to have eight surviving children, the first of these, Anne, only arrived in 1749, nine years into the marriage. This delay may relate to her husband's interests in the West Indies, possibly requiring his presence there for long periods. In any event, as part of a wealthy family, this child-free period no doubt enabled Frances to enjoy her first few years of married life with a certain amount of freedom of movement and entertainment. This changed significantly when her eight children were born in rapid succession between 1749 and 1760. As the family's story unfolds through the following generations, the birth of large numbers of children is a recurring theme, and contrasts starkly with the childless state of Samuel Pepys's own 17th century marriage.

Frances's marriage is central to our narrative, but whether it was John Cockerell or Frances who was more influential in deciding to give their second son the forenames Samuel Pepys is impossible to know. No doubt both were proud of Frances's connection with Pepys.

As context for their pride in this famous relative, any contemporary mid-18th century fame would have been through his successes in naval administration as Chief Secretary to the Admiralty and his literary interests, principally his impressive Library of some 3000 volumes. His Diary was only a small element of the latter and had been recorded in a very particular form of shorthand, effectively a code. As already noted, it was not until the early 19th century that passages were properly deciphered and transcribed, with the first published versions only appearing in 1825.

When John Jackson, Frances's father, had died in 1723 the extensive book and document collection amassed by Pepys, and bequeathed to John, was transferred to Magdalene College, Cambridge, and formed the Pepys Library. This would keep the Pepys name alive permanently, as well as making this tangible legacy accessible to the public, albeit initially only to an extremely small, interested, and educated section of the population. There is no evidence of a noticeable upsurge in public interest 30 years later which might have triggered or motivated the naming of Samuel Pepys Cockerell in 1754. We are left with the likelihood that John Cockerell and Frances simply had pride in the Pepys connection, which was still within the family's living memory, and wished to openly express this in the naming their second son. Their first son John had been given his father's forename, as was traditional, but it appears that the role as one of Samuel Pepys's successive heirs and guardians next passed to their second son. Having been given the name Samuel Pepys Cockerell this was of course entirely appropriate and perhaps planned many years earlier.

Frances died in 1769, and the text of her Will is on the public record. It explicitly treats male and female descendants equally in most financial aspects. Nevertheless, when Samuel Pepys's remaining physical legacies in the family's possession were passed down the family generations, this was predominantly through the male line. The text of Frances's Will notably references several deficiencies in her husband's financial management, with loose ends needing to be tied up before there was clarity about what Frances was able to bequeath. For example, one key phrase in the Will reads,

> *And whereas after our marriage it was discovered that the said lands and premisses were incumbered with a mortgage for the principal sum of five hundred pounds and with the Dower or thirds of Abigail Cockerell who is still living so that my late husbands of her estates and effects were as apprehended become liable to make good those deficiencies.*

While the inevitable formality of Frances's Will does not allow feelings to be openly expressed, there appears to me to be a sense of exasperation and resentment in Frances's wording about the state of her husband's financial arrangements. John Cockerell had died two years prior to her own death, and had left his finances in a complex state, including debts and mortgages which needed to be cleared. The wording of Frances's Will indicates that she had needed to use some of her own family's inheritances to pay off her husband's debts. So not only were Frances's parents financially embarrassed through involvement in the South Sea Bubble scandal, but her own husband's finances were also problematic. As it happened Frances, and particularly her children, were well provided for under the terms of her mother's and sisters' Wills already described above. Her sisters Susanna and Jane were spinsters and left money specifically for their nephews and nieces, Frances's children. It would appear from the limited evidence available that as well as the complexities of his financial situation, John's life itself was far from straightforward, as next outlined.

John Cockerell (1714-1767)

Born into a wealthy family, the sparse evidence available suggests John had a typical privileged 18th century upbringing and lifestyle, mixing country pursuits at the family's home in Somerset with at least one base in London for the fashionable season, which provided the ideal opportunities for matchmaking between families whose out-of-season main residences were spread far and wide across the country. It is in London that John and Frances would probably have met and developed their relationship. The family had interests in the West Indies, and although it is unclear how much time John spent there, it is certainly where he died.

Because of his marriage to Frances, which linked him with Pepys relatives and the associated celebrity, there is a danger that John Cockerell's own antecedents and family background are unfairly overshadowed. High quality portraits of the 18th century Cockerells evidence their gentry class and status. John's portrait below is attributed to Joshua Reynolds.

Portrait of John Cockerell, attributed to Sir Joshua Reynolds

As well as John's portrait, there is also a portrait (below) of his father, also called John, and these two portraits, which were owned by the Cockerell and Pepys Cockerell family through to the 21st century, give an impression of the family's social standing in the early decades of the long Georgian period.

John Cockerell (senior), attributed to William Verelest

John Cockerell senior's portrait indicates shooting or hunting as an interest, but this is so commonplace for late seventeenth and early eighteenth-century gentry that it tells us little about his character. In any event he belongs to the previous generation and our attention here is focused on his son.

The Cockerell family was a respected one in England at the time, but there are two aspects of John Cockerell junior's life which reveal chinks in his personal reputation. Firstly, in 1765, towards the end of his life, John was in the Kings Bench prison. This, if it were the only question mark against his character, would not be as surprising as it may appear. The Kings Bench prison often housed privileged individuals, but who had accrued some form of debt, often the result of a temporary cash-flow problem. It should be remembered that the sort of substantial financial assets commonly held by the wealthy at that time were often not easily 'cashed-in' at short notice. There was the additional challenge that some assets were physically held in other countries, for examples jewels in India, or certificates held on foreign markets. Unexpected adverse events could therefore cause short-term financial embarrassment to otherwise perfectly respectable individuals, and occasionally even result in a spell in a debtors' prison.

Jane Austen makes direct reference to the Kings Bench prison, and the social stigma associated with it, in the following passage from 'A Collection of Letters', one of her very early writings.

Lady Greville … was determined to mortify me, and accordingly when we were sitting down between the dances, she came to me with <u>more</u> than her usual insulting importance attended by Miss Mason and said loud enough to be heard by half the people in the room, "Pray Miss Maria in what way of business was your Grandfather? For Miss Mason & I cannot agree whether he was a Grocer or a Bookbinder." I saw that she wanted to mortify me and was resolved if I possibly could to prevent her seeing that her scheme succeeded. "Neither Madam; he was a Wine Merchant." "Aye, I knew he was in some such low way … Did not he abscond?" "I never heard that he did." "At least he died insolvent?" "I was never told so before." "Why was not your Father as poor as a Rat?" " I fancy not;" "Was not he in the Kings Bench once?"

The image below, although dating from early in the next century, caricatures the prison's unusual and ambiguous profile.

KINGS BENCH: *Tom & Bob taking a peep at* REAL CHARACTERS, *in the Abbots Priory*
London Pub.d by Jones & Co. Nov.r 15 1828.

The second negative aspect of John's life was his apparent involvement with slavery in the West Indies; indeed, he was in Antigua when he died in 1767. In the late 18th and very early 19th centuries, slavery was increasingly being regarded as morally unacceptable, attracting social criticism and hostile public reaction. Jane Austen's novel *Mansfield Park* has this as an underlying theme. There is evidence that at least some of the Cockerell family wealth was accumulated through West Indies investments, activity, and trade. When slavery was eventually abolished the Cockerells, like hundreds of others, appear to have been compensated for their loss of human 'property'. This compensation remains highly contentious, and the slavery itself rightly condemned. Its part in funding the 18th and 19th century British Empire, with a substantial portion of the wealth it generated being used to finance British estates and country houses, has been the subject of renewed research and examination in the 21st century.

John Cockerell and Frances produced a large family, and during the late 18th and early 19th centuries several of their children and grandchildren were to make significant national contributions in the fields of art, architecture and politics, as well as being influential in both military and commercial successes, most notably in shaping and supporting expansion of British India. Individually, these offspring clearly had inherent and substantial abilities, but their various impressive careers were no doubt assisted by their parents' social standing and valuable connections, a recurring theme in this narrative.

There are numerous archived letters sent between three of their sons, John, Samuel Pepys, and Charles, and these are featured in Chapter 6, not only evidencing their activities but also something of their respective characters, motivations, and interests. Unfortunately, there are no such archived sources for their parents John and Frances so, although we have their portraits, we are left with the fragmentary details set out above together with the bare facts of their births, marriage, deaths, the contents of Wills, and some of the locations where they spent their lives.

John having died in Antigua is surely a link with other records showing him having an interest in slave labour in the West Indies. Given that he was in prison almost certainly for falling into debt, however temporarily, perhaps he went to the Caribbean on some sort of financial rescue mission. Maybe he was going to dispose of some landowning interests there to raise money to pay off his debts, or to resolve some disputes which may have caused the debts. There is no clear evidence, but his death in the Caribbean would have left his family with many logistical, legal, financial and inheritance challenges. Indeed, as noted above, when Frances died just two years after John her Will refers to debts and mortgages, which she had been obliged to sort out. Fortunately, Frances had inheritances from her own Jackson family, and once the challenges resulting from John's death had been dealt with and debts settled, she would also benefit from her husband's remaining assets.

John and Frances both died young, leaving seven surviving children the eldest of whom were only teenagers. Given the somewhat chequered later years of John Cockerell's life, perhaps it is not surprising that three of their sons, born in 1752, 1754, and 1755, and their sister Elizabeth, born in 1758, were all motivated to carve out their own individual and distinctive paths rather than simply living off the wealth and status of their parents, as many did at this time. These four maintained very close contact throughout their lives, with mutually supportive relationships probably forged, or at least influenced, by the early loss of their parents. The diversity of their careers and life experiences perhaps also moderated any natural sibling rivalries. The letters between them showed concern and respect. Their stories now follow as part of coverage of the fourth generation, informed by far greater availability of personal details.

CHAPTER FIVE

Fourth Generation –
Forging Links with India

The historical context for this generation includes greater influences outside Britain, shaping career choices and domestic lifestyles. The opportunities described for the previous generation were being exploited with many new ones emerging. Expansion of foreign interests brought the prospect not only of wealth but adventure, with India especially having great attraction. As well as exotic plants, foodstuffs, fabrics, jewels and images being brought back from the East, returning travellers brought tales of radically contrasting and vibrant lifestyles and cultures. Portrayals of the sub-continents' architecture and landscapes by topographical artists, notably William Hodges and the uncle and nephew pairing of Thomas and William Daniell, gave the public a window into this distant and dramatically different world.

This fourth family generation, and subsequent ones, feature multiple Indian experiences and connections, including their impact back in England. Having an oriental aura and being out of sight of domestic scrutiny, some enigmatic and intriguing mysteries emerge. These relate predominantly to relationships, questions of paternity, and possible Indian 'marriages', puzzles not easily resolved simply from the raw information in publicly available official records. Fortunately, the family's letters, while often being the source of these puzzles, also provide clues to unravelling them, with most at least partially clarified, as outlined later.

At home in Britain, for many family members there was more time, wealth, and motivation to pursue cultural interests. The range of choices had also expanded in line with advances in travel and greater access to a wider range of knowledge and information, assisted by new and improved means of communication. This period also coincides with what is commonly considered the golden age of British portraiture, and we are fortunate in having portrait images of several family members by leading contemporary artists.

Before exploring the eventful lives of four of John and Frances Cockerell's eight children, namely John, Samuel Pepys, Charles, and Elizabeth, and how they fared in the late 18th and early 19th centuries, it is worth repeating that when their parents John and Frances died in 1767 and 1769 respectively, these four were all still very young. The younger two, Elizabeth and Charles, were only 9 and 12 when their father died, and 11 and 14 when their mother died two years later. While no doubt each of the four was affected differently by the loss of their parents, they all benefited from having supportive well-connected relatives and family friends, and they certainly had few financial worries. Nevertheless, their parents' deaths at quite young ages would have had an emotional impact and required a degree of resilience which they duly demonstrated. It is also clear that these four siblings formed a tight-knit group with frequent and mutually respectful communications, even when in distant parts of the world. From the nature and tone of their letters it is possible to gain insights into their respective and diverse characters.

Much less is known about John and Frances's other four children, Anne (1749-1760), Paulina (1751-1786), Edward (1756-1782), and Frances (1760-1784), but the latter three would also have been affected by their parents' deaths while they were still very young. All eight children were brought up in a family that continued to have great pride in the Samuel Pepys connection, which they were determined to keep alive. The eight are now considered in the order of their births.

Anne Cockerell (1749-1760)

John and Frances Cockerell's first child Anne, born on 12th April 1749, sadly died in 1760, not long after her eleventh birthday, and was buried on 3rd July that year. Whatever the cause of her death, this must have been extremely upsetting not just for her parents, for whom a first child would have held a special place in their hearts, but also for her young brothers and sisters, ranging in age from 8 down to 2 when she died. They no doubt looked up to Anne as the eldest child. While the cause is unknown, death at a young age was all too frequent at the time, even for wealthy families with access to good nutrition, living conditions and medical support.

Paulina Cockerell (1751-1786?)

Two years after Anne's birth, a second daughter, Paulina, was born on 29th July 1751, and baptised at Bishops Hull, Somerset exactly two months later. The family's direct descent was from Samuel Pepys's sister Paulina, and this choice of name was therefore particularly appropriate for one of their daughters. Her mother Frances was understandably proud of her descent from the Pepys family, underpinned by the role that she and her husband John Cockerell had as heirs of Samuel Pepys, and guardians of his memorabilia and legacy.

While we have little detail of Paulina's life, her Will does provide some information and insight into the close family relationships. Its wording indicates that Paulina was then resident in Lisbon, Portugal but, frustratingly, the circumstances and background to her being there are not clear from any available family letters or other documents. The mild climate made it popular for those with health problems, so that may be the reason, just as we know it was for her brother John's winter break a few years later. Some researchers have given her year of death as 1786, which may be correct even though her Will and grant of probate in 1793 would normally imply a date of death only shortly before this. Her Will, recorded in the Prerogative Court of Canterbury Wills [1793-1795] is as follows.

> *Items. to be observed as my will*
> *Paulina Cockerell. I desire the ring of cut diamond which my brother John Cockerell gave to me may be*

returned to him and that an handsome ring be made for him of my hair the miniature picture of my brother John and brother Charles be given to my sister Belli my brother Charles' picture and Sis. & Brs. Miniature to be given to Brother Pepys and? my books to be divided between brothers and sister Belli the few articles of plate which are my distinct property I desire brother Pepys will take except the tea pot and coffee pot and that he will take charge of my papers and arrs. and examine and settle them. I desire my sister Belli to have any other trifles and trinkets which it may have. My best cloaths and manmade muslins to be divided between herself and Mrs Pepys Cockerell my sister to chuse such as she may best like my servant Susannah Duchain to have my linen and common cloaths and an annuity of ten pounds pr. ann for her separate use and for her life . an handsome ring of my hair to be made for brother Charles an handsome seal to Mrs Belli : any share I have in my late uncle Jacksons property in my brothers right on? the first eight [eighth?] of the Hewer Estate to be given to my Aunts Susan and Jane Jackson for their separate lives

On the eleventh day of May in the year of our Lord one thousand seven hundred and ninety three administration (with the will annexed) of all and singular the goods with chattels and credits of Paulina Cockerell late of the City of Lisbon spinster deceased was granted to Samuel Pepys Cockerell the natural and lawful brother and next of kin of the said deceased having been first sworn duly to administer the Executor or residuary legatee being named in the said will.

Note that her brother Samuel Pepys Cockerell is simply referred to as Pepys, an identity he cultivated publicly and not solely in the context of a preferred family nickname as we see here. The Will also indicates his standing within the family, particularly among the siblings. Other Wills and documents show that he is frequently given responsibility for discharging legal and property duties, indicating his self-assurance, business acumen, abilities and trustworthiness.

If Paulina had died as early as 1786, cited by other researchers without definitive supporting evidence, it would be unusual for the Will to only be officially recorded, and probate granted, several years later. However, any such long delay, if genuine, could be attributable to her death being in Portugal, with associated logistical, legal, and bureaucratic challenges to overcome. As we have seen earlier, with Frances Cockerell having to sort out her husband's entangled finances, settlement of estates was sometimes a lengthy process. Indeed, in the next generation, sorting out the estate of Colonel John Cockerell, Frances's eldest son, only appears to have been finalised a similar seven years after his death, so perhaps Paulina really had died as early as 1786.

What Paulina's Will clearly indicates is the emphasis put on personal items, including those with purely sentimental value. As evidenced by other documents, having portraits of each other was important to the family, particularly when their lives took them to distant parts of the world. Not surprisingly, easily transportable miniatures (as itemised in the Will) were a favoured format. Portraits intended for their homes in England were often larger paintings intended to adorn walls. A few examples of such family portraits are interspersed in the text.

Colonel John Cockerell (1752-1798)

John and Frances's third child and first son, born in 1752 at Bishop's Hull, Somerset, was christened John, in line with family tradition of firstborn sons perpetuating their father's forename. Less traditional for a first-born son was his chosen career in military service, but it was a decision that led to achievement of high rank and profile, notably in India.

Colonel John Cockerell, c.1795 attributed to Sir William Beechey

John became Quartermaster General of the East India Company's Bengal Army under its General, Lord Cornwallis. With no blame whatsoever attaching to him, it was Cornwallis who had surrendered to the Colonists at Yorktown in 1781, effectively ending hostilities in the American War of Independence. With Britain's focus consequently switching to the East, he was seen as a solid choice for this key role In India. As his Quartermaster General, John Cockerell's own senior role carried with it overall logistical responsibility for the army's resources, including ensuring supplies of provisions and transport for the troops and their equipment in what was an especially inhospitable environment. The nature of these crucial responsibilities chime with Samuel Pepys's 17th century work on naval military efficiency, with his similar focus on logistics from ship building to staff planning.

The challenges for John were often unique to Asia and very different from those in Europe, including coping with extremes of weather, with unpredictable monsoons and droughts affecting rice harvests. Developing new skills such as tactical use of elephants was also crucial. These were formidable challenges in support of a military campaign across a vast continent, contending with the might of Tipu Sultan's army operating in the south on 'home territory', with all Tipu's associated advantages of fighting in familiar surroundings and climate. One element of this unbalanced dynamic was, however, self-inflicted by insistence on maintaining certain standards of living amongst the British officers, as graphically described in an extract from Alexander Frater's *Chasing the Monsoon*, cited by John Julius Norwich (2021, p175):-

> *We passed over the red roofs of Calicut, where Vasco da Gama made his first Indian landfall. Along here, in 1789, Tipu sultan had engaged the British in a famous campaign that demonstrated how mobile, fast-moving guerilla forces will always outflank a static army commanded by dull, conservative generals. Tipu, operating from a series of fortified hill-top droogs, ran rings around the British as they ponderously mounted the Ghats with their armaments – each cannon pushed by an elephant, while scores of men and oxen hauled on drag-ropes – and a stupefying amount of personal baggage. A typical captain went into battle with a large bed, several chairs, a folding table, two pairs of candle shades, twenty-four linen suits, several dozen bottles of wine, brandy and gin, tea, sugar and biscuits, a hamper of live poultry, a milch goat, seven trunks containing cooking utensils, cutlery, crystal and table linen, and a palanquin* [effectively a glorified sedan chair]. *The palanquin coolies were followed by a head boy, a lesser boy, a cook, an ostler, a grass-cutter and two bullock drivers for the four baggage bullocks.*

While in India, John exchanged numerous letters with his younger brother Charles, some of them while Charles himself was serving in India, and others with Charles back at their Hyde Park Corner house in London. There were also letters exchanged with his other brother Samuel Pepys, often referred to in the letters simply as 'Pepys', then living at his Westbourne House home near Paddington. These letters, featured in the next chapter, provide far more detail on his service in India. Although John was the eldest of the three, the letters make it clear that he relied on his younger brothers 'Pepys' (Samuel Pepys) and 'Carolus' (Charles) for non-military matters, notably finance and property interests, recognising their greater business skills and experience.

The letters evidence John's deep affection for his siblings and the wider family, but he never married, and any ambitions in that direction come across as passive rather than proactive. Although not an inevitable barrier to a conventional marriage, his arduous military career, frequently on active campaign across the subcontinent, didn't help. He did, however, have at least one liaison in India, perhaps an informal 'marriage', which produced four children. Such relationships were neither officially recorded nor formally acknowledged in Britain. Nevertheless, in his Will he does explicitly recognise and name his 'natural' children and makes provision for their care and education.

Such relationships were very common for East India Company personnel, and it is worth putting the paternity experiences of John and his brother Charles (see later) in context, because such liaisons didn't attract any significant criticism or condemnation at the time. Indeed, they were common, largely expected and, to some extent, encouraged. The following passage from Vyvyen Brendon's excellent book *Children of the Raj* (2006, p43) is illuminating.

If the evidence of family letters and memoirs is not always reliable, baptismal registers and wills provide more trustworthy data. At St. John's Church in Calcutta fifty-four per cent of the children baptised between 1767 and 1782 were Eurasian and illegitimate. And one in three wills made in Bengal from 1778 to 1785 contain bequests to Indian mistresses and their progeny. ... Historians estimate that about ninety percent of the British men in India by the mid eighteenth century had married (officially or unofficially) Indian or Eurasian women. The East India Company even encouraged the practice by giving a christening present of five rupees to the babies of soldiers married to Indian women.

John's time in India was extremely demanding, and as it was drawing to a close he began planning his return home to England. The family's main base was a very substantial house at Hyde Park Corner, able to host large balls and other social events, but far from ideal for the quieter lifestyle John envisaged for himself. He was keen to acquire a new home, independent of the Cockerells' London property holdings. Seeking a more relaxed and private environment, the property he chose was in rural Gloucestershire, in the North Cotswolds. It is no coincidence that it was close to Daylesford, the retirement house and estate of Warren Hastings, the first Governor General of British India, to whom both John and Charles Cockerell had ultimately reported in India.

The choice of Sezincote, near Moreton-in-Marsh, was guided by his brother Samuel Pepys Cockerell, architect to the East India Company and involved in many prestigious building projects, including elements of the rampant westward development of London. The Cockerells also had ownership and property interests as landlords in the Westbourne area of Paddington, and Samuel was well informed about property matters both inside and outside London. He had been requested to look out for potential locations for his brother John and identified the run-down Sezincote estate as having great potential. John's letters from India, many recorded in the next chapter, refer to his intent to purchase Sezincote and his plans for the house and its grounds. Once back in England, and having finalised the purchase in 1795, John progressed some substantive initial works, aiming to create a house in conventional contemporary style. However, his health deteriorated rapidly, works effectively stalled, and shortly after that, in 1798, John suddenly died.

John's marital status and intentions during the 1790s remain opaque. In his later years in India and about to return to England, he ponders a formal marriage in Britain but says that he doesn't believe marriage is for him. Another source claims that he had an Indo-Portuguese mistress, Estuarta, who returned to England with John and their children. However, in contradiction of this, the family letters in the Bodleian Library which this source cites as the main supporting evidence, clearly and repeatedly indicate that Estuarta is the familiar name the Cockerells use for Elizabeth Stuart Cockerell, the sister of John, Samuel, and Charles. There are many references to Estuarta in letters between John and his younger brother Charles, the context of which further confirms her identity, often explicitly linking her with her husband John Belli. There is also a reference to 'our dear sister, Estuarta'. If there weren't so many other references confirming her as their sister, and John Belli's wife, it might just be credible that the term 'sister' was being used here in the sense of the Cockerell family being fully aware of John's mistress and treating her effectively as notionally one of the family. However, the numerous other references – several cited below, and with yet more in Chapter 6 – decisively rule this out. 'Estuarta' is simply their sister's family nickname, clearly derived from her full name Elizabeth Stuart Cockerell, i.e. E stuart, with an 'a' added for phonetic neatness and flow.

Nevertheless, there **is** evidence of John having had an extra-marital relationship in India, references in the letters between the brothers alluding to 'unfortunate' children being born, and the context points to a mistress in India. John's Last Will and Testament, records John leaving money to four natural children, three of whom were male. If the surname Johnson, as evidenced in the Will, was a notional one, perhaps it was an obvious choice indicating in a literal sense 'son of John'.

The claim that Estuarta was his mistress and that she and the children were brought back to England is also at odds with the text of John's Will and other substantial clear evidence to the contrary, cited below and in more detail in the next chapter. The bequests made to his extra-marital children in his Will are expressed in Rupees which indicates that the children stayed, and were brought up, in India, at least at the time of him drafting the Will. There are also references indicating that their mother was in effect being bought off and left to fend for herself. Such liaisons in India, and even informal marriages there, were, as noted above, very common for East India Company staff.

There is also clear evidence within the Cockerell letters at the Bodleian Library that John's three 'natural sons' were sent from India to America in 1796 and that his 'natural daughter' remained in India, with a dowry granted to secure her future. The following extract from a letter of April 15th 1796 from John (having returned to England) to his brother Charles (still in India, and looking after John's remaining interests there) evidences yet again that Estuarta is their sister Elizabeth Stuart, and wife of John Belli, as well as crucially indicating in the letter's postscript the plan to send John Cockerell's three illegitimate boys from India to America.

> *Our dear Estuarta does not know of this 'Opportunity' to write Belli – but assure him from me, she is well, & all her children – she has a letter from him of Decr., by the Nonsuch. – but it is to be apprehended, all his letters to her for the Mary packet, must have been in the unfortunate boxes lost along side her by Shirborne. – She knows he is well – & hopes to hear ere long, that Belli will go to TurmCoke/TamCoke??, – I pray for it heartily – so say, with my best affections. –*
>
> > *Your commissions shall all go on the Thetis –*
> > > *the curricle, &c &c –-----*
> > > *God bless you – my dearest Carolus,*
> > > > *I am your ever affecte. Brother*
> > > > > *Jn. Cockerell*
>
> *Charles Cockerell Esq.*
> *PS.*
> > *Sir Ralph Woodford desired me to tell you he had letters from Lord Bute – or saw letters from him, I am not quite certain which, conceived on more favorable terms indeed to your Spanish Projects. –*
> > *I have read your letters of November about the disposal of the boys, to America – most satisfactory indeed, –*
> > > *Thanks – & thanks. –*
> > > > *J Coll.*   [John Cockerell]

Two weeks later in a follow-up of April 29th, John's next letter to Charles includes the two extracts below, which make it clear that the boys have departed India and he leaves the settling of his illegitimate daughter to Charles's discretion. In a reference to John and his mistress's progeny it also indicates that she was coloured.

> *– I have so many thanks to make to you, for correspondence, & for attentions to me, & to my wishes, that I know not where to commence. – the disposal of the children is the most material, and I am very happy indeed at the measure you have adopted. – nothing could have met my own choice more readily – & I think it must succeed to the future wellfare, comfort & prosperity of this little coloured progeny. – I shall wait for letters from your friend Mr. Pringle, ere I take any step of writing to him on this subject.*
>
> *Now, that the children are gone – I shall take into full consideration the business of the sum appropriated to their uses – I have already written a declaration to withdraw the Trust Charge of the Company's Paper, and have invested this Trust in Your House. – I am disposed to make such a disposition of this sum as shall leave you at more full liberty to settle the girl, if occasion should be favorable, and to make remittas. to America, in the full proportions for the boys – so to leave the residue at my own command, either for interest, or for remittance to England, as may be desirable:-*

The arrangement to send the boys to America is clearly regarded as a positive pragmatic solution to embarrassment about John's illegitimate children, but also evidenced is John's continuing concern for their welfare. As well as having earlier included them explicitly in his Will, a further letter to Charles of July 21st 1796 evidences his ongoing support for the boys in their American 'exile' :-

> *Have written Mr. Pringle at Philadelphia, approving, & confirming him in his Plans for the young Indians – & advising he will write C. Cll. Of his sentiments as to any augmentation of funds in America to their uses. –*

The reference to them as 'young Indians' again indicates that his mistress was probably of Indian ethnicity. A final reference to the American arrangements, and John's continuing concern for his illegitimate boys ('*the Young Indians*') comes in a letter of July 26th 1796 :-

> *I have written to Mr. Pringle of Philadelphia. – which my last to you would notice I think approving entirely that he should act in the Trust, on his own judgement, & your instructions. – advising that he should address you on any suggestions he may wish to make in respect to the augmentation of property in America, for the object of settling the Young Indians. –*

It should be recorded here that there is one other intriguing, tantalising, but probably merely coincidental link with the surname 'Johnson' attached to these illegitimate children. The imposing portrait of Colonel John Cockerell at the head of this section, and attributed to Sir William Beechey RA, was probably painted in 1795/6 shortly after John's return to England. Coinciding with this, at the Royal Academy exhibition of 1796 one of the eleven portraits Beechey displayed was of "a young lady from the East Indies, Mrs Johnson" (Roberts, W. 1907, p48), matching the surname of the four children cited in John Cockerell's Will. However, there is nothing yet established to link the match of names between this portrait and that of his natural children. In the absence of further evidence, the match must be regarded simply as a coincidence.

Returning to the claim that John had an Indo-Portuguese mistress this may have been erroneously speculated because of some link with John's sister Paulina having lived and died in the Portuguese capital, Lisbon, or the fact that John later visited Lisbon. However, this visit in 1796 was explicitly for health reasons, and John's letters written from Lisbon solely reflect a lonely and disappointing attempt to alleviate his symptoms. Regardless of any conjecture, these references to Portugal underline one element of the historical context for this fourth generation, namely the expansion in foreign travel, trade and wider influences. Lisbon was a common transit port for long voyages to distant parts of the globe, and a recommended therapeutic temporary residence during the harsh British winters.

John's Last Will and Testament provides a little more insight into his life and family relationships, evidencing and acknowledging his responsibility for, and to, his illegitimate children. Equally clear is the lack of any provision for, or even mention of, the children's mother (or mothers). John presumably felt, or knew, that she (or they) could cope. Maybe he also felt that the facts of the children's births were a joint responsibility, and he was solely recording his share of responsibility.

Within the Will, once the commitments to his four natural children (a total of 80,000 rupees) and expenses of his funeral have been dealt with, he leaves each of his aunts, Susannah (sic) and Jane Jackson, the interest on £2,500 of Stock during their lifetimes. The remainder of his estate (including the property and land at 'Seasoncote') he bequeaths to his brothers and sister, namely Samuel Pepys Cockerell, Charles Cockerell, and Elizabeth Belli (nee Cockerell) in equal one third shares.

In summary, John's outlook on marriage, family, and children is far from straightforward. His letters show a strong desire for the companionship and security of 'family', and these letters also evidence his close friendship with several individuals both male and female. However, his choice of a military career made the possibility of a conventional marriage more challenging than for his brothers.

Charles, even though he similarly spent large parts of his youth and early adulthood in India, was operating predominantly in Calcutta, in contrast with John, often on military campaign, trekking across the subcontinent. Charles married in a conventional manner in India, but sadly his wife died not long after the marriage. It was only much later, back in England, that he remarried, had a family, and combined a settled domestic life with a high-profile public one, as outlined shortly. Contrasting with this, John's own comments on marriage indicate a reluctance to commit, and his preference to remain a bachelor.

By the time John was planning his return to England and retirement from the military, his letters frequently reference his declining health and energy. They also explicitly record his intention never to marry. His wishes are for a quiet and peaceful retirement, and his brother Samuel Pepys Cockerell, or simply 'Pepys' as his brothers called him, duly obliged in finding the Sezincote estate. It had great potential, and in its rather run-down state represented a project for which John expressed enthusiasm. Unfortunately, as noted, this was cut short by his death in 1798 with the project only in its early stages. Indeed, his ill-health had already caused work to be paused with only modest changes made, and it was his brother Charles who took over the project and steered it in a totally different and dramatic direction. It would become an iconic architectural landmark.

John's time in India, with huge responsibilities and onerous travel in an unfamiliar climate, put an enormous strain on his health – as it did for so many East India Company employees, whether operating in military or administrative roles. His letters from India to his brother Charles evidence increasing mental and physical fatigue, and they record his increasingly passionate, almost desperate, desire to retire back to England. The autopsy carried out after his early death aged 46, just 3 years after his return from India, reveals numerous physiological conditions which had obviously worn him down. The following details are recorded in the Cockerell family archive at the Bodleian Library.

An Account of the Appearances which were observed upon examining Colonel Cockerell's Body

The Head was first examined, & upon inspecting the Membranes of the Brain, one of them (called the Pia Mater) was found to be considerably thickened, & to be studded with very small white masses, not larger than the Heads of small Pins. – This change of Structure (which is very uncommon) did not extend over the whole of the Pia Mater, but was confined to that part of it, which covers the upper surface of the Brain. Under the Pia Mater, on the upper surface of the Brain, there was a considerable quantity of water, or serum, in some parts gelatinous, & in others bloody. The Dura Mater (which is another Membrane of the Brain), was sound in its Structure. – The Brain itself was healthy, except that it felt a little softer than usual, but there is great variety in this Respect in different Individuals. – The lateral ventricles (which are two considerable cavities in the Brain) contained nearly double the quantity of water which is usual in the healthy state – The other appearances connected with the Brain were natural. –– More than a pint of water or serum was found in the Chest, whereas, in the healthy state, no water whatever is found in that cavity. – The lungs were perfectly healthy, but the Heart was considerably enlarged beyond its natural size. – it was nearly a third part larger, & some of its valves, were become thickened by disease. –

Upon examining the Cavity of the Belly, the Liver was found to be harder than in its natural state, & was a little unequal upon its surface. – There was the beginning of a tuberculated or what is commonly called a Schirrous Liver, which in time would have formed a fatal disease – The anterior Surface of the Liver adhered also to the Diaphragm an Effect, which had been produced by some former inflammation in this Part – The Spleen may be said to have been nearly healthy; its coats were only a little thicker than is usual, in the most natural state of this part – The two Kidneys were a good deal smaller than usual, were harder in their texture than they ought to have been, & were studded upon their Surface with extremely small white tubercles – The other Contents of the Belly were sound. –

In reflecting upon these appearances, it is obvious, that the immediate cause of Coln. Cockerell's Death, was the collection of water or serum upon the upper surface of the Brain, & in the lateral ventricle, which was stated by Dr. Blane & Dr. Bailie as being highly probable, when the fits came on.

The Water in the Chest, was the cause of the difficulty of breathing, & which was also apprehended to have taken place for several days before Coln. Cockerell's Daeth. –

The enlargement of the Heart had taken place very gradually, & probably produced many of those uncomfortable feelings, which could not be very accurately described . –

The disease in the Liver, had not advanced far enough to occasion much uneasiness, but in time, it would certainly have proved fatal. – The disease in the Kidneys is very unusual; what progress it would have made in time, it is difficult to say, but most probably it would also have laid the foundation of a Fatal Disease. –

It is unusual in examining Bodies, to find so much disease accumulated in different parts; & it is very satisfactory to the Medical Attendants, that they had formed a correct opinion, both concerning the difficulty of breathing, & the cause of the Fits, which immediately produced Death.

London July 8th. 1798   *G.B.–M.B–*

John was not the only one to die shortly after returning from the rigours of time spent in India. The following year, 1799, Charles Barber, whose commercial activities in India interlinked with John's brother Charles, returned to England already suffering from an undiagnosed illness. Passing away later that year at the Adelphi in The Strand, London, he died a very wealthy man, his estate being worth approximately £60m in today's money. He, like Charles Cockerell, had operated on the administrative side of the East India Company presence in India and, like Charles, had a private trading agency alongside his EIC post. There were several such agencies based in Calcutta, the EIC's main commercial and financial hub. The potential profits from such private trading activities far exceeded their official EIC salaries. By contrast, Colonel John Cockerell, like other EIC military staff, had less opportunity for accumulating wealth in this way, not least because of his frequent military campaigns across southern India away from the main commercial hubs, notably Calcutta.

The next chapter, describing correspondence between John and his brothers in this late 18th and early 19th century period, includes far more detail about his time in India and return to England, but for now we conclude this brief sketch of his life. Although he had died in 1798 the last part of Colonel John Cockerell's history is not recorded until 1805, and comprises an account of his personal Estate, which had evidently taken years to

73

finalise. After all other bequests, funeral expenses etc. had been settled, this account forms the basis of the splitting of assets into thirds for distribution to his siblings Samuel Pepys Cockerell, Charles Cockerell, and Elizabeth Belli (nee Cockerell). As with many financial inheritances within the Cockerell family in the eighteenth and nineteenth centuries, male and female recipients were treated equally. In this instance each of the three siblings inherited nearly £10,000, a very considerable sum at that time.

1805   State of the personal Estate of the late Col. J Cockerell
         with a view to the division in thirds

		£ s d
Cash in Bankers hands		475.. 1.. 7
Cash in C. nobles??		88.. 12..6
£20,300 – 3prCt. Consols	ac 58 _	11,774 .. .. ..
Cash received or appropriated to his own		
a/c by S.P.Cockerell out of the		
proceeds of personal Estate balance	4684..12..3	
Interest thereon from time of		
Receipt to 1805 about	991..6........	
	_____	
	5675.. 18.. 3	
Cash received or appropriated by		
C.Cockerell balance in England		
about	800	
Cash paid Ditto and for sundries charged in		
Jn. Walfords Acct. Ladyday 1801 &c.	289.. 5.. 5½	
Cash in India in July 1800	4864.. 2.. 7	
Interest from the time of Rect.		
to 1805 above	1405.. 1.. ...	
	_____	
	7358.. 9.. 0½	
Cash received by Jn Belli	2127.. 12.. 3½	
Interest from the time of Receipt	393.. 10.. ..	
	_____	
	2521.. 2.. 3½	
	_____	

	T3	27,893.. 3.. 8

	Each third is	£ 9297.. 14.. 6½

| Mr S P Cockerell's third | | 9297.. 14.. 6½ |
| D?. to Cash received &c as above | | 5675.. 18.. 8 |

Remains due to him		3621.. 16.. 3½
Mr C Cockerell's third		9297.. 14.. 6½
D?. to Cash received &c as above		7358.. 9.. 0½

Remains due to him		1939.. 5.. 6
Mrs Belli's third	9297.. 14.. 6½	
D?. to Cash recd. &c as above	2521.. 2.. 3½	

	6776.. 12.. 3	

| Total due carried forwards | £ 12,337..14..0½ | |
| Total due brought forwards | | £ 12,337..14..0½ |

Assets to pay the above

Cash in Bankers hands	457.. 1.. 7
Cash in C. nobles	88..12..6
3 prCent Stock 20,300£ at	
58prCent	11, 774..14..1

£ 12,337..14..1 = 12,337..14..0½

There is also a sum of £600 on a Mortgage of an Estate at Bath and years Interest due thereon.

John's death, just when he was about to enjoy retirement and the fruits of his tough life, feels particularly tragically ill-timed. Having read John's many letters to family members and friends, and the personal insights they reveal about his character and feelings, his early death as the eldest of this close-knit sibling quartet must have affected Samuel ('Pepys'), Charles ('Carolus'), and Elizabeth ('Estuarta') deeply. He had been their Indian trailblazer, and they would have been all too aware that his involvement in the subcontinent had opened up opportunities and delivered additional wealth for them and their children. Even in an era when death was arguably faced with greater equanimity, and perhaps psychologically needed to be, it was a bitter blow. He was no doubt regarded by them as an exemplar of personal effort, sacrifice, and family duty. The evidence available, with his behaviour and letters offering the greatest insight, reflect an honourable, traditional, but not especially imaginative personality, in stark contrast to the complex psychology and actions of his famous 17th century relative Samuel Pepys.

Samuel Pepys Cockerell ('Pepys') (1754-1827) & his wife Anne (1757-1843)

The portrait of Anne (nee Whetham) is a detail from
the double portrait described later in the text.

Script (not shown here) at the bottom of Samuel's print image above reads: *'Painted by Sir Wm. Beechey, R. A. / Engraved by Thos. Hodgetts. / London. Published Aug. 9. 1824 by Hurst, Robinson & Co. 90 Cheapside, and T. Hodgetts, Westbourne Green, Paddington.'*

Samuel and Anne lived at Westbourne House, Paddington. Other portraits of Samuel Pepys Cockerell include the following:-

Samuel Pepys Cockerell, attributed to Sir William Beechey (Courtauld & NPG)

Profile of Samuel Pepys Cockerell by George Dance, engraved by William Daniell

Born in 1754, the second son of John and Frances, he had no choice in the decision to have Samuel Pepys as his two forenames. However, as well as adopting Pepys Cockerell as his effective surname he was sometimes known as just Mr Pepys, dropping the Cockerell element entirely. Most minimally of all, he was referred to simply as 'Pepys' by his family and others. The deliberate allusions to their 17th century relative Samuel Pepys are manifold. Linked with this, as the next heir in line he also inherited responsibility for curating Samuel Pepys's legacy, both tangible and intangible, and no doubt felt fully entitled to act as the 'Pepys' flagbearer. He proceeded to incorporate 'Pepys' in the names of two of his sons and, as already noted, the Pepys Cockerell sequence of Pepys heirs was to survive for well over 200 years through to the 21st century. The various tangible Samuel Pepys memorabilia held by these descendants together with their own accumulation of Cockerell family legacies, including portraits, became known as the Pepys Cockerell Collection. The records of a few family portraits are explicitly noted by the Courtauld Institute and the National Portrait Gallery as being part of this Pepys Cockerell Collection.

Remaining in England, in contrast with his brothers John and Charles's Indian exploits, 'Pepys' nevertheless led a very active and successful life, and his marriage to Anne Whetham produced eleven children, securing continuity of the Pepys Cockerell family associations and legacy.

Samuel's entry in the Dictionary of National Biography reads :-

COCKERELL, SAMUEL PEPYS (1754–1827), architect, was son of John Cockerell of Bishop's Hall, Somersetshire, by Frances Jackson, his wife, and brother of Sir Charles Cockerell, M.P., of Sezincote, Gloucestershire, who was created a baronet in 1809. His mother was daughter of John Jackson, the nephew and heir of Samuel Pepys, and through her Cockerell became the representative, and inherited many interesting relics, of the great diarist. He was a pupil of Sir Robert Taylor, and soon rose to eminence in his profession, gaining an extensive practice towards the end of the century. He held the appointment of surveyor to the East India House,and was district surveyor under the building acts of parliament, besides filling other important professional offices. He first exhibited at the Royal Academy in 1785, sending some designs for ornamental structures in the park of White Knights in Berkshire. He did not exhibit again till 1792, from which year up to 1803 he was a frequent contributor, chiefly of designs for mansions and churches. In 1796-8 he rebuilt the church of St. Martin Outwich, London, his most important work, some of the designs for which he sent to the Royal Academy. This church was pulled down in 1874. He built several large and handsome residences, and was employed in altering many more, among those designed or improved by him being Middleton Hall, Carmarthenshire, Gore Court, near Sittingbourne, Kent, and Nutwell Court, near Exeter. Cockerell lived at the house at the corner of Savile Row and Burlington Street, and latterly at Westbourne Lodge, Paddington, where he died on 12 July 1827, aged 74. He married Ann, daughter and coheiress of John Whetham of

St. Ives, by whom he had six sons and five daughters; one of his sons was Charles Robert Cockerell [q. v.], a far more distinguished architect than his father. Sir William Beechey painted a half-length portrait of Cockerell, which was engraved in mezzotint by Hodgetts, and published on 9 Aug. 1834. There is also a profile by George Dance, engraved by [William] Daniell.

[Redgrave's Dict. of Artists; Graves's Dict. of Artists, 1760-1880; Diary and Correspondence of Samuel Pepys, ed. Bright, Appendix; Builder, 26 Sept. 1863; Evans's Cat. of Portraits; Catalogues of the Royal Academy.]

It is a little surprising that although Sezincote House, Gloucestershire is mentioned in the entry above, his role as its architect in what was a ground-breaking project is absent. Sezincote, which he remodelled for his brother Charles, remains the only Indian style country house in Europe.

Detail from a painting of Sezincote by Thomas Daniell RA who collaborated with Samuel Pepys Cockerell on the project. (See also the rear book cover image.)

Samuel became a famous architect at a time when this occupation, although reasonably clearly understood, was not yet precisely defined or properly recognised as a formal profession. It was still very much the preserve of what could be termed gentlemen-designers. Its professional status in Britain was only formalised in the 1830s. The Cockerells, and particularly Samuel Pepys and his eldest son Charles Robert, were leading figures in the move towards formal professional recognition. Indeed, in 1848 Charles Robert Cockerell would be the first Gold Medal recipient of the newly formed Royal Institute of British Architects. As well as being architect to the East India Company and surveyor to St Paul's Cathedral, Samuel Pepys Cockerell also designed several London squares and other developments in the rapidly expanding West End. It is clear from letters between the brothers that he often took the lead in managing the family finances and property matters, including speculative purchases on their behalf.

In sketching his character there is ample evidence, as for the 17th century Samuel Pepys, of enthusiasm for the wider visual arts, including the theatre. The famous tragedienne actress Sarah Siddons was a tenant of one of his properties, and there was some friendly and jocular correspondence between them. A letter from Sarah Siddons sold at auction in 2008 is one such example.

SIDDONS SARAH: (1755-1831) British Actress. A.L.S., S. Siddons, three pages, 4to, Westbourne Farm, 28th March 1806, to *'My dear kind Mr. Cockerel'* (apparently Samuel Pepys Cockerell 1754-1827, English Architect and Siddons' landlord). The actress writes *'I am almost persuaded to flatter myself that you will lend a gracious ear to my petition, and send Bacephlus [*Bucephalus was the famous war horse of Alexander the Great*] to snort and champ and paw the ground, where he may not disturb the repose of your simple cottagers; If you do not, depend it I shall very soon call upon you to perform your promise of nursing me, for he will certainly make me ill for want of sleep. Now this woud be very bad for us both, no less dangerous to me, than troublesome to you, my dear friend, as I really want not that additional proof of your amiable disposition to make me love and esteem you very much already. But to come to the point, like a woman of business.'* and continues *'Seriously, now my dear Sir, as I hope if it please God not only to pass many years, but to finish my eventful life*

*under this roof, you cannot but see and feel that it is
a circumstance of great moment to my comfort and
convenience, (independent of the annoyance I complain
of) to be mistress of the whole space which it covers, and
in one word I shall be most happy to make you any
reasonable compensation, for that part of it which is now
a stable and with which I hope and believe your goodness
will contrive to accommodate.'* In a postscript Siddons
further states *'I know not how to speak or write upon these
subjects therefore pity any ignorance and do me the justice
to think I mean well. I will roof the house at my own
expense or pay an additional rent for the stable, whichever
your wisdom and justice shall determine.'*

It is clear from this that Sarah Siddons and Samuel Pepys Cockerell
were close friends and this is corroborated by Samuel Pepys
Cockerell's archives containing a ringlet of Sarah Siddons's
hair. Another close friend of Sarah Siddons was Humphry
Repton, the landscape architect, who worked alongside Samuel
Pepys Cockerell and Thomas Daniell in creating the Cockerells'
dramatic Indian Mughal styled Sezincote House and gardens. In
reference to these three high-profile and imaginative designers as
'prophets', influencing the slightly later Brighton Pavilion,
Musgrave comments,

> *'The Indian movement in this country had its nerve centre
> at a house near Moreton in Marsh in Gloucestershire
> called Sezincote. … Here were gathered, as at a sort of
> Regency Bauhaus, all the prophets of the new enthusiasm.'*

> [Musgrave, C., *Royal Pavilion*, 1951, p49]

The artist Sir Thomas Lawrence, with romantic links to Sarah
Siddons and her daughters, was also a friend. Samuel was clearly
well connected in London society at the turn of the 19th century
and commissioned or arranged several family portraits by well-
known artists, as well as purchasing paintings and prints on
behalf of other Cockerell family members. There are references
to these artworks in letters sent back and forth between England

and India in the 1780s and 1790s written by the three surviving Cockerell brothers, the third and youngest of whom, Charles, is considered shortly.

Samuel Pepys Cockerell's Will provides some additional information on family relationships. Much of the text concerns his estate at Woolley in Huntingdonshire, the rents and profits from which he leaves to his *'dear beloved wife Anna* (sic) *Cockerell'* for the rest of her life. The estate and its proceeds are then left to his sons in priority order of age. In a grant of discretion to his executors, they are given power to dispose of the estate or exchange it for another but only if the replacement is within 70 miles of London. He leaves specific monetary amounts to his sons and daughters, and for his three unmarried daughters he essentially also leaves them the lease on House No. 7 Burlington Street for as long as they or any one of them remains unmarried. One section of the lengthy Will is cited here, as it evidences just some of Samuel Pepys Cockerell's many property interests, in this case various leaseholdings.

> *I give and bequeath to my son Charles Robert Cockerell my two other leasehold houses No. 8 and No. 9 Burlington Street for the term unexpired of the leases thereof at my death subject to the payment of the ground rents and to the performance of the covenants of the said leases the garden now extending the whole breadth next to Saville Row being held by separate leases with the three several houses No. 7, 8 and 9 are to belong to each severally according to the respective leases by which I hold the same.*

As well as these specific property interests and his estate at Woolley, numerous other property holdings are itemised. Managing all these must have taken up much of his, or his associates, time and attention. Alongside these property interests is, of course, his profession as an architect, and in his Will he pays tribute to his architectural mentor, the eminent Sir Robert Taylor.

…. and whereas by the non-retroactive Will of my late honoured friend and Master Sir Robert Taylor deceased the affectionate profound support of my early steppes and to whom under providence I was chiefly indebted for my first advancement in life I am entitled to the sum of one thousand pounds payable out of his estate on the contingency of his son Michael Angelo Taylor Esquire dying without issue I do hereby give the said contingent legacy to the said Michael Angelo Taylor if he be living at my death and so request his acceptance of twenty pounds for a ring

Without reviewing all the details of his Will here, some summarising comments are appropriate. Firstly, it is clear from the nature and scale of bequests and legacies that he was a very wealthy man, having accumulated substantial property ownerships and interests together with significant disposable financial assets. Secondly, he was determined to make provisions for the wide family network for whom he felt responsibilities. Having had eleven children and with several of these themselves producing children, with potentially more after his death, it is no surprise that his Will is lengthy and complex, aiming to cover both current and future family needs and benefits.

As previously indicated, there is a strong indication that he was central to much of the wider family's management of financial matters. Taken together with other indications of his abilities and talents as an architect and property developer, networker, and patron of the arts, all the evidence suggests he was the family's ringmaster, particularly so with his brothers pursuing their careers in India. While his death therefore left something of a vacuum, younger family members subsequently proved themselves perfectly capable of filling this void and leaving their own indelible marks on the impressive family narrative. One of Samuel Pepys Cockerell's intangible legacies was his enthusiasm and talent for the visual arts, both as practitioner and sponsor, and this passion was passed on to, and admirably developed by, his sons and grandsons. Their stories are outlined shortly.

Sir Charles Cockerell ('Carolus') (1755-1837)

A young Charles Cockerell, in a portrait dated 1786

Born on 18th February 1755 at the Cockerell's family home in Bishop's Hull, Somerset, Charles was the younger brother of Colonel John Cockerell and Samuel Pepys Cockerell, and fifth child of John Cockerell and Frances Cockerell (nee Jackson). His early life had its challenges; aged 10, his father was in prison in London, died in Antigua when Charles was just 12, and two years later his mother also passed away. He was educated at Winchester School and probably grew up physically somewhat distant from his parents. This would not have been unusual at the time, and like many other upper middle-class children his upbringing would have encouraged and developed determination, resilience, and self-responsibility. He certainly squandered little of a life full of ambition, enterprise, and success in several diverse fields and environments.

Charles had close and positive relationships with his elder brothers John and Samuel Pepys but rejected following either of their military or artistic career directions. However, John's earlier decision to join the East India Company would have given Charles, three years younger, an insight into the potential opportunities that the Company offered. John's departure to India also resulted in his brother Samuel ('Pepys') assuming responsibility in Britain for their famous relative Samuel Pepys's legacy, leaving Charles free to choose his own path. It is clear from his future achievements that Charles was bright, willing to take risks, able to exploit family connections and would have had many career options both in Britain and abroad. The lure of India at that time, with its exotic aura, promise of adventure, and tales of rapid wealth creation, was an obvious magnet and, with his elder brother John already established there, perhaps the many well-known risks of going to the subcontinent seemed less daunting. The potential rewards were certainly well documented and already realised by family and friends.

An administrative post was the standard route to leveraging the financial potential, and Charles was to embrace and capitalise on this to a degree that few others matched. So, like John, he entered the service of the East India Company and rose to be a prominent and influential figure in its increasingly dominant trading, military, and administrative operations in India. Arriving in India in 1776, he started, like so many others, as a 'writer' or lowly administrator, attached to the surveyor-general's office based in Calcutta. Perhaps through existing family connections or those established in India by his elder brother John, he was befriended by Warren Hastings and Richard Wellesley, 1st Marquess Wellesley. With their influential support he rose rapidly through various senior positions to become Postmaster General of Bengal in 1784, holding this post until 1792.

This prestigious position was well remunerated, but his main accumulation of wealth derived from private trading activities, which he operated in parallel with his official duties. In 1784 Charles became a partner in the agency house created by William Paxton, and subsequently managed the Calcutta house, trading as Paxton and Cockerell. This later became Paxton, Cockerell and Trail, *'the most successful agency concern of its time'*(ODNB). Charles was a shrewd and increasingly influential figure in the commercial world of Bengal. As Fiona Spear comments :-

> *Charles was a great networker with friends in high places. These included the first Governor General of India, Warren Hastings, and Richard Wellesley, older brother of The Duke of Wellington. Wellesley later became Governor General and was notorious for his military expansion in India. The agency house of Paxton, Cockerell and Trail financed Wellesley's campaign against Tipu Sultan in the Fourth Mysore War 1798-99. Charles was rewarded for this by Wellesley supporting Charles's elevation to Baronetcy in 1809.*

As well as links with Warren Hastings, the Cockerells were on very friendly terms with the Blunt family, as evidenced by several Cockerell family letters. In March 1789, in his mid-thirties and now well-established in Calcutta society, Charles married Maria Tryphena Blunt, daughter of Sir Charles William Blunt, 3rd Baronet.

Tragically, Maria died in November the same year. The psychological impact of this must have been huge, and one consequence may have been that Charles threw himself even more determinedly into his work and the pursuit of his ambitions. Even after he returned to England in 1801 it would not be until 1808, in his early 50s, that he married again on February 13th, to the Hon. Harriet Rushout, daughter of John Rushout, 1st Baron Northwick. Between 1761 and 1796 John Rushout was MP for Evesham, a position that Charles would eventually emulate.

Maria Tryphena Blunt, Charles Cockerell's first wife

Charles and Harriet had one son and two daughters. His children from that marriage, born into an educated, wealthy, and stable family environment, flourished as the long Georgian period ended and the Victorian age dawned. As well as these formal marriages, there is evidence from letters between the brothers (see Chapter 6) that Charles, like his brother John, had a relationship in India which produced illegitimate children. As previously noted, such relationships were very common for East India Company personnel.

Having returned to England and left such matters behind, Charles's business focus continued to be primarily as a partner in the agency house Messrs Paxtons Cockerell Trail & Co., a commercial organisation operating with matching offices in India and Britain. Such 'agency houses' were commercial organisations facilitating trade and transmission of funds between India and Britain, treading carefully to avoid East India Company business and monopoly interests. Fiona Spear provides an excellent summary:-

After the India Act 1784, EIC servants were no longer permitted to trade privately. To compensate, their salaries were increased substantially. Previously, they had conducted their own business deals and remitted money back to Britain using the Company's financial channels. It had been a very lucrative side-line.

With Company business channels closed to them, EIC servants had to find a new way to invest savings and send money home. This gave the perfect opportunity for free merchants, like William Paxton, to set up a new commercial organisation, the agency house, offering banking facilities and remitting money back Britain. Free merchants were allowed to trade as long as their interests did not interfere with the EIC monopoly, instead they dealt in 'country trade', i.e. opium, cotton, indigo, and salt.

Agency houses would have a sister house in London, which would sell cargoes imported from India and invest the profits or make payments to investors or investors' relations in Britain. The investor would be given a bill of exchange which could be cashed in at the sister agency house in Britain. At that time it was extremely difficult to exchange foreign currency. People travelling back to

Britain would have had to find other means of carrying convertible currency such as diamonds or gold which could be sold once they reached their destination. These would have been difficult to keep safe on the long journey home. Bills of exchange were easier and safer to carry or send on.

The sister agency houses in London were often managed by partners who had retired home from India. The Agency House proprietors became a powerful interest group in the East India Company's Courts of Proprietors and Directors.

By providing financial services to EIC employees, agency house proprietors, like William Paxton, became very important people in the community, indispensable to the wealthiest and most powerful officials. Paxton, Cockerell & Trail financed Governor-General Richard Wellesley, older brother of Arthur, Duke of Wellington, in the war against Tipu Sultan of Mysore in 1798-1799. This conflict dramatically increased the territory of the EIC.

[https://botanicgarden.wales/2020/01/paxton-agency-houses/]

The third member joining the Paxton and Cockerell core partnership was Henry Trail. In March 1776 Henry went to Quebec as chief assistant to the Purveyor General of the Hospitals in Canada, Mr William Barr, and remained there till Oct 1782. He returned to London in December 1782, but before long he was travelling again, sailing for India on 12th March 1783. Arriving in Calcutta on 8th September, he joined Mr P Delisle's House of Agency, and on 1st August 1787 became a partner in the United Firms of Paxton, Cockerell and Delisle. Mr Delisle died in 1788.

Having flourished in India for nearly twenty years, Henry Trail set off for Europe on 19th December 1802 with his wife, daughter, and son. The voyage from India took several months and after arriving in London on 26th May 1803, he took his place as a partner of the Agency House of Paxtons, Cockerell & Trail, with offices at No. 57 Pall Mall (see image below) and 8 Austin Friars. In addition to its trading activities the partnership also operated effectively as a bank, issuing its own credit notes from 1813 to 1820. The 1814 example here is from the British Banking History Society website.

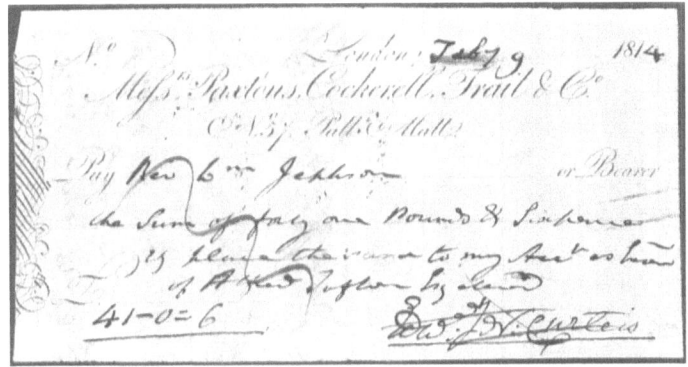

The other partner, Sir William Paxton, had links with Charles's brother Samuel Pepys Cockerell ('Pepys'), employing him to design the neo-classical Middleton Hall, Paxton's country residence in Wales, built between 1793 and 1795. 'Pepys' also designed the nearby Paxton Tower, built in a prominent position to reflect Paxton's pride in his achievements and status. The site now hosts the National Botanic Garden of Wales, encompassing the remaining part of the Cockerell-designed Middleton Hall. Paxton Tower still sits proudly overlooking the site.

Fiona Spear notes that after Charles Cockerell returned to Britain in 1801,

he kept his business ties with India, overseeing the British arm of the agency house. He was a stockholder in EIC and was Commissioner of the Board of Control in 1835 and 1837. Charles had various business interests in Britain including, along with William Paxton, directorship of The Gas, Light and Coke Company. Another of Charles's business interests was the establishment of passenger ships travelling to India which were partly steam powered, making journeys faster.

Sir William Paxton

These latter interests illustrate Charles's enthusiasm for moving with the times, seizing and exploiting new opportunities made possible by the dramatic development in technologies emerging over his lengthy, active, and eventful life.

There is a wealth of evidence that Charles Cockerell was an effective and shrewd operator, particularly influential and successful in the world of business and finance. Combining interests in India and Britain, he accumulated substantial wealth, enabling him to purchase and develop a prestigious estate and marry into a socially well-established Cotswold family, combining his 'new wealth' with historic inherited assets. He had succeeded in erasing any social shame attaching to his father's questionable West Indies commercial and financial affairs, establishing for his family a solid foundation of wealth, social status, and political influence. In doing so, he was happy to forge his own identity, leaving the links with his famous 17th century antecedent Samuel Pepys, and the diarist's various associated legacies, to the care of his brother Samuel Pepys Cockerell.

Charles had always forged his own distinctive and dynamic agenda, constantly seeking, adapting to, and exploiting new challenges. At the same time as his family life was flourishing, the political phase of his multi-faceted life was gaining ground. Now settled back in England, he was MP for various constituencies between 1802 and 1837, was created a baronet in 1809, served as Mayor of Evesham in 1810, again in 1833, and was Sheriff of Gloucestershire, 1814-15. In being elected MP for Evesham (as his father-in-law had been), his financial clout had played a part, as it did in most election processes in Georgian England, and he rewarded his key supporters accordingly.

1819 medal, with Evesham image,
presented by Charles Cockerell to his political supporters

*Sir Charles Cockerell, by George Taylor (1780-1873),
incorporating a large painting of Evesham,
for which he was MP*

Approaching old-age, Charles must have felt that he had achieved his main ambitions, which always had at their heart financial business interests, political influence, and social status. The large portrait below of a thoughtful, perhaps reflective, Charles with his family, by Sir Thomas Lawrence, also hints at the confidence and pride of a successful man.

91

Sir Charles Cockerell and family
Part of a painting by Sir Thomas Lawrence RA

While he was fortunate with the opportunities and advantages inherited through his family and upbringing, many Georgian gentlemen frittered away similar good fortune whereas Charles showed great determination and resilience, not only in risking his life and future in India but also when confronted with the early deaths of his parents and, most tragically, his first wife within a year of their marriage.

Much of the Cockerells' wealth in this fourth generation was generated by their commercial 'agency house' which exploited the opportunities for Indian trading. The agency house partnership emerging eventually as Messrs. Cockerell Trail & Co experienced many changes of partners from the late 18th century through well into the 19th, and a document clarifies the position in April 1824. Explicitly noting that Sir William Paxton had died, one of the new partners is John Cockerell Esq, but it is not known for certain whether this is Charles's nephew John Cockerell (1789-1869), which seems most likely, or another family member. An extract from the document gives key details :-

Messrs. Cockerell Trail & Co.   *Instrons. for Articles of Copartnership*
April 1824   Between   *Sir Charles Cockerell of the   1st part*
                                      Henry Trail Esq. of the   2nd part
                                      John Cockerell Esq of the   3rd part
                                      George Gerard de
                                      Hochefued Larpeul Esq. of   4th part and
                                      William Lumley Esq. of   5th part

Reciting that Sir Charles Cockerell Henry Trail John Cockerell George Gerard de Hochefued Larpent & Wm. Lumley have for several years carried on business in Copartnership with Sir Wm Paxton under the Firm of Paxton Cockerell Trail & Co which Firm in Consequence of the death of Sir Wm Paxton will cease on the 30th April instant

Also that said Sir Charles Cockerell Henry Trail John Cockerell George Gerard de Hochefued Larpeut and Wm Lumley have agreed to continue the said business for the Term of 5 years from 1st May next subject to such alterations and stipulations as after mentioned

It is Witnessed that said parties shall continue Copartners for said Term of Five years if all the parties or any two of them shall so long live and said Copartnership shall not be sooner determined under the Powers after contained

Proportions of Capital Viz.
Sir Charles Cockerell	*52000*
Henry Trail	*52000*
John Cockerell	*38000*
George Gerard de Hichefued Larpeut	*36000*
William Lumley	*26000*
	£ 204,000

The Firm "Cockerell Trail & Co"

That all debts Contracted or owing by said Copartners on account of said joint Trade or losses or Damages which may

*happen or the Gains or produce thereof by bad debts or
Losses and all House Rent Taxes Salaries & other Expences
shall be borne by the profits or by said Copartners according*

*To their respective shares and that all profits shall be
divided between the said Copartners and their respective
Exors &c. in the proportions in after mentioned*

*That Partners shall not release Debts nor purchase
Stocks &c. in without the consent of the other Partners*

*Books to be kept and annual accounts made up on the
30April in each year and subscribed by the partners*

*And upon completing such accounts there shall be set
apart out of the net profits of the said Business as a Fund
for securing or meeting any loss by bad debt or otherwise
26/128 parts of such profits and after the setting apart the
same the residue of such profits to be divided into the
remaining 102 parts as follows*

Sir Charles Cockerell	26
Henry Trail	26
John Cockerell	19
George Gerard de Hochefued Larpeul	18
William Lumley	13
	102
Appropriated as above	26
	128

Charles died in 1837, and having lived in the reigns of George II,
George III, George IV, and William IV, Charles failed by only a few
months to survive into the Victorian period. The text of Charles's
Will gives some additional insight into his life and family relations.
It is far shorter and less complex than many of the other family
Wills and leaves his wife with possession of his main estates,
together with the income from them, until she dies or remarries,
at which time his son inherits. The opening section of the Will
provides helpful information about the Cockerells' property
ownership, and the following passage emphasises how important

family portraits, mainly hanging in their own properties, were regarded. It specifically notes that,

'I am entitled to an equal share with my late brother Samuel Pepys Cockerell of all the family pictures which belonged to or were in the possession of my late aunts Susan and Jane Jackson and which I have permitted to remain in the house at Westbourne Green and which I still wish to remain there during the occupancy of the house by Lord Hill the present tenant thereof should he continue such up to and after my decease',

... going on to specify what should happen to his half share of these pictures. This indicates that a significant volume (if not all) of the family pictures coming down both the Jackson and Cockerell lines had latterly been in the possession of the two Jackson aunts (Susanna and Jane) featured earlier, and that these were still hanging in the large Westbourne Green house, which had been the main home of his brother Samuel Pepys Cockerell (1754-1827). Several of those pictures in the half share which went to his brother, and his brother's heirs, eventually ended up in the ownership of the last of the Pepys Cockerell branch of the family, Elizabeth Pepys Cockerell. As noted elsewhere, after her death, and with no obvious heirs, the remaining Pepys and Cockerell artefacts were sold at auction in 2019.

In Charles's Will there is also an instruction that if the *'curious picture of Samuel Pepys'* falls within his half share, it should go to his nephew Samuel Pepys Cockerell (1794-1869). This 'curious picture' is probably the rather odd one reproduced in the front of the 1926-published 'Private Correspondence' and explicitly noted as being then in the possession of J Pepys Cockerell Esq., having passed down through the family generations.

Although the lives of the three brothers John, Samuel Pepys, and Charles were so eventful and well-documented that focus on them naturally takes priority, the other siblings, and particularly Elizabeth Stuart Cockerell, deserve their share of coverage. Continuing to work chronologically through the brothers and sisters, Edward is next.

Edward Cockerell (1756-1782)

Edward was the sixth child and fourth son of John and Frances Cockerell. Born a year after Charles on 1st November 1756, Edward wasn't baptised until 14th April 1757. One secondary source gives his year of death as 1837, the year of Queen Victoria's accession to the throne, the year his brother Charles also died. These two brothers were very much of the Georgian upper middle class and, although sad, their joint demise at the end of that era and the dawn of the Victorian era would seem somehow appropriate. However, the limited evidence available makes the claimed date of death of 1837 extremely unlikely.

He was certainly still alive in 1770, as he appears in the granting of administration of his mother Frances's Will at that date. Another secondary source gives Edward's year of death as 1782, aged about 25, and this seems more likely because no marriage or other records of life events of any sort have been identified, and nor does Edward feature in the review of various Cockerell correspondence archives, or indeed in the Wills of his siblings. His relatively early death would also tally with the fact that he is not mentioned when pivotal moments occur within the wider family, such as Charles's buying out of his siblings shares of the Sezincote estate after the death of John Cockerell in 1798.

Elizabeth Stuart Cockerell ('Estuarta') (1758-1842)

Elizabeth was born on May 28th, 1758, and baptized on August 28th that year at Bishops Hull, Somerset, the Cockerells' main home. We know little of her childhood, but she would have had all the benefits accruing from her family's social and financial status. However, along with reaching adulthood came the expectation of achieving a suitable marriage, and this wasn't always easy, as the pool of potential suitors was limited when impeccable social standing and financial security were deemed essential. Marriages were often arranged between related families or very close existing family friendship groups. Where this failed, or better opportunities were anticipated elsewhere, the net was often cast wider, sometimes outside Britain, and this was Elizabeth's route in search of a marriage.

*Elizabeth Stuart Cockerell (later Mrs Belli), aged 18 or 19
by Horace Hone ARA, and dated 1777*

Following in the footsteps of her brothers John and Charles, and presumably encouraged by their initial positive reports, she embarked on the long and arduous voyage to India. She first married Bryan Glover, a free merchant, in Calcutta, Bengal, on 9th April 1779. This marriage may have been proposed before she sailed. Going to India to seek an advantageous marriage, or execute one that had been pre-arranged, was a well-established practice at this time, and Jane Austen incorporates an example of this exact scenario in her early writing. East India Company ships carrying numbers of such single aspiring females, aiming to catch a suitable husband, became known colloquially as 'the fishing fleet'.

The potential for positive outcomes, whether advantageous marriages or accumulation of wealth, had to be weighed against the considerable risks, not only those posed by the long voyages but also, after arrival, constant dangers to health from the impact of unfamiliar diseases, climate, and environment. Death rates were extremely high, and Elizabeth's husband Bryan Glover unfortunately died on 18th March 1780, less than a year after their marriage. Unlike her brother Charles, also suffering the loss of a spouse in India in the first year of marriage, she would soon remarry. Young single females from respectable British families were well-positioned to find partners among the East India Company community, and the following year, aged 23, Elizabeth married the 41-year-old John Belli on 20th November 1781 in Lucknow, Uttar Pradesh.

Elizabeth's second marriage was a particularly attractive match, at least in financial and status terms. John Belli was Secretary to Warren Hastings, Governor General of British India. Elizabeth's brothers, John and Charles, were already forming connections with powerful figures in India, and her marriage strengthened Cockerell family links with the most influential individuals at the heart of the expanding British military, trading and administrative network. The Cockerell family letters reference portraits of Elizabeth and John Belli after their marriage, but these have not been traced. The portrait of Elizabeth in her late teens at the start of this section is the only one of either of them so far identified. As noted earlier, in their informal family letters Elizabeth Stuart Cockerell is frequently referred to as Estuarta, the family nickname apparently derived, as noted already, from her first initial and second forename (E Stuart) with an 'a' added for phonetic neatness. Occasionally, they referred to her in letters using the even shorter name 'Stuart'.

Elizabeth and John Belli had seven children between 1783 and 1791. The first, Elizabeth, named after her mother, was born in 1783, and Paulina followed in 1784. The third child, Mary

Frances, was born in either 1783 or 1784 and was perhaps a twin of either Elizabeth or Paulina. In due course, each of these three daughters secured a prestigious marriage and lived in privileged circumstances, not only in comfort and wealth but also mixing in high-profile and cultured society circles. These three daughters, as well as marrying well, also feature in some fine portraits (shown later) by leading contemporary artists, Elizabeth's and Paulina's by Thomas Lawrence in the very early 1800s, and Mary Frances's by Margaret Carpenter slightly later. The next child was John Henry Belli, born in 1786, followed by George Lawrence Belli (1787), William Hallowes Belli (1790), and Charles Almeric Belli (1791). Their stories are related in Chapter 7 covering the next generation.

After Colonel John Cockerell died in 1798, his siblings Elizabeth, Charles, and Samuel Pepys inherited equal shares of John's Sezincote estate, and Elizabeth was presumably a willing participant in the associated family agreement which saw Charles buy the Sezincote shares of both her and her brother Samuel Pepys. This is an agreement that most sources allude to, without any mention of the other siblings, notably Edward. Again, it seems almost certain that he had already died.

Elizabeth's husband, John Belli, having returned to England, died in 1805, and Elizabeth lived thereafter as a widow, the terms of her husband's Will leaving her well provided for, stipulating that she should receive all the income and profits from his personal estate, comprising both properties and securities. Before his death, Elizabeth had lived for some time in a property John owned in Southampton. While John was still in India, she and her young children had also lived for a short period with her brother Colonel John Cockerell at Hyde Park Corner. After John's death there is evidence that she maintained residences both in London and Addington Park, Surrey, with an extensive and wealthy family network for support and companionship.

Later in life, Elizabeth appears in the Land Tax returns in 1833 with her residence given as being in the parish of St George Hanover Square, London, but her last years were spent at yet another location, and a very special one. In the 1841 census, Elizabeth Belli is entered as age 83, residing with her daughter and husband, the Archbishop of Canterbury, at the prestigious Lambeth Palace (his official residence). Described as living by 'Independent

Means', it appears she was residing at Lambeth Palace only for the last two or three years of her life, presumably on health grounds or simply old age frailty, so that she could be cared for by her daughter Mary Frances Howley (whose life is covered in the next generation). Mary is recorded in this 1841 census as aged 55, with her 75-year-old husband William (Howley) described as head of the household at Lambeth Palace. In the census he is entered as Wm. Cantuar, his correct legal title as Archbishop of Canterbury, Cantuar being the Latin for Canterbury.

Also included in this same census for Lambeth Palace is Henry Carrington, age 25, and whose profession is entered as 'The Church', so he appears, through family connections, to have secured a prime ecclesiastical post at Lambeth Palace early in his church career. He is almost certainly Elizabeth's grandson, son of her daughter Paulina, who had married Sir Codrington Edmund Carrington. Their stories are covered in later chapters focused on the next two generations.

After a long and eventful life, Elizabeth Stuart Belli, nee Cockerell, died in 1842 and was buried at Holy Trinity Church in the Parish of Clapham on October 29th that year, with the burial record giving her age as 84. Her official abode was given as Addington Park, Surrey, Elizabeth having retained its ownership while she was being housed and cared for at Lambeth Palace. Her Clapham burial reflects the Cockerell family's long connection with this location from at least the 1600s, as indicated earlier.

We are fortunate in having access to Elizabeth's Last Will and Testament, which gives valuable insights into her life and family. Her Will was proved on 14th December 1842, with probate duly granted, and her residence recorded in a codicil as '*late of Eaton Square but now residing at Lambeth Palace*', so she obviously had previously lived both in London and at Addington Park in Surrey, representing her 'Town' and 'Country' residences.

The Will and its two codicils are very long and detailed, evidencing the large numbers of relatives and the close personal links between them. There is a sense of mutual respect and pride, and the document explicitly records Elizabeth's strong desire to recognise all these individuals in what was to be her last earthly statement. Although her children and their descendants carry her husband's name Belli, therefore forming a distinction from the Cockerell and Pepys Cockerell family branches, there was at least one marriage connection between these different branches in later generations.

Elizabeth outlived most of those in this fourth generation and would have suffered much grief and mourning following the early death of her first husband and many deaths of family members during her lifetime, not least her second husband John and her daughters Paulina and Elizabeth. However, she lived long enough to see many of the next generation, including her surviving children, growing up, maturing, and establishing themselves as influential historic figures. It was a lifetime which encompassed many significant events and changes both within her wider family circle and in the world around her. The Industrial and Agricultural Revolutions were dramatically impacting on multiple aspects of day-to-day living including more efficient food production and variety, and new labour-saving machinery and devices. The range of imported goods was constantly and impressively expanding, and travel became much easier, with improved turnpike roads and the introduction of the railways.

When William IV died in 1837, it had been Elizabeth's son-in-law, William, as Archbishop of Canterbury, who formally informed the young Victoria that she was now the new monarch. Although Elizabeth lived the last five years of her life in this early Victorian age, much of the elegance of the Georgian period still prevailed at her death, at least in the environments frequented by her social and economic class. Hers was a richly varied and privileged life both in India and England at a time when Britain was emerging as a world leader. In this context, her husband's role as Warren Hastings' Private Secretary in India had been significant, and his life is now briefly traced.

Disappointingly, and surprisingly given his status and influential position, no image of **John Belli (1736-1805)** has been identified. His entry in the Dictionary of Indian Biography is as follows:-

Born in England, of a noble Italian family, probably of Viterbo, his mother being a lady of Spanish origin named Bivar: entered the E. I. Co's. service and became Private Secretary to Warren Hastings, about 1770–5: he married a sister of Sir Charles Cockerell; his daughters married Dr. Howley, Archbishop of Canterbury; E. Horsley Palmer, M.P. and Sir C. E. Carrington (q.v.)

Brought up in a family with illustrious European heritage, John Belli led a colourful life. Like many other young men with an eye to opportunities for advancement, he joined the East India Company and sailed out to India. Through invaluable connections and his own abilities, he established an influential position as Private Secretary to Governor General Warren Hastings at the heart of the rapidly expanding Company interests in the subcontinent. During his lifetime the ethics of these interests were increasingly being questioned by politicians back in Britain, but the private legal status of the Company meant that Government interference and control was extremely limited for much of the eighteenth century. This changed with the passing of William Pitt the Younger's India Act (1784), which established the dual system of control by the East India Company and the British government. The Company retained control of commerce and day-to-day administration, but important political matters were reserved to a secret committee of three directors in direct contact with the British government. The actions of the East India Company, and Warren Hastings in particular, became a highly emotive political issue, and Hastings was the subject of a lengthy trial after his return to Britain. As his Private Secretary, John Belli's records and memories of Hastings' conduct in India were important pieces of evidence. Hastings was eventually acquitted, after proceedings which lasted for several years – the longest political trial in British history.

John Belli and the widowed Elizabeth Stuart Glover (nee Cockerell) married on 20th November 1781 in Calcutta, Bengal. John Belli died aged 68 on 20th February 1805 at Baker Street, Portland Square, and was buried on 27th February at Holy Trinity Church at Clapham, a location with particularly strong Cockerell family connections, and where Samuel Pepys, the diarist, had spent most of the last three years of his life.

As well as the above information, we have the text of John Belli's Will which potentially could have shed more light on his life and particularly his relatives. However, while it evidences substantial property holdings, it does little to provide any personal insights, other than confirming equal treatment of his sons and daughters when leaving money after his death. He leaves his wife Elizabeth all the income from his assets for the rest of her life, which was standard practice at the time. The assets themselves were not within her control. It also evidences that his main property was at Southampton, providing further corroboration that his wife Elizabeth Stuart (Belli, nee Cockerell) is one and the same person as the Estuarta referenced in her brothers' Cockerell letters as living for long periods with her children at Southampton. Specific bequests in the Will are substantial, reflecting the wealthy status of the wider family.

Frances Cockerell (1760-1784?)

Frances was the last of the known children of John Cockerell and Frances (nee Jackson), and she is another for whom the records are sparse. Official church records note her birth on 11th February 1760 and baptism on 4th August that year. Beyond that, no other official records have been identified, although other genealogical researchers state her death as being in 1784, without any specific or decisive supporting evidence. Again, this early death would tally with the evidence that Samuel Pepys, Charles, and their sister Elizabeth, were the only siblings surviving through to the time of their brother John's death in 1798.

Having outlined skeleton profiles of the key characters in this fourth generation, mainly comprising Samuel Pepys's great great nephews and nieces, several letters between the brothers not only provide further factual details of matters affecting them but also include personal and family insights. The next chapter is devoted to these family letters, after which the chronological approach is resumed with the Fifth Generation.

CHAPTER SIX

Family Letters

Letter writing was a routine, often daily, activity for the educated classes over an extended historic period before other communication methods became available. Given the sheer volume and frequency of letters written during this later Georgian period, a high level of survival would have provided a wealth of information about the individual family members. Although the vast majority of these have been inevitably lost or disposed of over time, some collections of accumulated letters and associated documents have fortunately been deposited in publicly accessible archives, notably at the Bodleian Library in Oxford and the RIBA Library in London. Between them, these archives hold a substantial number of letters from John Cockerell to his brothers Samuel Pepys Cockerell and Charles Cockerell. These include many references to other family members and friends, and provide glimpses into the priorities, thoughts, and concerns of these wealthy, well-connected, and well-travelled members of society in the late 18th and early 19th centuries.

A selection of extracts from these letters is given here, chosen to provide an overview of the topics which reflect their way of life and mindsets during a period of dramatic global change, politically, militarily, economically, and culturally. Letters to and from India form a large portion of this chapter, and many of the selection set out here follow John through the critical years of his active service in India, his return to England, and the last few years of his eventful life. A chronological approach is followed as far as possible.

Letter Extracts

During John Cockerell's early years of service in India with the East India Company army, he has the rank of Captain and appears in a formal letter dated '10th Feby. 1779' from the army's camp. His brother Charles, who was also then serving as an administrator in India, is also referenced. The extract evidences the influential status of the Cockerell brothers, and their connections with Warren Hastings.

To the Honble. Warren Hastings Esq. Governor General &ca. Members of the Supreme Council, Fort William Gentlemen

At Ten days sight please to pay this my first Bill of Exchange (the second and third of same tenor and date being unpaid) to Lieutenant Alexander Apsley, or order, the sum of Current Rupees Two Thousand three Hundred and Nineteen, fourteen Annas, three Pic (Ct.Rs. 2319.14.3) for value received into the Honble. Company's Treasury as per? Advices from

Gentlemen
Your most Obdt. Hble. Servant
Camp 10th Feby. 1779   *[Signed] Thos Goddard*

On reverse of same paper document :-
Pay the contents to Capt. John Cockerell or order —--
A. Apsley
Pay the Contents to Mr Charles Cockerell or to his order —--
Jhn. Cockerell

By 1781, John has been promoted to the rank of Major. One large formal printed and annotated document lodged amongst the Cockerell papers at the Bodleian Library and personally signed by Warren Hastings and Edward Wheler, acknowledges significant amounts owed to Major John Cockerell. It dates from May 1781. The following extract captures the key points.

[Official Red Wax Stamp]

KNOW ALL MEN by these Presents, that We the United Company of Merchants of ENGLAND trading to the East Indies, are held and firmly bound unto Major John Cockerell in the penal Sum of Current Rupees Eighty Thousand of good and lawful Money of Bengal aforesaid, to be paid to the said John Cockerell or his certain Attorney, Executors, Administrators, or Assigns; for which Payment well and truly made, We do hereby bind ourselves, and our Successors firmly by these Presents; IN WITNESS whereof Warren Hastings Esquire the Governor General, and Edward Wheler Esquire Counsellor of the said Presidency of FORT WILLIAM, acting on the part and behalf of the said United Company, have hereunto and to two other parts hereof of the same Tenor and Date herewith, set their Hands and caused the Seal of the said United Company to be affixed this Sixteenth Day of May in the Year of Christ One Thousand, Seven Hundred, and Eighty one

WHEREAS the said John Cockerell on the Day of the Date of the above written Obligation, hath well and truly paid into the Treasury of the said United Company at FORT WILLIAM aforesaid, for and on the account of the said United Company, the Sum of Current Rupees Forty Thousand (as equal to the Sum of Pounds Sterling Four Thousand of lawful Money of Great Britain aforesaid, at the rate of Exchange of Two Shillings the Current Rupee) and which Money hath been paid on a proposed Remittance to Europe, upon the Terms, and Subject to the Stipulations herein after contained.

....
Signed SEALED and DELIVERED   *Warren Hastings*
                                                              Edwd. Wheler

*(where no Stamps are in use
or to be had) in the Presence of*

                        D Anderson
                        C Cotter
                        John Benn
                        John Rathay
                        Edw C Crosley

The inherent difficulties of managing financial affairs in India were exacerbated by other global factors, with wars between European powers causing nervousness for all concerned. The following extract from one of John's letters to his brother Charles, sent from Bombay and dated 3rd July 1781, reflects this apprehension. The Dutch War referred to is the Fourth Anglo-Dutch War (1780-1784) and resonates with the Anglo-Dutch Wars a century earlier with which the diarist Samuel Pepys had been so closely associated. This latest conflict, contemporary with the War of American Independence (1775–1783), broke out over British and Dutch disagreements on the legality and conduct of Dutch trade with Britain's enemies in that war. The letter also highlights the issues as to what counted as safe and easily exchangeable assets, whether in the form of physical assets such as diamonds, coinage, or more intangible assets such as loans or bonds. This was particularly challenging when troops were owed arrears of pay in conjunction with the '*Scarcity of Specie*', a phrase typically meaning coinage or readily exchangeable silver or gold.

Since I came here Yours of the 26th of April has arrived safe, covering the Power of Attorney, which I now transmit with this, to Paxton, properly executed. – I hope to God you did not leave the loan to Mr Ross in the Dutch Company's Treasury.

I conceive the declaration of the Dutch War, will affect all property so Concerned in a great degree, & publick of course more than private. – And I cannot now afford any further deductions from my Property.–

Advise me of this Dutch concern as soon as possible, Mr Ross's Character & property are both respectable, but still I must be under uneasiness until I hear from You.

If Scott can procure diamonds for me, I would even prefer their security to the Company's Treasury, altho' I expect it will be necessary for them to Consolidate in another Year if the War continues so long; – If Diamonds are not to be had, Even then I shall prefer the Company's Security to any private property whatever. – We are in the utmost distress here for money; You may judge of it, when the Arrears to the Madras Troops cannot be paid off nor a resource to be found – The Bengal Detachment are four months, & the Officers are all Eight months in Arrears. – Where we are to be paid from or How, I cannot divine by any means whatever. – So great a Scarcity of Specie here,

*& so low the Company's Credit, that the Treasury Bonds
cannot be discounted at even 12 pCent.*

As it happened, the Dutch loan referred to was redeemed
successfully as noted in the following passage in a letter from
John to Charles sent from Bombay on August 28th, 1781. It also
evidences that some letters were sent overland between India
and Britain as well as via the long sea voyage. Neither postal route
was rapid, nor entirely secure or reliable. The other reference in
this short extract is to '*Paxton*', one of the three partners in what
would become the profitable agency house of Paxton Cockerell &
Trail, already referenced.

> *I have also written to You overland since I came to
> Bombay. – The Information you give me of the Dutch loan
> being paid into Paxton's hands, was most gratefull News,
> and I approve of your disposal of it in the Company's Cash.*

In the same letter a later paragraph, in amongst military updates,
references their sister Elizabeth Stuart Cockerell, referred to
simply as 'Stuart' here, and as 'Estuarta' in later correspondence.

> *I have at last heard from my friend Scott. – Whilst he
> attends to my interests, I ought not to be vexed at his
> silence – I shall write him soon. – He tells me Stuart is well,
> & generally Esteemed at Lucnow – He even hints she has
> but to make choice, of many admirers. – If I may judge by
> her former Conduct her present silence might induce me to
> think She is preparing to make another Choice. – Assure
> her of my warmest wishes for her happiness, in whatever
> Station She may resolve upon. – I will not predict any more,
> I was too true, & too unfortunate in my last. –*

Elizabeth, who had followed her brothers to India in search of a
husband, did indeed '*make choice*' for a second time (as alluded
to in the letter), and an excellent choice it was. As noted
previously, the fortunate man was John Belli, Warren Hastings'
private secretary. Elizabeth's first husband, Bryan Glover, had died
only a few months after the wedding. Given the intriguing last

phrase in the above extract, perhaps John Cockerell had predicted that her first marriage wouldn't last, either through him sensing it a bad emotional match or maybe because Bryan Glover's health was already of some concern before the marriage.

Most of the accessible financial documents relating to the Cockerells' accumulation of wealth In India reference cash amounts, whether pounds sterling or current rupees, much of which was effectively transferred back to England. However, other valuable assets were also being removed from India, as the following archive extract reveals.

Capt John Cockerell in Account Current with Sir Robert Barker Bart. [1778-1781]
   Detailed account schedule, with the amount Cockerell owes Sir Robert being offset at the bottom 'By sale of Diamond Bulse No. 32 for £1,260.16.-'

This indicates frequent sales of batches [Bulses] of Indian diamonds by Sir Robert on Cockerell's behalf. Another entry in the Schedule reads,

'Oct 30th 1781 To Insurance of 4,000 Pounds on Ships …. at 30 Guineas per cent of Policy £1,260.12.-'

This high insurance premium, whether coincidentally or not, almost exactly matches the figure for the sale of a batch of diamonds above. Perhaps the diamonds were sold to pay the insurance on a much more substantial cargo. Nevertheless, this substantial insurance amount (31.5% of the value of goods) reflects the high level of risk for the long sea journeys involved. There is an interesting follow-up document which evidences these very real risks of loss or damage of ships sailing between India and England, and the further risk of delays, as outlined in the following :-

Extract of Sir Robert Barker's letter to Major Cockerell. Dated March 15th 1783. White Hall.
   With this I send your account with me, made up to the present time, you must have heard from Bengal that your

other Bulse of Diamonds were returned with the ship to Bengal to refit, this has been very unlucky for you, as they wou'd have arrived just now, at the best Market we have had for this eight years past.

The next extract, from a letter of 1783, highlights John Cockerell's sensitivity and frustration over recognition and financial recompense. John, then still holding the rank of Major in the East India Company army, writes to one of his superiors with influence over finances, politely but assertively requesting proper reward for his efforts and recognition of those under his command. It gives an impression of the interaction of the practical, financial, and political factors involved for army officers conducting a military campaign in the vast and unfamiliar environment of the Indian subcontinent.

Letter from Major J. Cockerell to
J. Bristowe Esq.   *Camp May 10th 1783*
Sir,

I have been favoured with yours of the 22nd of Febry. And beg leave to assure you of my thanks for your willing acquiescence to my solicitation in Behalf of Abdulrahman Cawn.

Col Morgan having deemed it Expedient for the Welfare & Convenience of this Detachmt. , in General, to direct the immediate March of the Candahar Cavalry towards the Banks of the Jumna, I am induced again to trouble you with my correspondence.

....

The steady attachment of the Corps throughout this distant and severe service, their cheerful Resignation in all the difficulties Troops labor under, from heavy arrears of Pay which in this part of India, when they have little Audit or Resource in themselves, and when all articles of provisions are at a most advanced price, may be accounted a misfortune of much greater magnitude than in any situation in Bengal, & their ready obedience to the commands of every Officer with whom they have been detach'd, has deservedly Entitled the Cawn to the good opinion of the difft. Commanders of this Detacht. and merits from me every Effort to obtain Him such Recommendations as shall insure Him the protection & favor of his Excellency the Vizir.

Permit me to make use of this opportunity of soliciting your attention to the circumstance mentioned in Col. Morgan's Letter, relating to the Charge I have held of his Excellency's Corps of Cavalry since the Junction with this Detacht. at Corah in April 1778. In this Charge, Every Transaction, Every Order, Their line of Duty, their Accts. Of Pay &ca &ca has wholly passed thro' me to the Com.g Officer. It has been my unremitting Study to Support this Corps in every Right & Respect, that the Honble. The Comps.? Troops could claim. I have had the Satisfaction of Conciliating their attacht. and Steadiness to the Public Service, and I have reason to believe I have acquir'd their Confidence & Regard by my attention. The Cawn Himself can but speak of this Point.

....

Happy as I should be to owe to your private Friendship and Civility, whatever Success may attend this application. I yet Trust my Claim will appear so reasonable to you, that the Influence of your Public Character at the Vizir's Court, may also be Exerted in favor of my Pretensions. I am not without Hopes that the Inclination which the Nabob formerly Expressed to Serve me, in Consequence of a Recommendation made of me by Sir Robt. Barker may be an additional motive for his attention to me in the present Instance.

> *I am Sir*
> *with regard & Esteem*
> *Your very obdt., Humbl. Servant*
> *[Signed] Jn. Cockerell*

While John Cockerell was accumulating capital from his military pay and organising for this, together with batches of diamonds, to be transferred back home, he needed someone to check safe receipt in England. This was entrusted to his commercially savvy brother Samuel Pepys Cockerell and several documents, including the following, evidence this financial arrangement.

London 5th February 1787. Received of S.P. Cockerell Esq. the Following Effects belonging to his Bror. Major John Cockerell Vizd.

A Bill on the East India Company for £.s.d 1211.0.9 and another for £928. – both due 12 Septr. 1787 with one Year's Interest thereon

A Bill on Messrs. Palmer Holmes drawn by the Exors of Lieut. Henry Hening [?] for £100 … but not accepted. & an East India Bill for * £1562: 10s payable with 3 Years Interest the 28th July 1788 and a draft on Messrs Raikes for * £341:13:4 and in Cash ** £2131. 16:2 –--------This is Davy's Debt –------

*this is Davy's Debt. –---------

** this was the balance at Coutts

Another document cited here is from 1790 and, as well as setting out John Cockerell's accounts at that time, shows that he has been promoted to the rank of Colonel, '*commanding the Bengal Army*'.

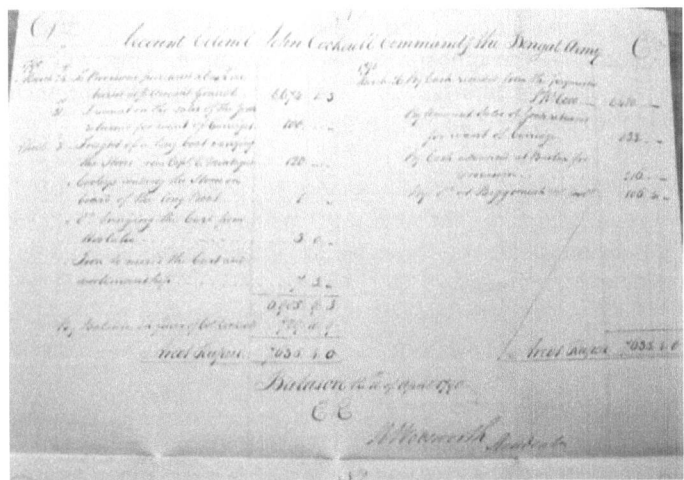

The following year, 1791, an extract from a letter to his brother Charles of February 20th, reveals that he had fathered several illegitimate children. This was not at all unusual for unmarried men serving on the subcontinent, far from home and with freedom from domestic constraints. John bemoans his ill luck with a further unwanted pregnancy but, despite callous references to '*the little Urchin*' and '*the other Unfortunates*', he does at least take financial responsibility for their long-term future welfare.

> *… well : my Evil Stars are yet working for me. – Be it so : It will be your care to help it, to all necessary wants. – & should Fate dispose of me, to let the little Urchin stand Entitled to one equal proportion of my Property, (share & share alike,) to the Sums devised to each of the other Unfortunates, respectively. – If male – the same sum as each of the males. – If a female, the same sum as bequeathed to the female & in all respects the same, Maintenance, Education, Trusteeship.*
>
> *This Memorandum I have made on a Camp Will, of this date, as Codicil. But this writing will be dated for a Soldier's Will.*

In the same letter John reverts to military matters with reference to the accumulation of the massive forces being assembled in Southern India in preparation for the assault on Tippu Sultan's main fortress at Seringapatam. The use of elephants and camels was a key part of Asian military logistics.

> *I wrote you to adjust my Balance to Mr Lautris' Estate of the 2 Elephants & 2 Camel. – the memo of which I left with your house in writing. – This to be paid to the Elephant Contract partners. –*
>
> *The Great Guns, are just passing my Tent to their Ground. – All up. – I hope, great as the noise is – their Thunder will be dreadfull to Tipp –*

In his next letter of April 18th 1791, John refers to the action against Tippu Sultan in the context of increasing tensions in Europe, which would soon lead to the Napoleonic Wars.

We are told ye war with France & Spain is inevitable. –
altho' no express declaration is yet made.

It cannot affect this war I think, & we shall have done
the principal business, I hope, (of Seringapatam) before
the French can give Tippoo the smallest assistance. – If we
are to credit reports, we shall find the Capital as bare of
Treasure as Bangalore. – It is supposed to be all removed
to the strong hill Forts. –

The following day, in another letter to his brother Charles (based
at Calcutta) John includes further rather offhand reference to his
latest illegitimate offspring and their mother. However, we know
that he does honour his commitments for his illegitimate children
in practical and financial terms, both before his death and by
making provisions in his Will. At this stage he still doesn't know
whether the latest child is a boy or a girl.

The sooner we prosecute the War, the sooner a conclusion
to it, may be hoped; & God be praised, when it shall be
finished. – The Bengallies will rejoice in the glad sight of
the Gungah; men & officers. –

With regard to my monies, I leave to You my dear Bye
to act in their Employ, & disposal, as you may best
approve. – Whenever I go home, I shall undoubtedly wish
to take all my monies with me : excepting only the Sum of
One Laac of Rupees, which I will have at Secure Interest,
for the uses of some Charges I am bound to, & who must
stay in this Country. – I wish to hear from you about
the last born ; & how you have disposed of it, and of the
mother. – It is better to give her some money & take
the Child to nurse : – is it boy; or Girl?

This letter provides updates on the military situation, clarifying
that the assault on Tippu's fortress is fast approaching, while also
indicating that John is beginning to turn his mind to returning
home. Later letters build on this theme, with his tone increasingly
expressing a longing for rest after arduous conditions endured on
the long campaign in India – the peace and quiet of home life
becomes a repeated siren call.

However, the main military engagement was imminent and the following extract from John's letter of April 30th 1791 to Charles describes the build-up and anticipation.

I wrote you on the 21st. from the Camp at Vincatty ghurry. – on that day our Reinforcements all joined from Amboor, & we marched the 22nd: The 28th. we encamped near this place to receive our heavy Guns, Stores &c. for the Siege of Seringapatam : for which place we commence our march the 2nd. of May it is believed.

We have not a day to spare in respect to the Rainy Season, & the rising of the Cauvay(??) River by every account. – The 10th of the month we shall be in sight of this famous City and Fortress. & I wish to believe, the English Colours shall fly on the proud palace of the Sultan of Mysore, by the close of a fortnight after we open Ground. – The figure 2 has been a favorite this war, in sieges : – It is rather soon, but not altogether impossible, but the 22d. May may be a lettered day in your next Year's Almanack. – "Seringapatam taken". God grant it may ! & as fortunately successful as Bangalore ! –--

Whatever crosses have occurred, it is to be declared, to the honor of this Army, that no Body of Officers or men in any Country have shown more zeal & exertion to promote & assist the War than is now exhibited in this Army. – The Cattle of Public Departmts. have failed greatly, by the nature & severity of the late Junction, since we moved into the Mysore Country : – & officers & men have given an assistance in carrying of Shot & Stores, that exceeds the most Sanguine Expectations of his Lordship; & he has publicly granted warm thanks :

All Eyes are turned to Seringapatam. All are confident of the Capture; & all hope, it's fall will prove a material Event in closing the toils of this war. –

There is no doubt that life on military campaign in an extremely challenging environment, subject to extremes of weather and constant losses of life through disease, was physically and emotionally draining. However, even amongst the horror of war, for senior officers like John Cockerell, with valuable connections and support, some level of day-to-day comfort and luxury persisted, as betrayed by an extract from his letter of 1st May, 1791.

My own letters to you I enclose to Mr. Balfour at Madras, which is ascertaining their route so far towards You. – Your supplies of Madeira & Brandy by Robinson came to me: but I have not heard of any others since, nor of the good things of Bengal which you proposed to send me. – as Potatoes, Beef &c. &c. Tellicherry appears now the best chance of drawing supplies: – and if opportunity occurs of Vassoly?? Going from Bengal to the Malabar Coast, I hope it will not escape you to send me drinkables of Madeira & Brandy; and any thing of salted you think will be good. – Riced smoaked mangoe fish is a good side dish

The major engagement which John had been anticipating in his letters, and in which he had a pivotal role in charge of logistics as Lord Cornwallis's Quartermaster General, took place on 15th May 1791. The following records the British victory, including reference to a map illustrating the positions of the opposing military forces:-

SKETCH OF THE POSITIONS of the British Army Commanded by EARL CORNWALLIS, / And the MYSOREAN ARMY Commanded by SULTAN TIPPOO SAHEB, / In the ACTION of the 15th of May 1791. near SERINGAPATAM 1792

Etching and engraving; printed on paper; hand-coloured | Scale: 1:61,000 approx. | RCIN 735002.3

A map of the Battle of Seringapatam (also known as the Battle of Arakere), fought on 15 May 1791, between the British (British East India Company's Madras army, and Allied forces from the Nizam of Hyderabad), commanded by Charles, First Marquess Cornwallis (1738-1805), Governor-General of India, and the Mysorean army, commanded by Tipu Sultan (1750-99), resulting in a British victory. Third Anglo-Mysore War (1789-92). Oriented with north to top.

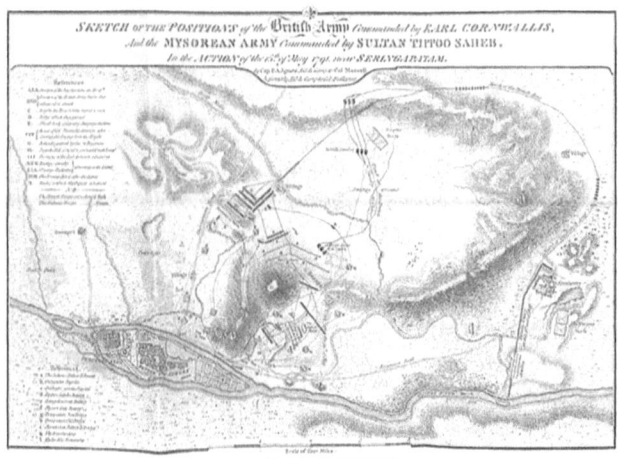

The next extract is from a letter John wrote to his brother Charles on August 6th, 1791. After conveying news of the ongoing tidying up of military movements and more minor actions in consolidation of the Seringapatam victory, it gives more general and personal comments, notably John's planning for his longed-for return to England. Meanwhile he continues to take an active interest in his horses back in Calcutta.

> *Your friends are all well & remember you, with congratulations that you are free of the late Villainous Explosion in Calcutta.*
>
> *On the 1st inst. I gave an order on you for the hundred Rupees to the family of a Servant: pay it, on presentments – It was in favour of a man of the name of anwear peadah. – I recommended to you to get rid of the Stock of Long Cloth, & Stockings, if they are either of them liable to damage in their Quality, by the delay that must, in the common course of events, happen to the time of my departure for the land of promise & liberty. – not even an immediate peace with Mysore can produce the Arrival of this wished for moment sooner than January 1793. –*
>
> *The deliciousness of this expectation I must strive to divert any thoughts from. –*

Do not think of providing any more horses for my Stud: – Your choice does not meet mine at all, Charles: – As to the Bombay horse, which I thought might turn out well, if he be so good for nothing as you describe, why are you at the expense of continuing Stable room & Groom to him?

I am inclined to judge you will persist in the trip to Europe, when you learn that the Swallow is for dispatch the first week in Septr. & shall expect to hear of you at Madras shortly. – J Dent is well – Give our regards to the family. – Adieu

> *I am Dr.[Dear] Charles*
> *Your ever affect/ brother*
> *[Signed] Jn. Cockerell*

As it happened, John's anticipated return to England was further delayed by a fresh flare-up of aggression from the proud Tippu Sultan. Although victory had been achieved in 1791, it turned out to be insufficiently decisive, and a further siege of Seringapatam was conducted the following year.

As the army was approaching Seringapatam for the second time in late 1791, ahead of the planned siege of 1792, John Cockerell was again looking beyond this second military engagement and planning his return home. The extract below is from a letter of 18th December 1791 and outlines his cautious focus on ensuring his finances are in a sound and prudent condition, together with links to Paxton outlined in the previous chapter. Also, it even more pointedly, almost desperately, sets out his weariness towards the end of his lengthy and arduous service in India. He explicitly rules out any future return to India once he has got through this last imminent military action and sailed back to England.

… of business, in regard to my Property in England. I have every confidence in the management of the Paxtons'. – aided by the attentions of Pepys Cockerell, to the securities &c. – I certainly must wish, however, my dear Charles, that you will allot a few moments to inspect into the state of all the monies. – & the securities under which the Interest is

accruing. – And that you will advise the most strict adherence to two principles of attention. – First: "security in loans themselves". – secondly, "that the manner of the loans do not hazard my being involved in Suits of Law of any sort whatever, whether friendly, or unfriendly Suits"; and lastly that I may hold a free command of my monies, when I may return to the management of them myself – You know my sentiments, my dearest Brother ! – nor ambition, nor the pride of power, can urge me to return to this Country :

I feel by anticipation, the gratefull blessings of peacefull retirement to a home – with the possession of independency, and I shall have earned my harvest, I think – after near Thirty Years of active toil, in the Service of my Country. –

In a letter from early 1792, John Cockerell reports both the success of the second siege of Tippu Sultan's fortress at Seringapatam, and his planned return to England, as well as his comments on his intended continuing bachelor status. Although he has had a relationship with a mistress, and has fathered illegitimate children, he expresses his intent to return, live modestly ... and alone. The letter is given in full as it records both a significant historic victory, the resulting peace treaty and more of John's personal reflections, which tells us much about his character and his determination to remain a bachelor.

Letter from Camp at Seringapatam February 28th 1792

My dearest Charles

If my letter of the 13th of this Month shall have run the Gauntlet clear to Madras, it will I hope get safe to you in England. – It will tell you of my being well – and gives you a general idea of our glorious success of the 6th. & 7th. inst. at that time we could scarcely suppose so speedy an Issue?? to this long Contest, and it was thought, I may say wished, that our haughty Opponent would dare the Siege of his Capital: But the terror of our prowess had began its' operation on his mind; & his Troops were probably dejected, to wait the further Issue ! – & Lakeels?? Were sent out, but their Conferences did not delay, or abate our preparations.

We had advanced our approaches almost to the point for our breaching Batteries, within 600 Yards of his walls, when on the 24th. the full preliminaries were Signed, & Exchanged: & a Cessation of Arms published to the Army. – and the day before yesterday the Hostages were received in Camp. – They are, the Second & Third Sons of this fallen Sultan, to remain with the English, until the full performance of the Articles of the Peace.

The Army in its' ardour, & in its resentments, feel a disappointment, that their Labors have not another glorious day and possibly a reward, in the Value of this famed City. – nevertheless, the business of the 6th & 7th, leaves us little to wish for – & the Peace, will no doubt be deemed as honorable in the moderation of the Victors, as it must prove in its' public Consequence; & every reason holds that it will be permanent. The outlines of this Peace are, I am told – the Payment of Three Corores and thirty Laacs in specie – And the Cession of one half his territorial possessions – to be selected at the pleasure of the Confederated Powers from his Rental Finance Records. – The Lord gave the Army the intimation of the Armistice in terms of Honor to themselves, & of humility to the Conquered. – He says the Enemy, "is subdued & humbled by their Valor and Discipline:". He promises too, to reward their Labors, by an handsome donation, from the Share of the Specie to which the Company becomes Entitled. –

Now, at length, my dear Bye, the prospect of our return to Bengall begins to open; & I think I shall be in time to bid adieu to India, on a February Ship next Year. – We can be in Bengall by the middle of Janry. I think – admitting that I get over Kistna & the Godauvery River, before June next. – We must canton near Vizag. & commence our march in October, when the Rivers of Cuttac/Cutlac?? Will all have subsided.

Our friend Capt. Madan is charged with the public dispatches, & has kindly proffered his Care of this to your hands. – He will be happy to meet you , & I am confident will be communicative with you on such particulars as you may wish to enquire into.-

I mean to write you a few lines for the latter Ship, sailing in April, by which time, our time of march & probable detention, will be known almost to certainty.

I must still resist all idea of extending my correspondence beyond yourself, and you must perform the good Office of my affectionate Remembrances to all our relatives and to my friends & intimates. – I wish to believe, Charles, that you will not revisit India; – yet should this be indispensable, to fullfill your promises, or to give greater stability to your House of Agency, I must express my hopes you will still be in England to the season of 1794. – because, not impossible, but I may defer my departure a season, if my arrival in Bengal should by any circumstances be delayed so late as March 1793. – I will however say, that you must not make your Establishments of House &c. (which you promised to prepare for my arrival) more than a requisite for a Bachelor of moderate Expense. – nothing I beg of Asiatic Ostentation & Vanity . – You already possess my sentiments, that I am fully of belief I shall ever be a Bachelor to the last day of this Stage, and reasoning, & time, serve to confirm me in this belief. Mighty well! – you will say.- John Rattray, Dent, Macleod, Welsh, & Wells, are all well, present my best love to Belli's, & Pepys's firesides. To James Street, & Spring Gardens – & make my sincere remembrances to Mr. Hallowes & Lady Barker.

> *Adieu my dearest Bye. I am your ever affectionate*
> *[Signed] Jn. Cockerell*

One consequence, cited in the letter above, of this more complete 1792 victory was that Tippu Sultan was obliged to hand over his two sons as a guarantee against further aggressive actions. A painting (below) by Robert Home (1752-1834) of this significant hostage handover includes the figure of Colonel John Cockerell, Quartermaster General, standing with Lord Cornwallis's other senior officers. As it transpired, an even more complete victory was necessary seven years later in 1799, which ended the Mysore Wars, but by this time John had departed India.

General Lord Cornwallis receiving Tipoo Sultan's sons as hostages, by Robert Home, c. 1793

A letter of 3rd May 1792, includes a summary of the military and political advantages of the recent success in defeating Tippu Sultan at his Seringapatam fortress. Competition with the French for control of India, commercially and strategically crucial, is also referenced.

Indeed it is Evident, that the whole Conduct of his Lordship, as well before the Peace, as since it was Concluded, has been so open, manly, & liberal, that even this Sultan appears to bear a respect, & confidence in his declarations, which is uncommon in his dealings with the English – I heard at his Lordship's a few days agoe, that the Vakheels had intimated the Sultan's wishes, for a plan of Commercial intercourse, & Establishment, between his Provinces, and the Carnatic. – I wish it may be Effected. – for independent of any advantages to the Countries, I conceive it may lead to the most desirable political benefits. & not the least that of shutting out the Connexions of our neighbours and Rivals, the French. – Such an intercourse, improved too, by the residence of the two Boys, our Hostages, amongst the English, may naturally be expected to Confirm, and reestablish, any lost faith of former transactions. – not unlikely, the Sultan's own reflexions, since this sudden

*destruction of his Airy Castles of Universal domain, may
shew him the better policy of a sincere friendship with the
English nation, preferably to other Connexions*

John's correspondence in 1792 increasingly anticipates his return
to England, and in another extract from this same letter of May
3rd he feels equally able to focus on non-military, non-political,
domestic family matters.

*I send home by ... ship two pieces of remarkably fine
Longcloth [in the care of] the Chief mate, Mr. Studd. – I beg
you to present one piece to Mrs Pepys, & one piece to
Stuart to make a summer gown for their eldest girl. –*

As well as evidencing John's thoughtful gifts, the manner of reference
to the two female recipients is instructive. 'Mrs Pepys' is John's sister-
in-law, the wife of Samuel Pepys Cockerell who, as previously noted,
was often referred to as 'Mr Pepys' or simply 'Pepys'. There are other
letters in which family members, as here, refer to his wife as 'Mrs
Pepys' again indicating their willingness to perpetuate the historic
connections. 'Stuart' is John's sister Elizabeth Stuart Belli, and her
eldest daughter is also called Elizabeth. This daughter's eventful life,
and those of her siblings and cousins, are covered as part of coverage
of the next, fifth, generation.

The following extract from another of John's letters, dated June
15th 1792, to his brother Charles, who was on his way back to
England, reflects the harsh reality of the war and the rigours of
military campaigning, leading to the suicide of one participant,
recorded here. In fleshing out John's character the extract highlights
his care for those under his command, and his humanity.

*You may remember a Young Lad of the name of Coleridge,
living with my lamented friend Archdeacon, & who came
round to my Detacht. just before you sailed. This young
man, in a melancholy delusion, after Severndroog was
taken, destroyed himself – Archdeacon had the Care of his
Property; but he too, was fated to die in the last glorious
conflict with the Sultan. I had given the Lad, a Watch some
years agoe, & I got it reserved, to be conveyed to his*

Mother in Devonshire. It will go to you by the Dutton [an East India Company ship]. *– superscribed to you – but an ??? address to Mrs Coleridge. – You must take the trouble to send it to her; & you must also have it accompanied by a Mourning Ring, or breastlocket – to be made plain, at my cost, Charles : – for which, the enclosure contains a Lock of his Hair, the date of his demise, & the address of his mother. – The Circumstances of the family are very slender, & you must consequently be attentive to bear all Charges of the conveyance of these articles to Mrs. Coleridge. –*

A further extract from this letter expresses his desire that both he and Charles should bring their respective stays in India to an end. It also says much about his own state of mind and limited expectations for his remaining years. It specifically records '*the great improbability*' of him marrying, linked with a Shakespearian allusion, evidencing his educated upbringing.

I certainly wish, my dear Charles, that on an Examination, & adjustment with Paxton, you may not find it necessary to return to India. – I most sincerely wish it, Charles ! – because, I hope your resolve to continue in England, may & I hope too, will lead you to look, once more, to an Establishment for Life. –

You know my sentiments in respect to myself, my dear Brother. – Reflexion confirms me in the determination : – My pursuits in Life, & the manner I have been accustomed to, these 25 Years past, in the military line, all forbid the idea of change, at this late day. –

If Happiness be not my lot :- as a bachelor it is with myself only. – & I have Enow [enough] *of Philosophy to bear up against the demon :- Therefore, altho' I have not the hardiness to deny the possibility of an alteration in my sentiments, I do most stoutly assert the great improbability, that I shall become a Benedick**. – No! the Winter of Life is coming on apace:-*

[** Benedick is the wilful lord in Shakespeare's *Much Ado About Nothing*, recently returned from fighting in the wars, who vows that he will never marry, but eventually does. This passage in John's letter therefore evidences his knowledge of Shakespeare, and stresses *'the great improbability'* that he will follow Benedick's example.]

Direct military action was not the only threat to life on the subcontinent during this extended conflict. John's responsibility for the welfare of the large number of troops under his command and care is also explicitly evidenced in his letters. The stress of this responsibility over a prolonged period goes a long way to explain the toll on his health, both physical and emotional. The following extract from John's letter of 11th July 1792 highlights one specific logistical challenge, also making horribly clear the devastating effect of famine on the local population in regions the army was traversing on their return from Southern India to Bengal.

> *I paid a visit to the Lord* [Lord Cornwallis] *at Madras in the last week of June, to secure his prove for my journeying towards Bengal, and every previous arrangement is now making, of forming Depots of Grain on my route of march, by sea conveyance: so that I assure myself to march from this Cantonment before the close of September & hope to arrive at Ghyretty by the middle of January. – My route the same as that I came. – But we shall have a most deplorable waste to go through, from the Kistra as far as Ganjam, in all which Extent the Famine has raged to an extraordinary degree. –*
>
> *These Districts are computed to have lost half their population, this has compelled the Governmt. to provide for the Support of my Detacht., Followers &c. (in all near 20,000 men) by sending Rice from Madras, by Sea conveyance and forming Depots on my route. –*

A month later, in a letter of 26th August 1792, as John plans his long trek back from southern India to Bengal with his 20,000 troops, he again expresses concern for the general populace.

> *We are prepared to encounter the most distressing Objects of famine, & consequent depopulation, in the whole of the Northern Cucais, even to Ganjam – But we shall not add to their Evils, & I hope we may even afford some small relief, by Charities, & Surplus Grain.*

John's letters contain dramatic contrasts of subject matter, from the horrors of the conditions surrounding him and his troops at one extreme, to far more refined topics at the other. The Cockerell family always had an eye for art, particularly that of personal interest, often family portraits or scenes of locations with which they had a connection. In a letter of July 21st1792 John refers to orders for certain subscription artworks, and names the family members and friends they are intended for. An anxious desire to return to England is again at the forefront of his mind.

My dear Charles

The Dutton is full in Madras roads, & her departure is now fixed for the 1st. August. – You will receive two Letters by her Packet from me of dates the 15th June, & the 11th. inst. – This is to enclose you an order for two Setts of Views in the Mysore Country publishing by a Capt. Allan of the Madras Establishment, for which the full Engagement is paid by myself – & to Acquaint you that an Order will be transmitted to Pepys's address, by this same Packet for three Setts of Views, which are publishing by Lieut. Rob. Colebrooke, half of which Subscription may possibly be demanded on delivery to You, which must be paid – The amount will be for the three Setts, One hundred & Eighty Arcot Rupees. – I have already paid the first half of this Subscription to Mr. Colebrooke. – his Plan contains twelve Plates of views in each Sett. – & you will find them greatly Superior in taste & execution to the other Plan. – Capt. Allan's plan contains twenty Plates in each Sett. – You will receive all these :- make Belli a present of One of Colebrooke's Setts, reserve the other for myself – of Allan's Setts give Pepys one – give one to John Devaynes, and give the third Sett to our good aunts** in James Street. –

... I am in the best health possible – but feel nevertheless the most anxious desire to be amongst my friends in my own Country. –

[** Susanna and Jane Jackson, Samuel Pepys's great nieces, who were frequently referenced in family letters, and clearly much loved.]

Details and images of two of the Mr. Colebrooke 'Plates' referred to by John Cockerell are given here. The description and context fits very precisely with John's ordering of three sets of the views, and his direct personal connections with the scenes portrayed.

Sewandroog and Ootra-Durgum, Robert H. Colebrooke,
Antique Print Pair, 1793
Robert Hyde Colebrooke (1762?-1808) (after)
John William Edy (act. 1780-1820) (etcher)

Captain Allan's images, also referenced in John's letter, are also well-documented.

> *This uncoloured aquatint is taken from plate 19 of Captain Alexander Allan's 'Views in the Mysore Country'. Srirangapatna is on an island in the Kaveri river 20 kilometres from Mysore, and was the seat of one of the best-known rulers in South Indian history, Tipu Sultan (1753-1799). The town's name derives from Sri Ranganatha, an incarnation of Vishnu, whose temple towers can be seen in the distance. Tipu's adventurous and able father Haider Ali (1722-1782) had become the leading power in Mysore in 1763 after the death of the Hindu raja. Tipu in turn built up the kingdom into a strong and prosperous state stretching over most of South India. The power of the so-called Tiger of Mysore inevitably clashed with British intentions and the Anglo-Mysore wars reflected this. Ultimately, Tipu died fighting and the British were victors. The figures seen on elephants are Tipu's sons, who were taken hostage in February 1792 when Srirangapatna fell to Lord Cornwallis, concluding the third Anglo-Mysore war.*

SERINGAPATAM

Another of these plates shows one of the 'droogs' or hill forts.

This uncoloured aquatint is taken from plate 10 of Captain Alexander Allan's 'Views in the Mysore Country'.

NUNDY-DROOG

Nandi Hills, Bangalore – 1794

After all John's forebodings about widespread famine on his march back to Bengal, a subsequent letter is more upbeat. Even though the famine had been severe, it had then abated. Positive reports on weather, travel progress, and supplies are followed by an interesting personal insight into his priorities before he returns to England. John is concerned that any imminent restructuring of the East India Company army may prevent him consolidating the rank of full Colonel, which he treasures, admitting a degree of vanity for his retirement status and its associated military uniform once back in England. He is determined to secure his position before leaving India.

My last letter by the Ganges [a ship sailing for England] – & by my fellow traveller Dick Scott, you will certainly expect that I shall be very shortly embarking for my native Country. – All is promising to offer me the Opportunity. – The affairs of the Vizag district did not detain me, & I am far on my route North. – We were greatly favoured, in respect of weather & of roads, far exceeding my own expectations – which differed much from the Common report I received at Madras – most fortunate too – the seasonable fall of Rain, & the still more favourable supplies of Rice by sea from Bengal, had jointly cast a ray of returning prosperity over the past wretchedness of all the Northern Provinces, & I have derived ample resources of Grain from the Country People on my route – almost to superceed the Public Depots lodged at Stations for my use.

This has made our march gratefully pleasant, & to add the more, we have a most charming cool Climate, & are blessed with health to keep us contented. – Now, my Bye – doubtless you look for my declaration of Embarking for England ! – The inclination is strong with me, nor do I relax in the least of this intention. – I have resigned my Office of Quarter Master General, from time past in favour of my friend Sam Dyer – & your old Chum, James Pringle, has gained the confirmation to Dyer's Office of Deputy QMGl & out of the Provinces – so that two good

People are benefited ! – But for myself, Charles, I defer my ultimate resolve to go – 'till I can be ascertained, whether my absence from India, at the time, when the talked of Changes & Alterations in the Military Establishments of the E. India Company, shall take place – may prejudice those Rights & the Station I have been so many Years labouring to arrive at. – The moment is Critical in the situation of the Army of the Company. – & prudence urges me to act with caution – & with deliberation. – It is not that I have a thought, the most distant, of seeking Employment again in my profession. – but I have, I avow, an Ambition to return home in possession of what I have served for. – & a right to wear the Appellation I have always studied to merit. – It favors a little of Vanity, possibly ! – but it is Excusable : – an Old Soldier – like an Old Coachman – remembers his former calling – & fancies a respect in his Coat & Cockade – as well as the Curricle In his Stable. – I am expecting answers from Calcutta to this point – if the Lord [Lord Cornwallis] *shall be candid to give me his sentiments, I have no hesitation in the decision – to go this season, – or to wait another. – If he is disposed to withhold a fair answer. – It amounts to the same thing. – You shall hear from me, by the succeeding ship – to a certainty. –*

John eventually arrived back in England in Autumn 1793. His next letter in the archives is dated 13th November that year, sent from Brighton to his brother Charles, also returned from India, at No. 7 Saville Row, London. It focuses on one of his passions, namely horses, and his return to London.

My dear Bye,

Since I wrote you by the post – Joseph the Groom represents that both the horses from Mr Hall had best go to Town, as the Brighton horse's back is tender from the use of the side saddle, & his own saddle not fitting well – therefore Young Joe takes them to Town – tomorrow morning – and Joseph Senr. will stay with me, & keeps your

*Arab – I do not mean he shall keep the road way with me &
Blane, so do not be uneasy for him –*

*Now, if you come to Tunbridge on Saturday to meet us,
you may ride to Town again with us on your own horse. –
Joe's turnpike account is paid in full, to this day – and he
has received for his personal expenses from the Three
Guineas, you sent to Town. –*

*I am my dear Charles
Your affecn. Brother
[Signed] Jn. Cockerell*

Unsurprisingly, back in England John Cockerell's focus turned to
matters of a more domestic character. He is living at the
Cockerell's prestigious house at Hyde Park Corner, and the next
year a letter of 26th June 1794 to his brother Charles (then
travelling to Plymouth on his way back to India) goes into some
detail about the housekeeping arrangements. The letter then
goes on to relate some embarrassing confusions about a portrait
of Charles, the original and copies of which are intended to go
to different nominated females. One of those nominated is
'Eliza' of whom we know little in detail, but for whom Charles
clearly has some responsibility and which, now he is returning
to India, he has left John to manage as best he can. Eliza's
position appears to be a sensitive one, as evidenced by the
following extract. The other intended portrait recipient is
Charles's sister-in-law Sophy Blunt. It appears that neither Eliza
nor Sophy are meant to know of the other also receiving a
version of the portrait.

But if she [Eliza] *still refuses Mrs Crosland is to
recommend a steady old Lady to stay with her, in place
of her mother. –------- And her sister will also stay with
her I suppose – rather than go to service, or to the
Country. And if otherwise, then Eliza must have a
servant maid.*

*I am very anxious to see her settled, before I go from
Town, & I hope it will be so.*

She is very solicitous about your health, & she was most thankful for your letter which I brought to Town, and read to her –---- the Picture is in hand for her – but when I called at Eddridge's to bespeak the Copy for Sophy Blunt [Charles's sister-in-law], *I found myself too late – she had enquired by letter at Eddridge's and was told you had not been to him.*

I am returned therefore to tell her candidly what was intended, of a Copy, (that is, from Lady Barker's, that she may not ask questions) since you could not give time to sit – and she have choice of that, for the Copy, or of the one that Lady Blunt has of you – which ever she prefers. –--- As this has happened, I cannot leave Plymer's with Mr Eddridge, lest any of them may call in, & discover the one which is for Eliza. –-- I am sorry it has turned out this unfortunately. –-- But the best remedy must be applied that can be, & what I propose appears to me the best –--- The loss of the Frame & the Glass of Eliza's is most unlucky. –-- Your stay at Plymouth would enable you to get a Glass that would do for the Passage, in Your Cabbin, and Plymer is preparing a new frame with two Plate Glasses as you desired. –-- which shall be forwarded to you by Mr Chas. Lambert, if I could possibly find him out. –-- If not, I must get it sent by some other person, – both these ships [Royal Admiral & Lascelles] are to be dispatched immediately – & may leave Portsmouth by Sunday it is said

[Henry Edridge (or Eddridge) and Andrew Plimer were prominent contemporary artists.]

A follow-up by John on the confusion over Charles's portraits notes that John had to come clean about any deception.

Eleven O'clock Thursday evening. I am come home from Ormond Street, & they are all well. –-- I spoke to Sophy of the disappointment, & told how it was to be arranged

> *since you could not give time to sit to Eddridge. She .... will be glad to have a copy by Eddridge, & will make choice of her mother's, or Lady Barker's for the purpose – Eddridge will do it – & this will be put in hand before I go out of Town.*

It seems that the intention had been for there to be two distinct portraits, one by Plymer (more commonly spelt Plimer) and one by Eddridge (with perhaps a small number of copies of one or the other), but that Charles had not found time to sit to Eddridge before departing for India. Therefore, some intended recipients apparently had to settle for Eddridge making copies of an existing portrait. It is this sort of pragmatic arrangement which makes attributions of portrait paintings at this period potentially such an inexact science. Although this is a slightly unusual situation with one prominent artist seemingly being commissioned to make a copy of another prominent artist's original, it must have been common for copies of artists' own originals to be made (perhaps by their assistants in the studio) to satisfy several relatives and friends.

A later extract from John's letter of 26th June 1794 gives more context for the intriguing relationship between Eliza (Wails) and Charles Cockerell :-

> *You may be assured of my attention & kindness to Wails – and I am sufficiently preproposed in her favor to believe, she will deserve the care, & protection you have desired. – She speaks with confidence of improving herself – & as I hope by the time I return to Town, she will be in some forwardness of reading, & possibly writing, for I trust in her good understanding to attend to her Books; I will get her such other masters in music as she may fancy most –--- She has been very busy with Betsy Crosland all yesterday, & today, getting a letter wrote for you, which I am to post under this cover –*

With a first name Eliza and the theme of a well-intentioned male arranging improvements to her deficient education and sophistication, it is hard to avoid comparisons with the much later theme of Eliza Doolittle in George Bernard Shaw's 1913 play *Pygmalion*. Whatever Eliza's relationship with Charles Cockerell, it is clearly a close one, and the Cockerell family are clearly keen to help Eliza avoid social embarrassment by providing her with the necessary education and skills. Other references in the letters between the brothers indicate that the relationship between Charles and Eliza was probably an intimate one.

Another part of the letter from John to Charles carries the news of their brother 'Pepys' and his wife Anne, who has just given birth to another child.

> *Pepys Cockerell has taken the drawings & dimensions of all the rooms, & assured me he would take them to the City today, in Duplicate – one for the Royal Admiral* & one for the Lascelles*. – You can then determine which rooms to provide the matts* [carpets] *for –-----*
>
> *You have got another Young Nephew in that family, born yesterday Se[v]ennight. –-- the Lady gives candle**, & both her & the Child are doing very well.*

* These are the ships carrying Charles's party to Bengal. Charles is to purchase carpets – 'matts' – in India to furnish rooms in one of the Cockerells' London properties. Providing copies of these drawings and dimensions for each ship reflects the risk of one or other ship not reaching India.

** At a baby-naming ceremony or christening, a candle was sometimes lit for the newborn as a sign that the child's loved ones want the baby's path through life to be illuminated by a spiritual source.

The birth referred to was that of Samuel Pepys Cockerell and Anne Cockerell's seventh child, and third son. He was named Samuel Pepys Cockerell, exactly mirroring his father, and lived through to 1869. His life is sketched as part of the next chapter covering the fifth generation.

The following day, 27th June 1794, John writes, "*I am in low spirits & almost lost in the large house – but I will try to like it when I come to Town for the Winter – altho' I think I may prefer one much smaller*". The Cockerell's Hyde Park Corner house was enormous, with a ballroom capable of accommodating large gatherings. John ends this letter with a final word on the confusion and deception over Charles's portraits.

> *You will see by my other letter, that Sophy B. was with Eddridge before I applied him – a discovery of our intended deception, of course followed, but she is well pleased to have a copy by Eddridge & she is to make choice of her mother's – or of Lady Barker's, whichever she approves. – I feared to send Plymer's to Eddridge, after I found she had been there.*

In a letter of 15th January 1795, John tells Charles that "*Estuarta trusts to me to convey to you her kindest affectn. regards, & to say all her flock are hearty & merry*". Their sister Elizabeth Stuart Belli (nee Cockerell) has by this time had 7 children, a flock indeed, aged somewhere between four and fifteen at the time of the letter. She is interchangeably referred to as Estuarta or simply Stuart in the Cockerells' family letters. As already outlined, there has been a suggestion by researchers at University College London that Estuarta is John Cockerell's Portuguese mistress, but there are multiple references in the Cockerell letters (several given earlier) that confirm Estuarta is Elizabeth Stuart Belli (nee Cockerell), and two extracts from this letter of 15th January provide yet more confirmation of this. John writes, citing both Estuarta and her husband John Belli, and their girls.

> *But it is out of my power to state to you the periods or the vessels by which my letters have gone. – They will I hope find their way to India ! – & at this moment I hastily write you a short note, for an opportunity Mr. Shields has promised me a conveyance for – & I send a note from*

Estuarta, with it, for Belli. – with my own assurance that she is as well as I have seen her since my return to England – I may say, in better health & spirits – which have just been heightened by a short letter from Belli – an overland Communication of 18th August last.

At Hyde Park house, little alteration has occurred – The new Kitchen is nearly finished – but will be used only as a wash house until you return. – I have almost determined Estuarta to take up her residence there, with me – & I think she will adopt it, for the benefit of the Girls – & I hope too, her own Comfort. – But my next letter will tell you all about it.

In a letter of 16ᵗʰ February, John provides the update promised. The interchangeability of 'Stuart' and 'Estuarta' as names for their sister and wife of John Belli is again corroborated in the following few letters.

Assure Belli, with my best affections, that his dear Stuart, & his Children are all in the best health, & preparing to leave Bath – Our plan of living together, in your house at Hyde Park Corner being fully settled :- There is no time to send to her for a letter to this opportunity. – She recd. Belli's overland letter of the 19th August.

The letter also gives Charles an update on his Eliza.

Your Eliza, my Bye – suffered much from her Eye and has been compelled to undergoe an Operation by Doctor Wathen. – She is now pretty well – & has every prospect of a perfect cure. – She sends you her best & gratefull regards & love.

A letter from John to Charles opens with confirmation of their sister Elizabeth Stuart Belli's settling in at the Hyde Park house, and the associated domestic arrangements, with confirmation sent to her husband John Belli.

Hyde Park Corner   *April 11th. 1795*
My dearest Carolus

> *I came to Town two days agoe from the Westward &
> brought Estuarta along with me. – She & all her flock with
> the Exception of the two Eldest boys are now settled in
> Your house. – & all in exceeding good health, you may
> safely assert to our worthy friend Belli. – I told you my
> arrangements for them. – The family occupy the whole bed
> room floor – & I have converted the front parlour into a
> bed Room for myself, papered & ornamented with Ward
> Robes, & Prints. – Your letter writing closet is my dressing
> room.*

Meanwhile, Warren Hastings's lengthy trial is coming to an end,
and a further letter of 29th April lets Charles know the outcome.
This nationally important news – the lengthy high-profile and
widely-reported trial had become almost a national obsession –
immediately transitions into more domestic family matters,
reporting the positive outcome of the ongoing saga of delivering
acceptable versions of Charles's portraits to the intended
recipients.

> *On Thursday last Mr Hastings trial ended – The Lords gave
> Judgement in Open Court upon the Separate Charges – &
> this persecuted servant of the public on a Ninth Year of
> trial, was Acquitted by a considerable majority of all the
> high crimes & misdemeanours charged against him by the
> Commons of Great Britain. – It was a grand, & awefull
> sight – and I am much pleased to observe the General
> impressions of Joy, which appeared to affect most visibly
> the Great Assemblage of the Audiences. –*
> *At last your peace is made with Sophy Blunt – Mr
> Eddridge has finished the Copy of you from Lady Barker's –
> It is well done – & Sophy is pleased & obliged*

The letter provides an update on John's purchase of the
'Seasincote' estate in Gloucestershire, and a light-hearted
commentary on one of the servants at the Hyde Park house.

I am not yet put in possession of the Estate in Gloucestershire – of Seasincote – but it is agreed for – and the Paxtons have promised to give me the aid of six thousand pounds on your account and under sanction of your letter to the house.

I have got a Complete set of new servants in the house, & even the Boy Joe, is to leave me – as he thinks himself Capable of the station of a valet I fancy, since I left him in Town to learn hairdressing –

There are innumerable references to domestic arrangements in these letters which exemplify late 18th century lifestyles and priorities among the upper echelons of society. A detailed account is not appropriate here, but two extracts put luxury items of wine and art at the forefront of John's focus.

Our wine commission to Spain is only partly fulfilled – Four Hogsheads of Sherry are all that is yet come to England. They are in my cellars – and I am to get Paxton's people to fine & bottle them directly, that they may be delivered in equal proportions to the Subscribers. – for I do not like the Care of them.

I have also subscribed for two prints for you of Loutherbergs In Pallmall. – Subjects the sea action of 1st June and the siege of Valenciennes –

*Lord Howe's Action, or the Glorious First of June,
by Loutherbourg (right)*

I have also subscribed to Brown's Picture of 1. June but think it much inferior to Loutherberg's –

I have not yet been able to get the Marquis to set down in the Library for half an hour; to the Pencil of Mr. Brown- but he has promised me he will

The latter reference alludes to the intention for the artist Mather Brown to execute a portrait of Lord Cornwallis. The reference to 'Pencil' probably reflects the normal process of an initial life sketch being made over a few hours, with the artist later working up the full colour portrait in the studio. The references to the 1st June relate to the major naval engagement in 1794 commonly known as the Glorious 1st June when Lord Howe defeated a French fleet in the Atlantic.

If any further proof was needed, the letter also once again confirms Estuarta's identity as John Belli's wife, Elizabeth Stuart Belli (nee Cockerell), John and Charles's sister :-

Your relatives are all well – & send loves to you – tell Belli – his dear family – now, mine** – are charmingly well. His Estuarta is in better health & spirits – than I have seen her.

** because Estuarta and her children are now temporarily lodging with her brother John at the Hyde Park house, while her husband John Belli remains in India

There is a letter from the enigmatic Eliza Wales/Wails, with whom Charles Cockerell patently has a very close relationship, the precise nature and background of which are never quite explicitly clarified. Its contents are given here in full and point to the connection being an intimate one.

Letter from E Wails/Wales to Charles Cockerell

May 8. 1795

My dear Charles

I heard with inprexpressible [sic] delight that the Ship in which you sailed was arrived safe in India, and sincerely

hope you are well, and at the time I am writing this you preparing for your return to England. I mentioned in my last letter that I had suffered greatly with my Eye, but thank God it is getting well very fast, but still a little weak which must be expected for some time yet. Almost a twelvemonth is lapsed my Charles since my widowhood commenced but I hope my time has not been lost during that long space but improved as much as my indifferent state of health has permitted. I am working very hard to make up for the time I have been obliged to lose. I am upon leaving my house, as my time is expired, and it is so replete with inconveniencies that I am not in the least inclined to renew it. I am not yet settled where I shall go, the Colonel being still at Bath, he has commissioned a person to seek me one on the outskirts of London. I dined last Tuesday week with Mrs Wood for the first time since your departure. Mr W is expected to sail about May she seems in tolerable spirits and desired me to give her Compts. When I wrote to you. We have still very cold wintry weather, I begin to think we shall never have any other. my Dear Charles, I have been hindered lately from writing but I now sit down with pleasure to inform you, that I am again settled in another House close to Brompton Chapel. I have had a Young Person to live with me, but as I made no progress in my Learning of her, I have parted with her for she was very unsteady which did not suit me, so I have got the same Person I had at first. My Dear Charles my Mother & Brothers & Sister all desires their kind love to you and my Brother grows a fine Youth I think you will be delighted with him because he resembles your Dear Eliza so much. my Dear Charles I am expecting some of your kind Letters every day now May is come it is the time that I look for that Pleasure, next May I hope I shall have still greater Pleasure in beholding those dear hands that write them, and then shall I bury in oblivion the heart felt grief that oppressed me when I was tore from those Arms that protected me from all the Miseries that this World surrounds me with, does not the returning Season bring that tender scene to

*your mind it is ever present in mine but when we meet
never to part no more that felicity will fully make amends
for the sorrow that parting has occasioned us. My Dearest
Charles I am just agoing to bed with these pleasing Ideas
shall not I see your lovely Image in my Dream so farewell
and may you be blessed with Health and all the Happiness
that the sincere Heart of her wishes who is yours truly and
affectionately*

Eliza Wales

A letter from John to Charles of 28th May 1795 provides an
update on his intended purchase of the Seasoncote estate. In a
light-hearted comment it also notes the antics of their sister's
children in the Hyde Park Corner house, and a desire for a quiet
life.

*I told you I have completed my bargain of Seasoncote
Estate. – the first ten thousand is paid.- I am to have six
thousand from the Paxton's on your account, & with the
recovery of monies at mortgage, I hope to be able to make
good all the purchase money, within the times I am
engaged for – It is called a remarkable good purchase and I
hope it will prove so. ....*

*Estuarta is vastly happy & contented, in her change to
scene, with all her little flock, – and she is in better health
& spirits, than I have known since I came home – she
desires me to say, that she & hers, are doing all they can
to prepare you amusement on your return to Hyde Park
Corner –*

*The furniture will certainly require to be replaced, she
thinks. – after all their dancing, jumping, and rioting! –*

*Upon my word Charles, if I had not been able to
persuade Estuarta to this plan of making her residence
here, I should certainly have locked up the house. – Now, I
will persist in living in it, at all & every expence, until you
come home:- Then, I shall make a new arrangement for my
self, & resign Hyde Park to your arrangement:- for, even if
my fortune should warrant a greater expence than I think*

*now, it will:- still it could not possibly meet your means:-
nor meet your wishes, and your pursuits:- I am disposed to
more of quiet, & more of privacy, than you are. –*

The next letter highlighted is one from the mysterious Eliza to
Charles of 16th June 1795 containing another intriguing, and
almost comical, extract about their relationship. Yorkshire
puddings are not normally thought of as an aphrodisiac, but Eliza
says ...

*I am always thinking of what passed when we parted,
and how I enjoyed the Yorkshire Pudding the night before,
little thinking of what so soon followed, if please God we
live to see each other again we will have another. Nay
Dear Charles I pray constantly for your safety and
preservation, and my earnest hopes are fixed on your
happy return. Let me hear from you as often as possible,
but never doubt of my fidelity. Farewell my Dear and may
the wisdom of God direct you and his providence be your
guard. Is the sincere prayer of her who prefers you before
all the World.*

All the indications are that Eliza and Charles had a truly
affectionate and intimate non-marital relationship. What is less
clear is what other relationships he had, either in England or
India. There was certainly one in India, the natural children from
that relationship appearing in copies of certificates of the baptism
of three children subsequently included by Charles in his Will.

*Copies of Certificates of the Baptism of the Three Children
described in the body of my annexed Will December   1782
[Charles Cockerell]*

*28th – Eliza Clara, natural Daughter of Mr Charles
Cockerell, Factor in the Honble Companys Service – Bapd.
At Bhauglepore by the Revd. William Johnson.*
(Signed) William Johnson
Chaplain

NB: The above is extracted from the Register book of Christenings in the Out Settlements

(A true Copy) [Signed] C Cockerell

Baptisms – 1784

Paulina Frances, Daughter of Mr Charles Cockerell of Boglepore Factor baptized 10th Feby. –

NB – This Baptism is extracted from the Revd J Blanshards Register of Baptisms &ct, when he was Chaplain of the Garrison

(a True Copy) [Signed] C Cockerell

Baptized the 27th Novr – 1791.

Charles, Edward, Stuart born 11th Decr – 1790 parents unknown

God fathers. Jn Cockerell & Willm. Logan
God mother Mrs E Mowbray
(Signed) John Christ: Diemer   Clerk
A true Copy

[Signed] C Cockerell

So, both John and Charles appear to have had extra-marital relationships in India, with several children resulting in both cases. Equally, the evidence indicates that both John and Charles were reasonably caring and honourable in their respective treatments of these children. As an aside, John's natural children were given the surname Johnson, and Charles's natural children were baptised by the Revd. William Johnson, but no link has been established. It is a common surname and probably no more than a coincidence.

It is striking that one of Charles's illegitimate children has been baptised Paulina Frances, directly referencing Charles's descent from the 17th century Paulina Pepys, Samuel Pepys's sister, while also honouring his mother's name Frances.

Returning to the correspondence between John and Charles, a letter from John of 2nd July 1795 makes more reference to artworks.

I believe my former letters told you, that the Great Picture was gone to Mr. Brown's – & the Marquis has promised me to call in upon him, that his likeness may be perfected. Pepys has bought two Pictures in oil, at Hodges sale, (who is quitting London) to be put over the Drawing Room Doors. – They are called good Paintings. –

Once again, the 'Pepys' referenced here is their brother Samuel Pepys Cockerell. The 'Great Picture' is a large portrait of Lord Cornwallis by the artist Mather Brown with John Cockerell heavily involved in ensuring the commission is executed well. As we know, John was one of Cornwallis's direct reports during their joint time on military campaign in India.

The second reference links directly with, and adds detail to, accounts in the publication '*William Hodges 1744-1797 – The Art of Exploration*', the catalogue to the exhibition of William Hodges's art at the National Maritime Museum, Greenwich, July-November 2005. On page 7, the editor, Professor Quilley, notes that 'Hodges's European, British, historical, and literary subjects are now substantially untraced: many were sold by Hodges in the hasty and dismal sale of his works following closure of the 1794-95 exhibition (Christie's, 29 June 1795) and remain unlocated'. John Cockerell's letter extract above, written just three days after this '*hasty and dismal sale*', therefore locates two of them at that time.

Hodges did much of his work in India, and it is entirely fitting that 'Pepys', architect to the East India Company, purchased two of his paintings. It is even possible that the two paintings purchased were the famous, or infamous, polemic pair by Hodges entitled '*The Effects of Peace*' and '*The Consequences of War*', seen by many contemporaries as critical of Britain's global warmongering. The Cockerells probably hung the purchased paintings at their Hyde Park house, but their current whereabouts are unknown.

John's personal expenses for 1795 include transport of a painting, and monetary amounts paid to Paxton (the Cockerells' business partner) relating to the purchase of John's intended home and estate of Seasoncote, Gloucestershire. His accounts for January to April 1795, also include the following :-

'St James' Club subn. 1795	*£4.14.6*
2 subns. of Louthenbourg's Paintings (1/2 paid?)	*5.5.-*
Ditto of Mr. Brown's ditto (1/2 paid?)	*1.1.-*
Debretts Bill Book	*3.1.6*
Edridge's miniature (SB)	*7.7.-*
Private Trust acct. E.W.	*40.3.11'*
Also payment of £400 to Lady Blunt.	

Alongside John's annual subscription to his gentlemen's club, three entries indicate continued interest in works of art, with references to subscriptions for Mr Louthenbourgs Paintings and Mr Brown's Paintings, and a miniature by Edridge, the bracketed initials SB presumably identifying it as the portrait of Charles for Sophie Blunt. The entry 'Private Trust acct, E.W.' for the considerable amount of over £40 probably relates to the money John is spending to look after his brother Charles's female companion, and possibly mistress, Eliza Wales/Wails, during the time Charles is still in India. Further evidence of a close relationship between Charles Cockerell and Eliza is provided in a letter of 8th December 1795, in which John notes that *'Eddridge writes me he will undertake the miniature of Eliza, and I am going out to settle with her to attend Dufour's place tomorrow. He promises to have it ready by the 15th'*. This miniature is to be sent out to Charles in India, another example of the Cockerells commissioning portraits of family and friends.

One significant passage from a letter of 26th April 1796 confirms that John will not return to India and has formally retired. It also evidences the role that his brother 'Pepys' performs in managing the family finances and property dealings. In a throwback to the much earlier family origins, the extract also references '*the Hewer business*', the ongoing lengthy resolution of which is a legacy of Hewer's close involvement with Samuel Pepys in the late 17th century. 'Pepys' is now, a century later, finalising the division of those inherited assets, and John is anticipating his share.

Just to tell you, that I am at length determined to continue in England. – I have finally resolved on this, my dearest Bye ! – and have accordingly wrote into the Court of Directors, that I am so determined. – & am to avail myself of the option, the Court gave to a petition I was a party in, which claimed our right of pay on 25 years service, without returning to our stations. – The Court could not resist the reasonableness of our claim – but they have accorded our Retiring Pay, under very shabby restrictions. – They give us the pay of the rank in which we left India. – & we retire the service. – Duncan, & Maitland, will accept the terms as well as me. – so will Eyres. – but those of the rank of Captain, and who by the arrangements must be Lieut Colonels – will I suppose revisit India. – Duff goes out by a later ship & I believe Burnett – but I know not Mark Wood's plans. –

Here then, my Bye, for the first time, I begin to consider myself, as set down from all further bustle of public calles of employ. – and shall set about the management of all my own affairs, heartily & seriously. – you will agree with me, it is high time ! But really, I am so restrained in my knowledge of money concerns by the various blends of property in Pepys's hands, in mortgages, my landed purchase, & the family legacies, that as yet I have no particulars sufficiently arranged to encourage me in a beginning. Pepys at length promises a considerable division of the Hewer business, very soon. – and any settlement of this property will of course bring all the rest of my monies in Pepys's management, into some determinate regularity.

The fate and future of the illegitimate children John has fathered in India is clarified in a letter three days later (29th April) from John to Charles, who has now returned to India and is sorting out John's outstanding affairs there. One important part is securing the future of John's illegitimate children. The three boys have gone to America, and John is instructing Charles that their shares of the monies set aside for them are duly sent to America. In parallel, John gives Charles discretion to ensure the daughter, remaining in India, is likewise financially provided for.

I have so many thanks to make to you, for correspondence, & for attentions to me, & to my wishes, that I know not where to commence. – the disposal of the children is the most material, and I am very happy indeed at the measure you have adopted. – nothing could have met my own choice more readily – & I think it must succeed to the future wellfare, comfort & prosperity of this little coloured progeny.

Now, that the children are gone – I shall take into full consideration the business of the sum appropriated to their uses – I have already written a declaration to withdraw the Trust Charge of the Company's Paper, and have invested this Trust in Your House. – I am disposed to make such a disposition of this sum as shall leave you at more full liberty to settle the girl, if occasion should be favorable, and to make remittas. to America, in the full proportions for the boys – so to leave the residue at my own command, either for interest, or for remittance to England, as may be desirable

Having had these sensitive and challenging responsibilities resolved by Charles, John is able to focus on himself and what he is to do with his later years. However, further decline in health was to limit his choices and he would only live for another two years. Nevertheless, all of that was in the future and in a letter of 26th August 1796 he was still a little concerned about Estuarta (his sister Elizabeth Stuart Belli) and where she will reside before her husband John Belli returns from India. John was also looking forward to establishing his own permanent home.

Estuarta will come to Town in the Spring, to help forward the education of the girls in musick chiefly, and in dancing. – and you know, my Bye, should the expence bear at all hard upon her funds – it cannot be a difficulty for a Brother to find some means of making this easy, which shall be both delicate, & friendly. – as for myself, Charles, I am equally unsettled as the moment I arrived – for I have not a home of residence yet – for the present I am commencing a repair & small addition to a farm house at my landed property of Seasoncote – heretofore a mansion, so to make up a moderate decent cottage – of two sitting rooms, & three or four good small Bed Rooms. – and where I purpose to have a good cellar. – Seasoncote is a mighty good purchase, – it is not in the very best part of Gloucestershire – for it is 3 miles N. of Stowe on the Wolds. – & on your maps of Glostershire you may find its name on the NW borders, between Bourton on the Hill, & Moreton in Marsh. – a good neighbourhood of a few miles – & Hastings's is about 7 miles by road, & 5 miles by Bridle from me, and I am well pleased to have my property proportioned between the Funds, & Land. –

All this family are very well & I am to send with this to Shields, a packet from Estuarta & her dear children, for Belli. – You may assure him, her health is most perfectly good, & so are all the children –

On September 21st 1796, John provides updates about his aunt and his sister and is more actively starting to think about his new property acquisition, intending to perpetuate memories of India by requesting sub-tropical plant seeds and curry recipes. The '*aunt Jackson*' referred to must be Jane Jackson (1720-1801), the other aunts having died before 1796.

… my aunt Jackson has been with Estuarta since the beginning of the month and I think I never saw her in better health, or spirits, than at present – Estuarta is vastly well, & so are the children –

I entreated you would send me assortments of all manner of seeds you can procure, & which are likely to keep. – of Fruits – of Trees – shrubs – plants, & flowers – that I may find myself employment at my Garden & Farm. But you must send descriptions of soil – growth, time of sowing – and general climate of each sort. – Send me good recipes for the different sorts of curries – Hindostanny Pilloaws – Kabobs – of Chuttny &c. &c.

Six days later, artwork is once again referenced.

You desire to pay £200 to our dear Sister, Estuarta, on the score of the Picture, I have communicated to her, & I shall pay this sum to her immediately on your acct. & as she will probably write of it to Belli, I think you should explain to him, that you have done so. –

The picture will be a long while in getting thro' all the Stoppages in an E.I. Warehouse – when it is received, I will tell you what I think of the likeness –

John's health raises its head again in a letter he writes to Charles ('Carolus') from a surprising location at the beginning of the following year. He also comments on the painting by Horne of his sister Elizabeth (Estuarta) and her husband John Belli.

Lisbon, January 21st 1797
My dearest Bye, Carolus ! –

Should this vessel make a very quick Voyage, not impossible, but the place of date may surprize you, but I have hopes that a letter I wrote you from my last post, Falmouth, in England may first arrive, or that my friends of Buckingham Street, will have told you of my travels to this Clime, & of the Cause which induced me to it –

I came here to avoid the Winter of England, which I feared to encounter, from a severe & continued obstinate cough, a little threatening my lungs. – But all these symptoms were so much removed 'ere I quitted our own Isle, that I felt not the actual necessity when I embarked in the Packet, & could I have foreseen the very little pleasure or gratification Lisbon has afforded me, I most certainly had not come at all. – Yet after all, I do not say, but perhaps, it was the better plan, for the Winter set in unusually severe, & I might have suffered by resisting physical advice. – I cannot say to you, my dear Bye, that I possess my accustomed good health. – for I am teased with a most provoking, & almost daily renewal of cough & of cold. – but in no shape to affect my lungs, or bodily health; more than that I am not in the same strength for exercise

Estuarta had recd. the Picture by Horne – the likenesses highly approved, as good, & striking – but Belli's had the most finish, & looked most animated

By the end of 1797, John reports in letters of 20th & 21st December that he has relinquished the massive Hyde Park Corner house for which none of the Cockerells currently had a use. It had been let out, first to Sir H. Vane, and latterly to the Earl of Chatham.

Our dear Estuarta is excessively well indeed. – she has received many of Belli's letters by this Fleet – but expecting many more; & the children are yet looking for their promised letters. –

Hyde Park house is now occupied by the Earl of Chatham. – Sir H. Vane having relinquished it – but it is let at a lower Rate – & this will still be far reduced by the new assessed Taxes – now carrying through – But, after all – it is all the better for being tenanted, & Pepys says, it is well taken care of –

In the early months of 1798 John is getting seriously concerned about his health but tries to project some optimism. His letter of 19th March reports as follows.

Why I have neglected you so long, I can only account for truly, on the fevre of spirits and I must fairly own to you Carolus, I have been very much below par in this respect, and altho', I hope, improving, I cannot even now say, that I am well. – My latest letters of the past Year, were more promising of returning health than the Event shewed me ; Incessant colds & coughs have fixed upon me from the Commencement of the winter and have weakened, and Enervated me very much. –

But my spirits have suffered, as well as my bodily strength – and at times I fancy the Energy of the mind also fails me. – but this sensation I consider as the natural result of the weakness of bodily strength – and I am in hopes now to overcome it – as the spring approaches.

Of wider concern to John in this letter is the war with Napoleon, and the threat of invasion.

> *Our gallic neighbours are more threatening than heretofore – & England is well prepared to resist, manfully I trust, whatever their mad Inveterate Envy, & Enthusiasm, can attempt. – I scarce can determine in my own mind, whether Invasion may be attempted. – But I cannot join in a belief, not uncommon, that it is a practicable thing : Indeed, I would pronounce the attempt impracticable almost, – notwithstanding the Enthusiasm of the Character of the People, & the Extraordinary Encouragement their successes hitherto must give them. – I am however singular in believing, that an Invasion will not be attempted. – and the Rulers of this Country seem to look forward to the possibility – Every preparation to discomfit our Enemy is devised, that can be thought of, & I have full confidence for my own part, that England cannot be overpowered in England, by any foreign power. – I will not suppose the Effects of disunion in our own land. – I hope it is less to be dreaded than some may imagine.*

John's '*singular*' belief that an invasion by the French '*will not be attempted*', proved correct. However, John didn't have to worry about such threats for much longer, as his health unfortunately declined rapidly, and he died in July.

Letters from John to his brother, 'Pepys'

The extracts above are predominantly from letters John wrote to Charles. Further insights into family matters and priorities are contained in letters of 1794-1798 from John to his other younger brother Samuel Pepys Cockerell ('Pepys'), mostly in the period after his return to England. The following letter extracts overlap chronologically with those from John to Charles above, but are deliberately cited separately below because they form a coherent set. Also, these have more immediacy than most of those above simply because writer and recipient are both predominantly in

England rather than one or other being in India, which for letters between John and Charles had usually involved several months delay between transmission and receipt of each letter.

In a letter to his brother of 4th October 1795, from Harrogate, John includes the following passage. 'Pepys' has clearly been encouraging John to consider becoming an MP, but John's response indicates that, while wanting to find a purpose in life after his army retirement, he rejects the murky world of politics.

> *On the business of your first letter, a seat in Parliament, I feel no sort of ambition towards it.- I should assuredly be desirous of having my mind occupied, with something like business, if I am to remain in England,? but I cannot fancy to attain happiness in the wily paths of a crooked political labyrinth – I abominate all species of Duplicity – whether in a public, or private line of life.*

In another letter of August 17th 1796, John includes the following extract about his birthday plans.

> *My birth day is on Sunday, & I must therefore put you to the expence of a letter to entreat you will call, or send, to the Venison Shop, bottom of Old Bond Street, directing a haunch of good venison (fit to be eaten on Sunday next the 21st) to be sent to me by to morrow evening's coach:- if there is not a good haunch, let it be a good neck.& breast.-*

And in another extract from the same letter, which gives a hint as to the dynamics of the three brothers' relationships, John expresses to 'Pepys' his concerns about their brother Charles's reaction to the decision to vacate the Hyde Park house and rent it out.

> *We shall be heartily blamed, & abused by him, when he finds Hyde Park house actually at rent – for he is half angry already at my letters which hinted it only.*

Also, not for the first time, John flags concern about his health.

The pain in my side does not shift, tho' I tried one hot bath [presumably at the Harrogate Spa] – I mean to try another to morrow, & then if it continues, I will take a little opening physic, but I am not so plagued with violent perspiration at night.-

In a follow up letter of September 21st 1796, John gives his thanks for a food and drink parcel.

As I am sending a packet of letters for India to Buckingham Street, it has just occurred to me, that my letter by post yesterday, began purposely to convey our thanks to you for a basket of game by long coach – & a hamper of 3 doz. of Pippin Cyder p.waggon, (both recd. on Saturday eveng.,) was unluckily finished with other matter, instead of what I intended.- The cyder I know to be from you.- for the game I am left to guess it:- my Aunt partook of the hare; & the girls with mama, & Uncle Coln. [presumably 'Uncle Colonel' is how John is familiarly referred to by his nieces] *, all smacked their lips at the partridges, & the cyder: but both hare, & birds were almost too good for their stomachs.- Therefore let me amend my forgetfulness of yesterday, by saying all our thanks to day – & with them, all our affectionate regards &c. to you & yours.-*

As already mentioned, John went to Lisbon for the winter of 1796/7, and there are many letters sent from there. While there, matters back in England obviously still dominate the letter contents, and in one dated December 29th,1796 the focus is on family artwork, a keen interest for the Cockerells.

I think I acquainted you Mr. Brown portrait painter, No. 20 Cavendish Square, kept Carolus's large picture to exhibit to his friends – when you go that way, I beg you will call in – & enquire if he has done all to it which he promised to Charles – I understand from a letter of Charles's – that he was to finish it more in the back ground – & make some alteration of the perspective, as well as to repair the cracked part in the bottom – When you may wish to replace it in the frame at Hyde Park Corner, Mr. B. will send it there.-

While in Lisbon, John is keen to send home items of food and drink more readily available in Portugal than in England. In a letter of February 25th 1797 to 'Pepys', he notes,

My dear Brother – I wrote you on the 21st obit. by the King George packet, & enclosed you a second Bill of Lading of my consignmts. Of two chests of oranges, for your flock, & for Estuarta's.- I hope they will get to you quickly, so as to be fresh & good –--

---- Another consideration is, my wines of Charles Cockerell's, which I have & am still, to commission – there is no room at H.P.C. [Hyde Park Corner] *cellars. The catacomb cellar is full – so is the opposite one, of casks – (you must remember Govr. Devaynes placed a Pipe of Port Wine of his there, & it stands with the end to the door –) I have already commissioned Five Pipes from Oporto – of Port & of which I have recd. the best recommendation.- They will all be consigned to you – & are ordered to be marked – viz. –*

One Pipe   *S.P.C. – for yourself*
Two "   *C.C. – for Charles Cockerell*
Two "   *J.C. – for John Cockerell*

The white wines I will attend to – & shall get it here. I mean to send two Pipes for you, Devaynes, & Dawes :- One for Charles & John Cockerell, and I will get you a qr. Cask of the best Malmsey procurable here for yourself, which will be about ten dozens bottled.

All this wine may arrive in England, in the ensueing May or June, I imagine; & you ought to think of a proper cellar to place it in, pro tempo.- but do not suffer it to go to a wine merchants' cellar, I entreat – & Paxton should be kept ignorant of this adventure – for he would certainly feel sore, I judge – The charges here of purchase,

(& insurance which it will be best to cover in Portugal I am told,) may be about twenty* guineas each Pipe, red & white;-

[In the margin is written *"* It may be twenty five pounds"*]

The duties & freight will be payable in England, so that we shall drink it more reasonable, & I hope better, than from Archy Paxton's cellars.-

These are considerable quantities of wine – a 'pipe' is about 550 litres.

John's letter from Chester dated September 1797, includes reference to visiting his new purchase of Seasoncote (Sezincote). As well as more comments on wines and fruit, it provides another example of the interchangeable use of 'Estuarta' and 'Stuart' for their sister Elizabeth Stuart :-

You must not forget to settle with Mr. Smith about my lodgings.- I wish him not to require a full year's engagement – because I mean certainly to go to Seasoncote at Lady Day, and stay there a month or six weeks to do every thing in regard to the furnishing the house, and arranging the offices, grounds, &c. &c. (The old landlord at the Lion at Stowe [Stow on the Wold] *will give me rooms, & meat, & drink, whilst I continue there.) – possibly he may be content with six months certainty. I hope the wines both from Lisbon, & Oporto, have arrived with you, in good cases.- Your own wines are marked distinct.- The hogshd. Of Malmsey for Estuarta & Anna, is marked J.C. No. 2.- remember – when you draw it off – remember likewise, that if you use pints – six dozens are to go to my aunt, if of quarts, three dozens.- the remainder to be equally divided to Stuart, & Anna, with my affections.*

I hope the Guimareen Plumbs may get to you safe, after all the changes of ships &c. & that there may be no change of boxes; as happened with the oranges.-

In a letter of January 15th 1798, John refers to choosing livery colours for the Cockerell family retainers – projecting an appropriate social status was clearly considered of some importance.

I have put on my Groom – a brown livery coat, with yellow buttons, and red collar.- temporary only – untill you have made the enquiries; & that we can settle a permanent colour, for all of us

The next letter is given in full as it expresses so much about John's state of mind and loss of self confidence in what would turn out to be the last few weeks of his life. It is largely addressing his brother Samuel Pepys's encouragement for John to offer his military experience to the local militia, during this Napoleonic War period :-

Stow April 26th 1798 ['Stow' is Stow-on-the-Wold, close to John's 'Seasoncote' estate]

My good Bro Pepys.- I do thank you for your letter of yesterday, heartily; but with every willingness, to do whatever I am capable of, in the present call for personal effort of every good subject, I cannot determine to follow your advice of making proffer to the Lord Lieutenant of the County.- I feel it too strongly implicating vanity.- I am a perfect stranger in the County and wholly unknown to every class of the inhabitants.- In what, consequently, might I hope to make proffer of? – positively and efficiently – the will of a well disposed mind – assisted somewhat by an arm too, tho' God knows sadly weak and debilitated, to what heretofore it has been.-

I have other difficulties to make proffer to the Lord Lieut. – that are serious to myself – my former profession, and the services I have seen, will no doubt encourage an expectation of public benefits from me, which I am too confident of failure in.- The duties of parades, and forming of soldiers, I have little habit of having attended to. My duties were always more in the direction of military arrangements, than parade duties – and I might possibly gain more applause in conducting a Detach., than in the disciplining of a Regiment.- My health also is too precarious to offer unlimited proffers of service.-

When the Lord Lieut. has planned his dispositions, some means may occur by which I could step forward . But till I see my way more clearly of being able to fulfill & accomplish that which I may undertake, it is most advisable to be quiet.- It would be folly to do any thing in a half way.- We have a Troop of Yeomanry, by subscription, from this part of the Wold – Stow Moreton & Campden – Parishes in this district.- & I have subscribed £30.- to the Estbt. The Troop is complete 80 strong – well mounted – well appointed – & well trained:- Seasoncote Parish is actually a Connexion of this Establishment and I hesitated not to put my name down the moment I was applied to. – & if I must do more, very likely I may pay in addition, personal service, as a Yeoman.- But I shall defer, to hear from you, or to have the happiness to take you by the hand – which I look for on Tuesday: the exercising day of the Cotswold Troop, at Stowe.

I am going to dine at Dalesford house .- by invitation.- Yet I had far rather stay at home – for my cold does not mend – & my throat is very troublesome.- Strength & spirits also much fail me – but I hope the approach of summer will do me benefit.

We have began to dress the Bank & the Pond – to drain &c. Labor & expence enough ! –

My love to Anna &c. – keep me advised of your motions this way –

> *I am your ever affect. Brother*
> *Jn. Cockerell*

S P Cockerell Esq

The invitation to dine at 'Dalesford house' [Daylesford] is from Warren Hastings, retired Governor General of British India, with whom the Cockerell brothers had had direct Indian involvement.

A follow-up letter from John to his brother evidences John's increasing interest in setting up, and furnishing, his proposed Seasoncote [Sezincote] home. It references Bourton-on-the-Hill, barely a mile north of Sezincote, where several of those engaged on the project were housed. The letter's postscript also includes reference to Christies, the well-known auction house. The final comment relates to dissatisfaction with the tenant farmer at Sezincote in the months before his tenancy was terminated:-

Your idea of a few bottles to lay up at the House is not bad.- The best way will be to send a note to Buckingham Street, & order a Hamper of 3 dozen – to be sent to my name, by Waggon – Seasoncote – to be left at the Inn, Bourton-on-the-Hill.- assortment, one dozen Brandy – one dozen port wine – one dozen Sherry – It will arrive soon enough by Waggon.- My affect. regards to Anna &c. &c.

> *I am your affect Brother*
> *Jn. Cockerell*

S P Cockerell Esq

PS. You have the List Memo of furniture.- & will by now & then casting your eyes over it, when Heath calls with Inventory, be able to give him directions, as to Glass ornamental Furniture, for chimney pieces &c. Articles often at sale – at Christies, and elsewhere. Think of this, Pepys! & keep Heath in memory to let no good opportunity pass – for Beds, Rooms &c. – for much is yet to be found & bought.- Articles of Furniture might be sent as they are ready – Don't you think the Drawing Room may as well be completed, New ? – & ordered:- The Paper should be thought of also – and the Chymical paint – if you approve it to be used at Seasoncote.-

I wish we have not been imposed on by Phillips.- One of the stacks was quite green, when carried: & is probably in a bad state.

> *J Cll.*

In one of his very last letters, dated May 27th 1798, John gives an upbeat report on works at Seasoncote, in parallel with a promise to seek further medical advice and assistance. His death just a few weeks later, on 6th July therefore feels particularly sad.

> *I was at Seasoncote yesterday – The Foundations are laying.- The mason is at work on fixing chimney pieces.- The Stone Masons are come from Painswick to set the stair case – & will go to work to morrow.-*
>
> *The Brick Makers from Stratford, begin to morrow – a most charming, & they say, a Superior Clay – fit for all & every kind of work, & easily tempered.- I shall make 5 clamps of 20,000 in each.- I shall make a conclusion of my own business here, after Tuesday's meeting, with Walford, & tenants:- and I will satisfy your solicitude, my kind Brother ! – & assure you, I will come to London :- to the object of getting medical advice & assistance.- for I am too sensible, that my state of health, requires more than what can be done, by nature, or by seasons.*

Concluding Remarks on John Cockerell's Letters

There are copious volumes of these letters, which could form a topic for a separate study, but the above extracts give some idea of the family's interests, priorities, concerns, and the frequency of letter-writing between them, only terminated by John's death in 1798.

Much of the focus in this and the previous chapter has been on the four Cockerell siblings, John, Samuel ('Pepys'), Charles ('Carolus'), and Elizabeth ('Estuarta'/'Stuart'). Unlike his three siblings, John does not seem to have a family nickname, perhaps because he was the eldest. When John died in 1798 he did not leave any legitimate children to continue the family line, but Samuel, Charles and Elizabeth certainly made up for this, raising large families, several of whose members were to make significant names for themselves as part of the Fifth Generation, covered in the next chapter.

CHAPTER SEVEN

Fifth Generation – Building Status & Wealth

Selective Approach

As we progress chronologically, the number of individuals in each generation naturally expands, particularly so in the 18th and 19th centuries, with large numbers of surviving children from each marriage being typical during this period. Increasing selectivity of those included in this Fifth and later generations has therefore been unavoidable. As part of this selection decision, the branch involving Sir Charles Cockerell and his descendants has deliberately been excluded.

Charles and his relatives largely left the guardianship and promotion of the Pepys connection to other branches of the family. Having formed a marriage alliance with the Rushout family, Charles and his descendants forged their own strong and separate identities. Their future marriages into high status families simply took them further away from any focus on the Pepys connections. Unlike other branches of the family, in which the name Pepys was frequently incorporated, no such use has been identified in the Cockerell/Rushout branch. So, although Charles's family and descendants have their own considerable historic interest, their stories are not pursued any further here.

With Charles Cockerell sidelined, and John Cockerell having died in 1798 without legitimate children, the focus of the Fifth and Sixth generations is principally on the children of 'Pepys' (Samuel Pepys Cockerell), and those of his sister 'Estuarta' (Elizabeth Stuart Belli (nee Cockerell)). The individuals highlighted in this Fifth generation were almost all born in the last two decades of the 18th century, with most living through beyond the death of George IV. They can therefore be considered the last family members truly of the long Georgian era. They would be influenced mainly by Georgian values but later in their lives, and those of their children, early Victorian attitudes emerged, with more formal and morally constrained social norms developing, at least on the surface.

This Fifth generation witnessed further dramatic transformations in the fields of transport, patterns of employment, food production, science, and communication. While these advances were theoretically available to a greater proportion of the population, in practice their benefits continued to be very unequally experienced. The wider Cockerell family members were at a level of the social hierarchy very much favoured by these transformations. Another notable feature of this period was mass migration from rural areas into the rapidly expanding towns and cities, a trend which accelerated throughout the Victorian era. These changes were interlinked with the accelerating Industrial and Agricultural Revolutions and the parallel rapid expansion of Britain's global commercial trading interests. The Cockerells and their East India Company involvement continued to contribute to, and benefit from, the latter.

Anne Cockerell (1784-1865)

Born on 6th September 1784, Anne was the first of 11 children of Samuel Pepys Cockerell ('Pepys') and his wife Anne (nee Whetham) who survived infancy. Brought up in the family's home at Westbourne House, Paddington, at that time a semi-rural and fashionable part of London, Anne enjoyed a long and fulfilling life as the matriarch of a highly successful and influential family, only dying in her eighties on 28th December 1865 at Rodbourne, Wiltshire. Anne and her brothers and sisters who feature in this chapter were again extremely fortunate to have parents who were educated, and from wealthy backgrounds. As children they consequently enjoyed a physically healthy domestic environment, good food, education, and access to the best and rapidly improving medical support then available. It is remarkable that eight of the eleven children lived beyond the age of 70, when life expectancy in the general population was roughly half that, highlighting the disparity in conditions between the poor and wealthy in late 18th and early 19th century Britain.

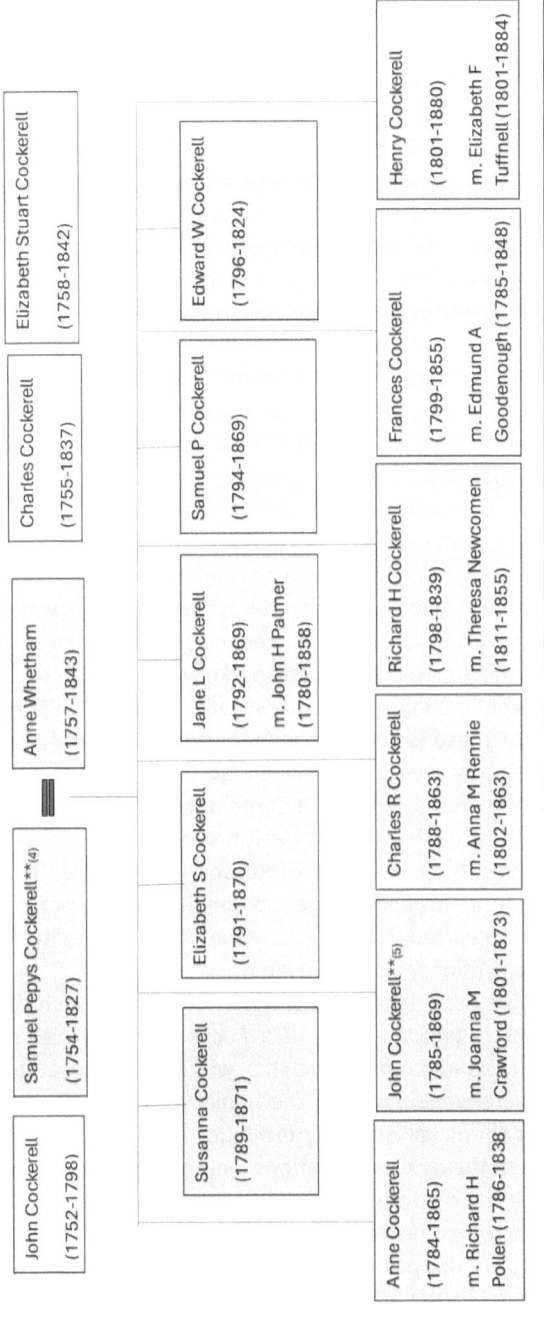

Children of Samuel Pepys Cockerell (1754-1827) & Anne Whetham (1757-1843)

John Cockerell (1752-1798)

Samuel Pepys Cockerell**(4) (1754-1827)

Charles Cockerell (1755-1837)

Elizabeth Stuart Cockerell (1758-1842)

Anne Whetham (1757-1843)

Anne Cockerell (1784-1865) m. Richard H Pollen (1786-1838

John Cockerell**(5) (1785-1869) m. Joanna M Crawford (1801-1873)

Charles R Cockerell (1788-1863) m. Anna M Rennie (1802-1863)

Susanna Cockerell (1789-1871)

Elizabeth S Cockerell (1791-1870)

Jane L Cockerell (1792-1869) m. John H Palmer (1780-1858)

Samuel P Cockerell (1794-1869)

Edward W Cockerell (1796-1824)

Richard H Cockerell (1798-1839) m. Theresa Newcomen (1811-1855)

Frances Cockerell (1799-1855) m. Edmund A Goodenough (1785-1848)

Henry Cockerell (1801-1880) m. Elizabeth F Tuffnell (1801-1884)

** Denotes Samuel Pepys's successive heirs   N.B. Of Samuel & Anne's 11 children above, the 6 on the bottom row feature most strongly in the text

163

Growing into adulthood, Anne and her siblings also benefited from a social network which afforded them excellent opportunities for advantageous marriages. In this latter, Anne was a perfect example, her choice of husband, or his choice of her, strengthening their positions and status in society, mirrored in many of the marriage alliances of her brothers and sisters. Securing a socially and financially advantageous marriage in the Regency and late Georgian period was something of an obsession among the middle and upper middle classes. It is no surprise that most of Jane Austen's novels, and much other contemporary literature, have this as the pivotal issue around which much of the action and motivation of characters revolves.

Another indication of the wider Cockerell and Pepys Cockerell families' status in society, and their associated self-confidence, is evidenced by the existence of portraits of individual family members. Photography only entered the scene in the mid-19th century. Before that drawings, paintings, and sculptures were the only means available to capture likenesses, and it is clear both from family documents and surviving known portraits that the family put great emphasis on commissioning such works. The fact that many of these were by prominent artists of the day – for example Thomas Lawrence, William Beechey, Mather Brown, Thomas Gainsborough, Margaret Carpenter and Henry Edridge – further emphasises the family's wealth, status, and connections. It also signals their own contributions, as patrons, to the contemporary artistic and cultural environment, in their case very much London-centred. Several family members also contributed directly as practitioners, outlined later.

The double portrait of Anne and her mother, from which the image below is taken, is part of a Pepys Cockerell history of portrait commissions and ownership which runs like a thread through several generations of the family. This double portrait, exhibited at the Royal Academy exhibition of 1809, was passed down through the family generations, only re-entering the public domain with the death of Elizabeth Pepys Cockerell in the early 21st century when many of her effects were auctioned. The re-emergence of this painting, and associated art-detective work, is described in Chapter 10.

Anne Cockerell, before her marriage to Richard Pollen

The Cockerells had connections and friendships with many influential figures in late 18th and early 19th century cultural circles. These include portrait painter Thomas Lawrence, landscape architect Humphry Repton, topographical artist Thomas Daniell, novelist William Makepeace Thackeray, and the multi-talented extensive Kemble family of singers and actors, including Sarah Siddons, already featured in coverage of the Fourth generation above.

A few years after the double portrait was painted, Anne would be married at her local church of Saint James, Paddington on

14th January 1815 to the eminently eligible bachelor, Richard Pollen (1786-1838), son of Sir John Pollen, 1st Baronet. Later that same year, Anne and Richard's first child, predictably named Richard, was born on 19th October 1815 into a period of relative European peace, almost exactly ten years after Trafalgar, and just four months after Waterloo. Many years later he would become Sir Richard Hungerford Pollen, 3rd Baronet. His baptism was recorded in Paddington on 1st December 1815 and, by coincidence, exactly one week earlier on 24th November in the very same Paddington baptismal record appears Adelaide Kemble, who would become a famous singer in the Victorian era. She was just one of the impressive Kemble family of actors and entertainers, well known to the Cockerell family. As noted in the previous chapter, Samuel Pepys Cockerell was a generous landlord to the famous tragedienne actress Sarah Siddons (nee Kemble), and there are friendly letters between them.

Anne's husband Richard was admitted to Lincoln's Inn, becoming a barrister, but sadly didn't share Anne's long lifespan, dying aged 52, and leaving Anne as a widow for more than a quarter of a century. The couple lived at his family home, Rodbourne House, near Malmesbury, in Wiltshire. Although widowed at an early age, Anne's long life allowed her the pleasure of seeing many of her direct descendants, and those of her brothers and sisters, flourish into adulthood and record notable successes in a wide range of careers. Several of their Pollen descendants had nationally important impacts in the arts, religion, and the military. These included Anne and Richard's second son John Hungerford Pollen, whose own long life, covered later, was to make a very significant contribution within the Victorian artistic community, not least as part of the Pre-Raphaelite movement.

In her early years Anne would have been made aware of her links with Samuel Pepys and the dramatic national events he witnessed and engaged with in the 17th century, no doubt with numerous family anecdotes embellished in the intervening period. Contrasting with any such tales from the 1600s, in her later years Anne would have witnessed modernity in the form of the railways, photography, and telegraph communication. Running through all this was her awareness that several family members in the generations after Pepys continued to be influential in national events. As already noted, in her own generation these included her cousin William Howley, Archbishop of Canterbury who, in 1837, had the duty of informing Princess Victoria that she was now Queen. Even closer to home, her brother Charles Robert Cockerell was celebrated for his pioneering archaeological adventures in the Classical Mediterranean world and for his later role as the 19th century's leading Classicist architect.

As with any first-born child, Anne would always hold a special place in the family. The fact that a leading portrait painter, one exhibiting at the Royal Academy and painter to the Royal Family, was commissioned to execute the much-praised double portrait of the young adult Anne and her mother indicates her family status. The portrait's gentle domestic style, much praised in contemporary commentary (see Chapter 10), points to a particularly close and loving relationship between mother and daughter.

The contemporary obsession with securing a favourable marriage, usually before a woman's mid-twenties, meant that when she married Richard Pollen in her early thirties the natural sense of joy was perhaps accompanied by some relief. He may have been equally happy and fulfilled to have found his life partner in his late thirties. Their ages made it extremely unlikely that Anne would emulate her mother in producing 11 children. In any event, having witnessed first-hand her mother's frequent pregnancies, with an almost annual pattern, no doubt with their fair share of challenges and fatigue, Anne probably had no desire to follow suit. Whether by choice or not, in an era of large family sizes the relatively modest number of four children would result. In contrast, as will be outlined shortly, her son Richard and his wife Charlotte would produce a large family in the early Victorian period.

Anne's husband Richard Pollen died in 1838, and she lived the last 27 years of her life as a widow. However, this would be no single or lonely existence, as evidenced by the 1851 and 1861 censuses. In the 1851 census, Anne, aged 66, and described as a widow of her deceased barrister husband, is firmly the head of the considerable household at Rodbourne House, with substantial associated responsibilities. With her are her son Richard Hungerford Pollen, aged 35, Justice of the Peace for Wiltshire, and his wife Charlotte, aged 24, with their four children. Richard, Mary, and Katherine were aged 4, 3, and 1 respectively, with baby Laura just 12 days old.

Clearly this was a busy household although, as well as having several servants, the pressures of looking after the young children may have been eased by having one of Anne's daughters, Jessie, aged 31, living with them. Also recorded in the census is one of her nieces, Annabella Goodenough, aged 25, who is there as a visitor at the time of the census, possibly linked with the very recent arrival of baby Laura. In addition to family members, there were ten servants and one of the housekeeper's nieces. The roles of the servants, namely butler, coachman, housekeeper, housemaid, cook, nurse, nurserymaid, kitchenmaid, scullerymaid, and monthly nurse, gives a good idea of how a substantial upper middle-class household with young children was run in the mid-19th century.

Ten years later, the 1861 census provides an update on how the composition of the household had evolved and expanded. Anne, aged 76, no longer head of the household, is described as 'widow of landed property'. Anne's son Richard Hungerford Pollen is now entered as the head of the household, but widowed. His wife Charlotte had sadly died since the 1851 census, but only in the late 1850s because their three daughters and one son appearing in that earlier census, have not only survived but been joined, and exactly mirrored, by three more daughters, Constance, Anne, and Helen and another son, Charles. Aged 3 at the time of the census, Charles is the youngest of these eight children, and the eldest, Richard, is now aged 14. The children are all described as scholars, education always being a priority within the wider family, from Samuel Pepys's 17th century time onwards.

Other family members and relations at Rodbourne House in the 1861 census are Louisa and Jessica, Anne's unmarried daughters, aged 44 and 41. Jessica is the Jessie appearing in the previous 1851 census. If these two daughters had not managed to secure suitable marriages it would be entirely natural that they are now present as part of this extended family household. Also present at Rodbourne in 1861 are Anne's unmarried nephew Frederick Goodenough, aged 33, described as a merchant at Calcutta, and her unmarried niece Lucy Goodenough, aged 34, described as a clergyman's daughter. A final extended family member present is Richard Pollen's unmarried brother-in-law Archibald Godley, aged 32, described as a land agent in Ireland.

To support the running of the household, still typically requiring the many formal daily routines and protocols expected at this time, there are now ten female and three male servants including Antoinette Chenaux, a nurse born in Metz, France, and Helene Emmell, a governess born in Prussia. One hopes they worked together amicably as part of the household without any of the national animosity leading to the imminent Franco-Prussian War. The total household comprised 20 females and 8 males and, even though it was a large house as described in the much later Historic England list description below, there would probably have been much sharing of rooms, particularly amongst the servants.

Rodbourne House is a Grade II listed building. The list entry below includes reference to the Hungerford Pollens, the Pre-Raphaelites, and the author William Makepeace Thackeray.

ST 98 SW ST PAUL MALMESBURY THE STREET, Rodbourne
WITHOUT (north side)
8/170 Rodbourne House
II

Detached house. Probable late C17-early C18 core with extensive
1859 additions and alterations (datestone on north-east tower)
carried out for Sir Hungerford Pollen. Squared and coursed rubble
with brick and stone dressings, ashlar copings and concrete tile
gabled roofs with tall triple stacks of brick and stone laid in
bands. Irregular plan with core ranges facing south and south-
west, C19 additions to north and north-east. North front of 2
elements: 4-storey tower with pyramidal roof to left of 3-storey
Cl9 section and earlier 2-storey and attic block to right with
advanced canted front. C19 section has ovolo-moulded cross-mullion
fenestration with tall 9-light windows to right of tower. Earlier
section to right has a 3-light French window to ground floor, a 16-
pane sash above and 2 gabled dormers; rusticated stone quoins.
Doorway to right of C19 section with part-glazed door. Interior:
inaccessible on resurvey but reputed to have a fine Arts and Crafts
staircase. The Hungerford Pollens were close associates of the
Pre-Raphaelites and the novelist William Thackeray is said to have
stopped here.
Listing NGR: ST9374883504

As well as the William Makepeace Thackeray connection at the end of the listing, there is a further intriguing link between the Cockerells, the Thackerays, and other prominent cultural figures. Anne Isabella Thackeray, William Thackeray's eldest daughter, also a novelist, lived at 16 Onslow Gardens, Chelsea, with Anne's nephew John Cockerell and his family at neighbouring 15 Onslow Gardens, as evidenced in the 1871 census. The head of the household at 16 Onslow Gardens was Leslie Stephen living with his wife Harriet, another daughter of William Makepeace Thackeray. When Leslie Stephen remarried after Harriet's death, the couple had two daughters who would, a generation later, become leading figures in the early 20th century Bloomsbury Group, namely Virginia Woolf the writer and Vanessa Bell the artist. This is revisited in a later chapter.

It seems that the nineteenth century Cockerell and Thackeray families were well acquainted, and both families made major contributions to the Victorian cultural scene. The list description above references the Pre-Raphaelite connections. Prior to his death in 1863, William Makepeace Thackeray had also lived near to Cockerell family members in London. He is noted as head of the household at 36 Onslow Square in the 1861 census and described as 'writer of novels – barrister not in practice'. His household in 1861 included his daughters Anne and Harriet, who had also been listed with him in the 1851 census at 13 Young Street, Kensington, when he was described as 'barrister, periodical writer'.

As well as these various cultural links, geography provided another, because W. M. Thackeray was born in India, as were so many of the wider Cockerell family. Notably, several of Anne Pollen's uncles and aunts had lived and worked in India in the late 18th century, as already set out in considerable detail. India also provides the backdrop to key characters in Thackeray's novel 'Vanity Fair'.

Four years after the 1861 census, Anne Pollen (nee Cockerell) died on 28th December 1865 at Rodbourne House where she had lived since her marriage decades earlier. Her Will was proved by the oaths of her sons Sir Richard Hungerford Pollen and John Hungerford Pollen. As noted, John was influential in the national cultural scene during the second half of the nineteenth century, particularly in relation to the Pre-Raphaelite and Arts and Crafts Movements, and his story is outlined later. In 1865 his address was given as 11 Pembridge Crescent, London, and he lived there until his death on 2nd December 1902. He truly epitomised and influenced major strands of Victorian artistic fashion, and it is appropriate that his life spanned Queen Victoria's entire reign.

In summary, Anne had been born in the late 18th century, and her son John would live through into the 20th. Also, as outlined earlier, her grandson Arthur Pollen, businessman, engineer and scientist, significantly initiated and influenced improvements to naval gunnery and strategy at the turn of the 20th century. Between them the Pollens experienced and enjoyed much that Britain's prominent global presence delivered in economic, scientific, and cultural terms during the 19ᵗʰ century. Undoubtedly beneficiaries, but also significant contributors.

John Cockerell (1785-1869)

Anne Cockerell was not an only child for long. Shortly after her first birthday, her mother gave birth to John who, like his sister, would live into his eighties. As the senior male child and next Samuel Pepys heir, in 1827 he would inherit the considerable responsibility for the substantial volume of Pepys private letters, documents, and various other legacies that had passed down to his father.

These historically important documents, while significant, didn't include the Diary itself, which was incorporated in the Pepys Library at Cambridge University, housing Pepys's massively impressive collection of books, pamphlets, and manuscripts. At the time of John's father's death in 1827, the value of Pepys's Diary was only just being recognised, the first version of its deciphered text only published two years earlier in 1825. With the associated growing public interest in Samuel Pepys as an important historical figure, John would have been even more aware of the importance of the family's legacy collection he now held as tangible evidence of their link with Pepys. The substantial collection of Pepys's private correspondence, and other memorabilia, later loosely termed the *Pepys Cockerell Collection* (see Chapter 11 for more details), would in turn pass to John's son, Andrew Pepys Cockerell (1830-1886), and eventually to his grandson John Pepys Cockerell (1866-1930). It was this latter relative who facilitated the publishing, in 1926 and 1929, of Samuel Pepys's private letters and correspondence covering the period 1662 to 1703, which the family had then held and safeguarded for over two hundred years.

In protecting and passing on the collection, John Cockerell (1785-1869) clearly accepted the inherited family responsibilities, and perhaps enthusiastically promoted their importance as part of the family's pride in the Pepys connection. Certainly, by naming one of his sons Andrew Pepys Cockerell, John was faithfully following the pattern established by his grandfather and father, namely incorporating Pepys as a middle name. The family's first-born sons were usually called John, but in this case it was the second son who was named John (1831-1877). Perhaps there had earlier been a first son named John who had died in infancy, perhaps even a twin of Andrew born in 1830.

Returning to John's earlier years, he had been admitted to St. John's College Cambridge on October 6th 1803, matriculated (i.e. was formally accepted as an undergraduate) in 1804, gained his BA degree in 1808, and was awarded his MA in 1811. Alongside his academic studies he was admitted to Lincoln's Inn on 5th April 1805. Like his sister Anne, John married at a late age for the time, 44 in his case, with his wife Joanna Mary Crawford being some 16 years younger. Joanna, the daughter of Brigadier-General James Catlin Crawford (often spelt Craufurd), had been born at the Cape of Good Hope on 5th March 1801, two years after James's marriage to Anne Elisabeth Barnard. The Barnard surname and South African context resonate with Christiaan Barnard, the cardiac surgeon carrying out the world's first human-to-human heart transplant in 1967 but exploring any possible family connection is outside scope here.

Joanna's father had an especially eventful military career during the Napoleonic Wars. Having been promoted to Brigadier-General on 26th July 1809, he died from a fever in 1810 at Abrantes, Portugal while on campaign in the Peninsular War. His death and its aftermath left Joanna, her sisters, and her mother in an extremely vulnerable financial position. Fortunately, Wellington intervened with a letter to the Secretary of State, the Earl of Liverpool, requesting financial support and Joanna's mother Anne was duly granted a £300 annual pension. However, this pension would end on Anne's death, so the family, still living in Sussex, remained in a precarious position. Joanna would therefore have been all too aware of the importance of securing a respectable, and ideally financially advantageous, marriage. John Cockerell, although much older than Joanna, was eminently eligible.

It is not clear how she and John Cockerell met, but whether it was any more a genuine love match than her mother's marriage (evidently largely one of convenience), it was a relationship with mutual benefits. Joanna's marriage to John on 24th September 1829 at St George Church, Hanover Square, was conducted by John's brother-in-law Edmund Goodenough, just one of several examples of Cockerell family marriages being conducted by clerical relatives. It appears that the marriage was enthusiastically celebrated by the respective families, with the official marriage record evidencing far more than the usual number of witnesses. On the Cockerell side these were Samuel Pepys Cockerell, Richard Howe Cockerell, Charles Robert Cockerell, John Horsley Palmer, Elizabeth Horsley Palmer (nee Cockerell), and Jane Louisa Cockerell. From Joanna's family, witnesses were James Craufurd, Isabella Barnard, A F Barnard and H W Barnard. Although there are frequent references to their initial Sussex residences, emerging from her father's military posting in Lewes in 1803, their son Andrew Pepys Cockerell and daughter Mary Theresa Cockerell were both born in London, Andrew in Putney and Mary in Paddington, probably at John's parents' house Westbourne House, in Westbourne Grove.

John is recorded as being a Justice of the Peace for Wiltshire and was the owner of Burton Hill House, a late C17 manor near Malmesbury, not far from the Pollen's house described above. Burton Hill House was destroyed by fire on March 14th, 1846, after which it was rebuilt. However, the couple clearly felt that Sussex was their natural home and fifteen years later the 1861 census record shows John and Joanna living at 9, Adelaide Crescent, Hove, near Brighton, with their daughter Mary Theresa, aged 24, and five female servants aged between 17 and 52.

Eight years later John died, and his probate record is given at the end of this section. Two years after his death the 1871 census shows the family still living at 9, Adelaide Crescent, with Joanna, aged 70, now the head of the household and described as 'fundholder', i.e. living off investments. With her are her son Andrew Pepys Cockerell, aged 40, described as the owner, and her daughter Mary Theresa Cockerell, aged 34. They still have 5 female servants, but all different from those employed in 1861. There was nothing unusual about such a turnover of servants.

When Joanna died two years later in 1873, the probate record gives a little more information.

COCKERELL Joanna Mary *(Effects under £1,500)*
*10 April. The Will of Joanna Mary Cockerell late of 9 Adelaide-crescent Brighton in the County of **Sussex** Widow who died 15 March 1873 at 45 Hertford-street May Fair in the County of Middlesex was proved at the **Principal***

> **Registry** *by Andrew Pepys Cockerell of 45 Hertford-street Esquire the Son the sole Executor.*

Clearly, sometime before her death she had moved from Brighton to 45 Hertford Street in Mayfair, the home of John's brother Samuel Pepys Cockerell (1794-1869), presumably so that she could be better cared for in her later years, with the wider London-based family and the best medical practitioners on hand. Her son Andrew Pepys Cockerell is also noted as living at 45 Hertford Street in the 1873 probate record. Although Andrew is resident in Brighton at the time of the 1871 census, he is also recorded as residing at 45 Hertford Street when his father died in 1869 (see below), so around this time Andrew clearly frequented family residences in both Brighton and London. Later records show both Andrew (in the 1881 census) and his sister Mary (in the 1891 census) living in London not far from Hertford Street at 11 Mandeville Place, an address that tallies with a later strand of our narrative.

Joanna's probate entry '*Effects under £1,500*' indicates that the value of her assets was just below this amount and, although by no means a fortune and less than several other family members, this was still a substantial amount at the time. As context for the value of £1,500 in 1873, an average farm worker's annual wages were around £35 a year, itself probably more than the wages of individual servants the family had employed in Brighton.

We now refocus briefly on John Cockerell who had died at 9, Adelaide Crescent, Brighton on 28th April 1869, 4 years before Joanna. Compared with many other family members, he has not left any high-profile personal legacies nor made his mark in any specific field but he does appear to have continued with several of his father's business interests. The probate record entry is given here.

> **COCKERELL John Esq.** *(Effects under £800)*
> *13 November. The Will of John Cockerell late of 9 Adelaide-crescent Brighton in the County of* **Sussex** *Esquire deceased who died 28 April 1869 at 9 Adelaide-crescent aforesaid was proved at the* **Principal Registry** *by the oath of Andrew Pepys Cockerell of 45 Hertford-street May Fair in the County of Middlesex Gentleman the Son one of the Executors.*

The value of John's effects is surprisingly modest for the eldest son of a family with such a high profile and social status. Perhaps he passed on some of his wealth to his children well before his death. John and Joanna's eldest son Andrew Pepys Cockerell's story will feature in the next chapter, including his role in inheriting, and then in turn passing on, the so-called Pepys Cockerell Collection of Samuel Pepys letters, documents, and other memorabilia.

Charles Robert Cockerell (1788-1863)

Charles was Samuel Pepys Cockerell and Anne's second son and while his elder brother John, as first son, inherited many of the family's assets and, notably, many of the historic Samuel Pepys documents and memorabilia, it was Charles who pursued his father's profession as an architect. Evidence indicates a strong bond between father and son, and high expectations of Charles. He not only met, but massively exceeded, these hopes. He had the help of investment in his development, and ongoing family encouragement but, just like Samuel Pepys a century and a half earlier, his innate talents were the paramount factors in his success.

Charles Robert Cockerell, RA, PRIBA Portrait by William Boxall (1800-1879)

Assisted by the family's impressive connections, his travels in Europe, with their archaeological significance, were widely reported in the British press, and made him a young celebrity, despite him neither seeking nor enthusiastically embracing such fame. As a character he was in many ways the opposite of his father, who had been opportunistic, ambitious, worldly, and focused on status and reputation. Charles was more introverted and academic, particularly when it came to the visual arts. Although designing some outstanding buildings of national importance, Charles was more interested in the artistic, aesthetic,

The young Charles Cockerell planning his Mediterranean tour, seated beside the Wellington Pillar at Sezincote, the Indian style house (in the background) designed by his father.

From a painting by Thomas Daniell RA, also responsible for the Indian detailing of the house.

archaeological, and theoretical aspects of architecture rather than commercial success, and he was a star member of what was only just being established as a formal professional body. Indeed, he was one of the Royal Institute of British Architects (RIBA) founders and had a major national influence on architecture during much of the 19th century. In the 19th century 'Battle of the Styles' between Classical and Gothic architecture, Charles was a key flagbearer for the Classical camp.

Because he was such a high profile and pivotal architectural celebrity, there is a wealth of source information, in contrast with the sparse information available for some of his close relations featured here. He recorded many details of his foreign travels in Southern Europe and the Levant between 1810 and 1817 in a journal, somewhat reminiscent of the record-keeping Diary of his famous predecessor covering the 1660s. Charles's journal was edited and published by his son (another Samuel Pepys Cockerell) in 1903, exactly 200 years after Samuel Pepys's death.

Letters between his father and Charles give an insight into his life and character. In one such letter of 1816, referred to in the Introduction chapter, Charles acknowledges his good fortune in being born into a wealthy and talented family, commenting, '*I exult in being one of so remarkable a family*'. By this time, Charles had already established his own positive reputation and degree of fame through his Mediterranean architectural and archaeological discoveries and commentary.

After departure from England in April 1810, reports of his adventures had been circulating in London throughout his absence. Some early letters home were carried by his friend Lord Byron on the ship transporting the Elgin Marbles to London which stimulated interest in all things connected with classical antiquity. His father, Samuel Pepys Cockerell ('Pepys'), writing to Charles shortly before his return in May 1817, refers at length to his son's developing reputation and celebrity, including the following passage.

> '*You have raised a name here so high that everything in perfection will be expected from you; at least in all that relates to taste in the arts, and in all the subordinate degrees of contrivances, as well as in decoration. ... Your friends Lord Burghersh and Lord Dillon proclaim your name without ceasing, and much is expected of you. The Duke of Gloucester has commanded me to introduce you to his acquaintance. You have been spoken of at Carlton House* [residence of the Prince Regent]*, where I have reason to think there is great likelihood of your being noticed advantageously ...* '

Such expectations were a burden to Charles, given his rather diffident and sensitive nature, but reflected a reputation to be celebrated because of its obvious merit, even at this early stage of his life. His artistic and aesthetic impact, particularly in the blossoming field of architectural theory, would flourish substantially as his influence took hold over the next half century. At odds with the vision his father had for him, there was some tension between their respective commercial and aesthetic leanings, but ultimately it was a constructive and amicable relationship.

Charles Robert Cockerell's passion was the Classical architectural style, both in theory and practice, leaning heavily on his archaeological investigations and discoveries in Southern

Europe. His contributions were nationally and internationally significant both through theoretical architectural writings, which contributed to his Professorship, and through an impressive portfolio of executed buildings. These latter were predominantly in Classical styles, with most surviving in the 21st century, an obvious example being the magnificent Ashmolean Museum and Taylorian Institute in Oxford. Notably and appropriately, considering Samuel Pepys's 17th century library and collections, Charles designed several 19th century public libraries and museums.

Charles was also Surveyor both to St Paul's Cathedral (and was buried in its crypt), and to the Bank of England, designing its branch offices in Manchester, Liverpool, Bristol, and Plymouth. One of his cousins was a Governor of the Bank of England. Charles won the first RIBA Gold Medal for architecture in 1848 and became its president in 1860.

While his impressive legacy doesn't have the impact or profile of Samuel Pepys's achievements a century and a half earlier, he certainly played a major role in keeping the Pepys name and family links alive in the public domain, not least through incorporating Pepys in the names of two of his sons, Frederick Pepys Cockerell and Samuel Pepys Cockerell, whose lives and achievements were to be of substantial merit. Their lives are outlined in the next chapter covering the Sixth generation.

On 4th June 1828 Charles married Anna Maria Rennie, the ceremony being conducted by William Howley, then Bishop of London, the husband of Charles's cousin Mary. Anna Maria was the daughter of John Rennie, a giant in the field of civil engineering who made a massive contribution to the extraordinary works transforming Britain's built infrastructure, including bridges, canals, docks, and lighthouses. The Oxford Dictionary of National Biography comments that, "*Rennie's crowning achievement was the trio of metropolitan bridges spanning the Thames: Waterloo Bridge, Southwark Bridge and London Bridge … Waterloo Bridge (1811-1817) was his masterpiece*". As an indication of his national profile and achievements John Rennie was buried in St. Paul's Cathedral, just as Charles himself would be.

John Rennie, as well as being Charles's father-in-law, provides yet another link with the Cockerells' Indian focus, as he was responsible for the design and building one of the largest docks in

London. In 1800, he was appointed engineer to the London docks and in 1803, engineer to the East India Docks. Rennie was also heavily involved in introducing steam-driven machinery in the royal dockyards, to speed ship repairs. Once again therefore, there is a strong naval connection back to Samuel Pepys and his 17th century work for the Admiralty, identifying and initiating improvements to the dockyards along the Thames. John Rennie was engineer to the Admiralty, and his son Sir John Rennie (Anna Maria's brother and C. R. Cockerell's brother-in-law) succeeded to that position from 1820 to 1831. Docks and shipbuilding yards comprised a large part of the Rennies' engineering work, and the parallels between his in-laws' 19th century dockyard work and Samuel Pepys's similar focus on 17th century dockyards would not have been lost on Charles, with such close family connections to both.

Susanna Cockerell (1789-1871)

Referred to in family correspondence as Suky, we know little about her long life, but she would have witnessed many momentous national and global events and conflicts as well as profound societal changes. She was born in the transport age of horses and coaches, but by the time of her death the rail network spanned several thousand miles of track, and her life spanned the period from the French Revolution to the Franco-Prussian War, with the Napoleonic and Crimean Wars in between. Other far-flung conflicts included those in India, in which her uncles and cousins had been actively involved. Like the rest of the family, she would benefit from greater access to the variety of goods being imported from the expanding empire.

Susanna never married and, like her sister Elizabeth Sophia (see below), she was living with her brother Samuel Pepys Cockerell at 45 Hertford Street, Mayfair, London in the parish of St. George Hanover Square as evidenced in the 1851 census, with Samuel noted as the head of the household. There were three female and two male servants.

Her nephew Andrew Pepys Cockerell was still living with her at the 45 Hertford Street address when she died on 5th May 1871. Her Will was proved on 26th May, describing her as a spinster, with her effects valued at just under £16,000, a very considerable amount at the time, equivalent to over £1m today.

Elizabeth Sophia Cockerell (1791-1870)

Younger sister of Susanna, Elizabeth was another family member who far outlived the national contemporary life expectancy, dying just short of age 80 on 16th November 1870 at 45 Hertford Street, Mayfair. As already noted, in 1851 she was living there with her siblings Susanna and Samuel. Apart from those sparse details, no other recorded information has been found despite searches in both family letters and more general genealogical sources. What is clear is that none of the siblings would be lonely, and they probably enjoyed a very comfortable lifestyle including refined social interaction. Having a large family network in London would have had many benefits, not only practical and emotional, but in the Cockerells case it also provided connections with some influential individuals.

During the 19th century, the family had two addresses in the West End of London which crop up frequently. 45 Hertford Street is one, the other being 11 Mandeville Place. The compact Hertford Street terraced house is very close to Hyde Park Corner, where a more imposing house had been the base for the late 18th and early 19th century generation of the Cockerell family. Some outline information and clues about the scale and grandeur of this latter house are described in letters sent backwards and forwards between India and London.

Jane Louisa Cockerell (1792-1865)

Jane, often referred to as Louisa or just 'Luce', her family nickname, was the third daughter and fifth child of Samuel Pepys Cockerell ('Pepys') and Anne (nee Whetham). Although remaining a spinster for most of her life she would eventually marry John Horsley Palmer, the widower of her cousin Elizabeth. Such tight family intermarriages, particularly in later life as was the case here, often had mutual benefits for both partners, aside from any emotional or romantic attachment.

Intriguingly, although only married to the widowed John later in life in 1841, and approaching her 50th birthday, there is evidence that there may have been some attraction between them some thirty years earlier. In a letter of 19th January 1811, written in Athens from their brother Charles Robert Cockerell to his sisters (including Louisa), he notes that he is replying to a '*delightful letter of Luce*'. Her letter had alluded to a possible engagement for their sister Anne, and he notes in reference to a different and more definite engagement, '*I am more than happy to hear that Old Horseley the worthiest of men is at last allied to our family, he is a prop & a tower we may all put our trust in and boast of, I wish to God it was as you say my Dear Louisa a still nearer connection*'. This is a reference to the engagement of John Horsley Palmer to their cousin Elizabeth Belli (nee Cockerell) which, although celebrated in Charles's comments, is accompanied by slight regret that John Palmer was marrying Charles's cousin rather than one of his sisters. Among those sisters, perhaps it was Louisa herself, then aged 19, who Charles had in mind in his 1811 letter. If so, any mutual attraction existing at that earlier time was eventually and happily rekindled three decades later, leading to Louisa's marriage to the widowed John Horsley Palmer in 1841. Marrying him in later life, after her cousin Elizabeth's death, would have been some considerable consolation for any disappointment Louisa may have experienced in her youth.

John and Jane Louisa were married on 8th July 1841 in the Chapel of Lambeth Palace. This prestigious venue was a natural one for the couple because Lambeth Palace was traditionally the home of the Archbishop of Canterbury, at that time William Howley, married to Mary Frances (nee Belli), who was both John's sister-in-law, and Jane's cousin. John's address is given as Hurlingham House, Fulham, Middlesex, and Jane Louisa's as Stratton Street, Middlesex. The witnesses of the marriage were her brothers John Cockerell and Samuel Pepys Cockerell. These brothers are not to be confused with the brothers of the same names in the previous fourth generation, covered in some detail in previous chapters. Repetition of names between generations is once again evidenced as a prevalent feature of the Pepys Cockerell family.

In the 1851 census, Louisa, aged 59, was living with her husband John Horsley Palmer at Hurlingham House, with John listed as the head of the household, aged 71, and his occupation given as 'Merchant East India'. Also recorded at Hurlingham House in the 1851 census are John's 29-year-old son Richard, from his first marriage to Elizabeth Belli (nee Cockerell). Richard was born in Fulham, and his wife Emma, aged 26, is recorded as having been born in Madras, East India – yet more Indian connections. Also living with them were Elizabeth, aged 34, and Frances, aged 30, two daughters from John's previous marriage to Louisa's cousin Elizabeth, who had sadly died in 1839.

John Horsley Palmer had purchased Hurlingham House around 1820 from the 3rd Earl of Egremont for £12,000. In the preceding decades, this prestigious house had been visited by several high-profile guests including Lord Admiral Nelson, the Duke of Wellington, David Garrick, Richard Sheridan, and Prime Minister George Canning. To give some idea of the running of the house in John and Jane Louisa's time, there were two male and seven female servants listed in the 1851 census, as well as there being a separate Gardeners House where the Head Gardener and his wife lived with their two sons and two daughters. Also supporting the operations of the main house were the head coachman, his wife, and daughter, housed in the Gate Lodge, as well as a second coachman living in the stables.

Focusing back on Jane Louisa, although she had previously had a comfortable upbringing and supportive family environment, this unexpected later part of her life must have been a particularly delightful experience, becoming part of a settled family enclave with as indulgent a lifestyle as she could possibly have hoped for. Her husband John died on 7th February 1858, and a few years later Jane died on 13th October 1865. Four years after her death, the grand Hurlingham House and its grounds, having been a private residence for many decades, became the Hurlingham Club. The Hurlingham Rules for the game of polo were introduced there in 1874.

Samuel Pepys Cockerell (1794-1869)

The succession of children from the marriage of Anne to Samuel Pepys Cockerell continued in 1794 with the birth of their third son, Samuel Pepys Cockerell, taking his father's exact name and perpetuating the naming link with his three times great uncle, the famous 17th century diarist. Within the family – evidenced by letters between his siblings – he was frequently referred to simply as 'Pepys', just as his father had been amongst his own siblings. Judging by comments in letters from his brother Charles Robert

Cockerell, in his youth this reincarnation of 'Pepys' was thought somewhat lazy in his own letter-writing, a social skill considered particularly important not just as the main means of communication between family members, friends, and business contacts but also evidencing a good education.

Whether or not Charles's criticism was justified, this latest 'Pepys' reincarnation had indeed benefited from a good education and became a barrister at the Court of Chancery. Privileged family circumstances and physical environment helped him to enjoy a long life. There is no record of him marrying and, as noted above, the 1851 census shows him as the head of the household living with his elder sisters Elizabeth Sophia and Susanna at 45 Hertford Street, Mayfair, near Hyde Park Corner, where the previous Cockerell generation's large prestigious house neighboured that of the Duke of Wellington.

At the time of his death, he was still living at 45 Hertford Street, and the probate record provides more details.

> **COCKERELL Samuel Pepys (*Effects under £10,000.* Resworn** *at the Stamp Office March 1871* **Under £18,000.***)*
> *26 February. The Will of Samuel Pepys Cockerell late of Lincoln's Inn and of Hertford-street Mayfair both in the County of **Middlesex** Barrister-at-Law deceased who died 7 February 1869 at 45 Hertford-street aforesaid was proved at the **Principal Registry** by the oath of Andrew Pepys Cockerell of 45 Hertford-street aforesaid Esquire the Nephew the sole Executor.*

As is clear from text above, the property at 45 Hertford Street was occupied by several members of the Cockerell family at various times, including Andrew Pepys Cockerell of the next generation as recorded by the above probate record in 1869.

Edward William Cockerell (1796-1824?)

Edward was the fourth son of Samuel Pepys and Anna Cockerell, and if one source relating to his death is to be believed then, unlike his many siblings, Edward unfortunately died in his late 20s and would have been much mourned by his parents as well as by his nine living siblings and their families. However, while there seems to be agreement that he was born on 31st January 1796 at No. 7 Saville Row, London, one of the two homes of his parents Samuel Pepys Cockerell and Anna Cockerell, details of his death are scant, other researchers noting it as being in 1824 at Sevenoaks Kent, but there are no official sources cited.

What is also slightly unusual is that in 1812 his father Samuel Pepys Cockerell made a deposition regarding the details of Edward's birth, seemingly to rectify some error in recording the child's baptism back in 1796. The handwritten copy of the deposition reads as follows :-

Samuel Pepys Cockerell of Saville Row in the parish of Saint James Westminster and Westbourne Green in the County of Middlesex Esquire one of his Majesties Justices of the Peace for the said County maketh oath and saith that Edward William Cockerell son of the said Samuel Pepys and Anna his wife, was born in their dwelling house No. 7 in Saville Row aforesaid on the thirty first day of January which was in the year one thousand seven hundred and ninety six at a little after two o'clock A.M. that the said Edward William was as this deponent believes very soon afterwards viz. on Saturday the twenty seventh day of February named by the officiating Minister of the said Parish according to the rites of the Church of England and that the said Edward William was shortly afterwards viz. on Thursday the thirty first day of March fully Baptized according to such rites, and this deponent is informed and believes that no register of the said Baptism hath been duly made in the Register of the said Parish, and is desirous that the same should now be made [Signed S.P.Cockerell] Sworn before me one of his Majesties Justices of the Peace for the City of Westminster at the Vestry Room of the Parish if Saint James Westminster this second day of January 1812 –-----------------

R Johnson
Entered on the seventh day of February 1812
Witness H J Bracken (?) in Orders and Registrar

It has proved impossible to establish, let alone verify, any details of Edward's life. He appears to have left little trace. Research continues. When searching for an Edward William Cockerell born in 1796, very little comes up apart from the birth and baptism details evidenced by the deposition above. However, a wider search on the name Edward Cockerell does throw up intriguing criminal records for an Edward Cockerell aged 29 in January 1826.

It should be stressed at the outset that the link is extremely unlikely, even though this set of public records could explain Edward's disappearance from any of the normal records. It is the Middlesex record of the 1826 January session at The Old Bailey in which an Edward Cockerell, aged 29 (which would match with 'our' Edward Cockerell having been born on 31st January 1796) is charged with forging County Bank Notes. For any of the Cockerells to be involved in crime would seem highly unlikely. However, younger sons did not always have an obvious career path but could still feel the pressure to be economically independent, and if finding themselves embarrassed financially may *in extremis* have resorted to a criminal action. If any of the wealthy Cockerells were to be involved in criminal activity it would be most unlikely to be things like petty theft or anything involving violence, and more likely to be a 'white collar' crime like fraud or forgery. The case, with category 'deception' and sub-category 'forgery' is recorded with a date of 12th January 1826, and the verdict of the court is recorded as guilty with the sentence of death, and the word 'executed' added. Although this could explain not only his 'passive' absence from the records but would also be an incentive for the family to proactively destroy any records or letters, other details of the case evidence that this was almost certainly not 'our' Edward Cockerell. It is, nevertheless, illustrative of the harsh penal codes existing at the time.

Assuming, as seems almost certain, that this convicted Edward Cockerell was not 'our' Edward William Cockerell, a more helpful approach might be to focus on the definite information given in Samuel Pepys Cockerell's deposition in 1812. The obvious questions are why Edward's father made the deposition, and what might have triggered this? The most likely reason was that, at that time, Edward needed to provide evidence for his age, and when his birth and baptism records presumably proved to be defective, or absent, his father had to make a deposition to get the parish records formally registered. One possible reason for Edward needing to evidence his age in 1812 may be entry to the military, with the ongoing Napoleonic Wars continuing to fuel demand for new military recruits. Edward was 16 years old and perhaps, with typical youthful enthusiasm, relished the exciting prospect that military conflict abroad promised. He would also have been aware of other family members having joined the military, not least his uncle Colonel John Cockerell. If Edward did enlist and was killed in action abroad this would explain his disappearance from any British records, but ultimately this is all speculation.

In any event, the fact remains that while there are well-documented details about his birth, because of his father's deposition, nothing else about his life and death has been identified. In contrast, his brother Richard's life, explored next, is reasonably well recorded, including his active naval service and his prestigious marriage, one resulting child later becoming Countess of Shrewsbury.

Richard Howe Cockerell (1797-1839)

Richard, the fifth son, was born on Christmas Eve 1797, and died relatively young, at the age of 41, in August 1839. However, his short life was one of some significance not only through his own naval career but also through his marriage on 5th June 1831 to Theresa Newcomen in Calcutta where he was to die just 8 years later, shortly after the birth of their third daughter. His wife Theresa was one of the eight illegitimate children of Thomas Gleadowe-Newcomen, 2nd Viscount Newcomen, and the Viscount's long-term mistress Harriet Holland. Theresa's life story follows shortly.

Richard provides the family's first active naval involvement since Samuel Pepys's 17th century Admiralty reforms. Other naval family connections would follow. Richard served in the Royal Navy and is described both as a Captain and Commander. He was made a lieutenant in January 1818 and appointed to the 21-gun ship *Dauntless*. On 18th November the same year he was appointed Captain of the ship *Honourable Valentine Gardner*, and on 8th March 1821 he became Captain of the 60-gun *Leander*, flagship of Sir Henry Blackwood, on the East India station, yet another Cockerell involvement in the Far East. On 3rd October 1825 Richard was promoted to the rank of Commander.

After this there is no record of Richard having any further significant naval service, probably because after Waterloo in 1815, which effectively signalled the end of the Napoleonic Wars, the scale of Britain's military commitment was substantially scaled down. The high cost of the wars contributed to economic pressures for many years afterwards, but while the impact on many ex-military personnel and much of the working classes in Britain was severe, Richard was more fortunate. On leaving the Navy, he was able to switch to pursuing the wider Cockerell family commercial activities in the Far East, including interests in Java. These commercial activities led to a court case, the pivotal issue being entitlement to dividends from the profits of a Java estate and plantation in which the Cockerells had a stake. The following extract from the 1840 court case documents gives the context. The John Palmer referenced may well be the John Horsley Palmer (already introduced above) who married Elizabeth Belli (nee Cockerell) as shortly described below, but this has not been confirmed.

> *That the insolvent firm, at the time of its insolvency, was possessed, jointly with the firm of Sir Charles Cockerell and Co., of London, of the beneficial interest in a large plantation in the island of Java, purchased and carried on for account, and with the joint funds of the two firms of Palmer and Co., and Cockerell and Co., but in the sole name of John Palmer, for the joint benefit of the two firms, in equal shares. ...... That the Plaintiffs directed their agents at Batavia (after the insolvency of Palmer and Co.) to take possession of the plantation, and dispose of it- for the benefit of the creditors of the insolvent firm, and remit the proceeds to the assignees for distribution.*

At first, the Cockerells' interest had been providing finance, but the operations they were financing collapsed. One consequence was that, as creditors, they inherited the plantations themselves. These Java plantations were initially growing mainly cotton, but this proved unprofitable largely because of the wet ground.

Subsequently they were primarily producing sugar for export. The main challenge was securing an adequate workforce for this labour-intensive crop, and this proved difficult. At this time the system of indentured labour was typically employed, and while not quite as reprehensible as absolute slavery, was not something to be proud of. The Cockerells eventually wound up their private commercial interests in the Far East in the mid-19th century. However, involvement with the East India Company carried on, and many of the wider Cockerell family continued to have roots in India.

After Richard's death his widow, Theresa Cockerell, remarried. Theresa Cockerell's second husband was Archibald William Montgomerie, 13th Earl of Eglinton and 1st Earl of Winton. The connections secured by this second prestigious marriage assisted in Richard and Theresa's eldest daughter Anna Theresa Cockerell securing a marriage which eventually saw her becoming Countess of Shrewsbury. Anna's life is covered later.

Refocusing on Richard Howe Cockerell, he died at the beginning of August 1839, on either 2nd or 7th, there being a difference between the secondary sources available. We are fortunate in having access to his Will, dated 14th May 1839, and this provides some additional information. The Will was signed not long before his death, so he was possibly aware of his imminent demise, perhaps implying a terminal illness. Richard's death appears to have triggered at least one complex legal dispute focused on commercial interests in Java, resolution of which is unclear, and outside our scope. In the Will he is described as living in Calcutta and being a member of the firm of Messrs. Cockerell & Company of Calcutta, merchants and agents. After his funeral costs and other associated expenses have been settled, his Will gives and bequeaths to his wife Theresa Cockerell the whole of the property which was settled upon her at the time of their marriage. Once monies owing to him have been collected and his debts settled, the residue was to be invested in East India Company stocks, known commonly as Company's papers, or alternatively in United Kingdom government stocks, with the interest to go for the benefit of his wife and three young children.

Two of the three children – Anna Theresa and Susan Caroline – are named in the Will but a space is left for the third daughter, Frederica, only very recently born on 20th April 1839, in Calcutta. She had presumably not yet been named when the Will was drawn up 24 days later or, if she had, there had simply not been enough time to add her name. The Will goes on to specify that on his wife's death, the three children will inherit their equal shares on attaining age 21 or marrying, whichever happens first. They will also benefit from the family's quarter share of lands and assets known as the Scotland Estate on Prince of Wales Island, presumably the one in Queensland, Australia, rather than that in Alaska. It is not known how or when the Cockerells purchased these lands and assets.

In summary, although dying young, Richard Howe Cockerell had an eventful life and was also pivotal to the family's entry into high society. His eldest daughter Anna Theresa Cockerell's path to becoming Countess of Shrewsbury, and her life in that role, is described as part of the next generation's story. His other two daughters also married into the nobility, and they too are covered in the next chapter, including a very specific connection that Frederica's husband has with other Cockerell relatives and their purchase of Sezincote two generations earlier.

Frances Cockerell (1799-1855)

Born on 10th May 1799, Frances was the fifth and last daughter of Samuel Pepys Cockerell and Anne. She married Reverend Edmund Addington Goodenough (1785-1845), 14 years her senior, at St. James Church, Paddington on 31st May 1821, with several named witnesses, including her relatives Jane Louisa Cockerell, Mary Anne Howley, John Belli, and Charles Robert Cockerell. The service was conducted by 'W. London', the official title of William Howley, then Bishop of London, whose wife Mary Anne was Frances's cousin. This is another example – and there are many – of Cockerell family weddings conducted by their relatives. In a further example, when Frances's brother John married Joanna Mary Crawford in 1829 the marriage service was conducted by Frances's husband.

Frances Cockerell. Artist not identified

Edmund and Frances were to have at least ten identified children, almost as many as Frances's mother. Sadly, one daughter died in childhood, another daughter in her teens, and a further son in his early twenties. Even for a family enjoying general good health and living conditions, such experiences of early death in the nineteenth century were a sad but all too familiar reality. The immediate family's grief would nevertheless have been acute and would also have been felt and mourned across the wide network of relatives. While we have no direct accounts of the funerals, these ceremonies in this early 19th century period were often extremely elaborate and formal displays, with attention to strict contemporary protocols being socially expected of wealthy families.

The 1841 census shows Frances and Edmund living at the Deanery, Wells, Somerset, with Edmund as the Dean of Wells Cathedral. With them are their twin daughters, Annabella and Lucy, aged 15, and their three sons, Frederick (10), William (8) and Leonard (2). The household is run with the considerable support of 6 female and 4 male servants. Edmund died in 1845, and the 1851 census sees the widowed Frances (51) living with her daughter Lucy (25) at 57, High Road, Loughton, Essex, with four servants.

The Goodenough descendants, like so many of the Pepys Cockerell clan, left their own distinctive legacies, including senior military contributions, perhaps the most notable individuals being Lt. Gen. Sir William Howley Goodenough, who served in India, Egypt and South Africa in the 19th century, and Admiral Sir William Edmund Goodenough, prominent at the Battle of Jutland during the First World War. Their stories and links with other Pepys Cockerell relatives are briefly taken up later.

Ten years after the death of her husband, Frances died of cholera on 5th August 1855, at Malaga in southern Spain and was buried there. Why she was there is not known, but perhaps for health reasons.

Henry Cockerell (1801-1880)

Henry, born on 8th June 1801 at Westbourne House, Paddington, was the eleventh and last of Samuel and Anne's children, and would outlive all his siblings, dying on 8th February 1880 at the Vicarage, North Weald Bassett, Essex.

Aged 18 he had matriculated at Trinity College Oxford on 17th December 1819 and later followed a religious calling. On 6th May 1827 he married Elizabeth Fanny Tufnell at Great Waltham, Essex. Like Henry, she had been born in the very early years of the 19th century and, as with so many of the wider family, her birth had been in India. They had four children, but their only daughter, Catherine Paulina, and one of their sons, Henry Edmund, died in their mid-twenties. Young Henry Edmund's death was a violent one, in India, described shortly. Catherine's second name Paulina was a frequent family choice, redolent of Paulina Pepys the 17th century diarist's sister from whom they were all directly descended. Henry and Elizabeth's two surviving sons were Francis Richard and Louis Arthur, the latter appearing in censuses through to 1871 when he is still living at home. Francis Richard Cockerell's story, largely in India, is outlined below.

In the 1841 census for Northweald, Essex, Henry Cockerell is living at the Vicarage, aged 39, described as Clerk, but there is no mention of his wife Elizabeth. She may simply have been away on the day the census was taken, appearing instead in the census recorded at wherever she was staying. Ten years later the 1851 census for Northweald shows Henry aged 49 and now described as Vicar of Northweald. His wife is recorded as Fanny Elizabeth (the order of her two forenames perhaps erroneously switched), aged 47, described as Vicar's Wife, and born at Seringapatam, India, a location already prominent in earlier text. The other entries record three servants, described as a cook, a housemaid, and a footboy.

Henry is listed as the head of the household in 1861, aged 59, living at the Vicarage, with his occupation given as Clergyman, and also engaged in farming 58 acres, employing 3 men and 1 boy. His wife Elizabeth Fanny Cockerell and son Louis Arthur Cockerell are listed, along with a footman, cook, and housemaid. Henry conducted several Cockerell family weddings, including the 1862 marriage of his nephew John Cockerell to Henrietta Frances Torrens, yet another family member who had been born India.

In the 1871 census, the family are living at 'Vickerage House' North Weald, Essex, served by a governess, cook, lady's maid, housemaid, and footman. Henry is head of the household, described simply as Vicar of the parish, no longer with any mention of farming. He is aged 69 and Elizabeth aged 70, which doesn't tally with her age of 47 cited in the 1851 census. The details do, however, tally with other records indicating that Henry and Elizabeth were both born in 1801. Elizabeth's birthplace is confirmed as 'Syrangapatam, India'. More usually spelt Seringapatam it is renowned as the fortress of 'the Tiger of Mysore', variously referred to as Hyder Ali, Tippu Sultan, Tipu Sultan, or Sultan of Mysore, a constant thorn in the side of British ambitions in India.

Just a few years before Elizabeth's birth a series of famous battles had been fought by the East India Company army at Seringapatam to take possession of this massively well defended fortress. Notably, as outlined earlier, Colonel John Cockerell, Henry's uncle, played a major role as Quartermaster General to Lord Cornwallis in the early campaigns and battles. John features prominently alongside Cornwallis in a large historic painting (shown earlier) recording Tippu Sultan handing over his two sons as hostages to ensure limitations on future threats to British expansionary interests in India. Elizabeth had presumably been born into a British settlement at Seringapatam established to secure peace at this iconic location and surrounding territory. Many children born to the British serving in India were repatriated to Britain as a more suitable place for their upbringing, and presumably Elizabeth was one such case. The Cockerells' Indian connections probably led to her marrying Henry Cockerell sometime after arriving in England. The initial introduction and connection may even have been envisaged and arranged while the young Elizabeth was still in India.

The 1871 census also shows Henry's son Louis Arthur Cockerell still living at home and now described as a Clergyman. There are two unexpected entries. The first is Margaret Cockerell, aged 13, 'granddaughter' (of Henry), whose 'rank, profession or occupation' is described as 'Civilians Daughter', with her place of birth recorded as Calcutta, India. The other interesting census entry is Rowland V. Cockerell, aged 36, described as a 'visitor', 'unmarried', born in Middlesex, with his occupation given as 'East India Civil Service'. This is Rowland Vyner Cockerell, Henry's nephew, the son of Henry's brother John Cockerell.

Shortly after this visit back in England, Rowland returned to India and died in a very strange and dramatic manner. This raises questions about the nature of Rowland's involvement with, and relationship to, Margaret. Rowland was based in Calcutta, Bengal, India, where Margaret was born, and she is an appropriate age to be his daughter. Although Margaret is described officially in the census as Henry's granddaughter, indulging in speculation, could Rowland be her natural father? It appears that she had been brought back to England to be raised and educated, with a governess (Agnes Wilson, shown in the census) appointed. Perhaps Rowland had arranged some of this through a feeling of responsibility. However, putting speculation aside he may simply have been staying with Margaret's family for a while at the time of the census, on leave from India, before returning there.

Sometime after the 1871 census, Rowland returned to India and sadly died on 9th October 1873. His death is described as happening near Simla, India, 'falling over a precipice in the

Himalaya'. Again, only speculatively, if there was some disgrace in fathering a natural daughter without ever marrying, and having now settled her back in England, combined with the very strange circumstances of his death shortly after returning to India, it is hard to exclude the possibility that he took his own life.

However, the other obvious possibility is that Margaret really was a blood granddaughter of Henry, with one of Henry's sons having been the father. One son, Henry Edmund Cockerell, born on 1st May 1831, was appointed a Civil Servant of the East India Company in 1852, was resident in India, and died on 15th June 1857 in Banda, Uttar Pradesh, just a few weeks after his 26th birthday, without ever marrying. The circumstances of his death are, like Rowland's, sudden and violent, as reported in connection with medals awarded to his cousin John Cockerell, which feature later. The text reads :-

> *At the outbreak of the Mutiny* [John] *Cockerell must have learnt with horror and rage the news of the murder of his cousin, Henry Edmund Cockerell, of the Bengal Civil Service. One night in mid June 1857, Henry, who had chosen to remain at his isolated post in the Banda district longer than was wise, decided there was nothing more he could do to enforce the Company's authority over the surrounding country. He ordered his syce to saddle his horse, and set out to seek the protection of the Nawab of Banda. But on reaching the Nawab's palace, he was treacherously pulled from his horse and hacked to pieces by the Nawab's retainers.*
>
> *Refs: Hodson Index (NAM); IOL L/MIL/10/67; IOL L/MIL/10/45; IOL L/MIL/10/65: IOL L/MIL/10/98; WO 76/550; WO 76/130 f. 76.*

If Margaret's age of 13 in the 1871 census is correct then she must have been born sometime between April/May 1857 and April 1858, and it cannot be entirely ruled out that Henry Edmund was her natural father and that she was conceived prior to his death. Even though such extra-marital relationships were almost commonplace in the East India Company, if the pregnancy had become known to Henry, could the shame have motivated him to take unreasonably reckless, almost suicidal, actions. It seems unlikely, and the fact that

Margaret was born in Calcutta and Henry was based in Uttar Pradesh tends to suggest he wasn't her natural father. His brother, Francis, was based in Calcutta where Margaret was born, so he is a more likely candidate as her father, and he is considered next.

Francis Richard Cockerell was born on 23rd August 1829 at the family home in Essex. There is an entry in the 1841 for the 'Free School' in the Hamlet of Brentwood, Essex for a Francis Cockerell aged 11 together with a Henry Cockerell aged 10, and this must be the two brothers. Like his brother Henry, Francis spent much of his adult life in India. He had been appointed a Civil Servant in the East India Company in 1850.

Francis is officially recorded as marrying Evelyn Lowther Powney Thompson on 16th November 1863 at St. Andrew's Church, Calcutta, Bengal, some 6 years after Margaret's birth. But did he have a previous marriage which could possibly have resulted in Margaret's birth in 1857? More research reveals that the answer is yes, Francis having married Alice Shakespeare Jackson on 24th June 1853. The name Jackson obviously springs out as matching that of 17th century Samuel Pepys's in-laws and his heir, John Jackson, but any connection may just be coincidence.

Alice had been born in India on 23rd July 1831, and much later she appears in the 1861 census for the parish of Upton With Chalvey living in the household of her father Welby Jackson. She is described explicitly as Welby Jackson's daughter, and a child then aged 3, named Madeline Cockerell is described as Welby Jackson's granddaughter, strongly implying that Madeline is Alice's daughter. This child's details tally with the Margaret Cockerell described above, and her identity appears to be confirmed when she is consistently thereafter called Margaret Madeline Cockerell, notably in the following census in 1871.

Sadly, Alice died very shortly after the 1861 census was taken, leaving the 3-year-old child in the care of her grandparents Welby and Elizabeth Jackson. By the time of the next census, and having lost their daughter Alice, Welby and Elizabeth were well into their 60s, and it no surprise to see that in the 1871 census, Margaret Madeline Cockerell, now aged 13, is instead living with Francis Richard Cockerell's family in North Weald Essex. Although he wasn't present, at least Francis was still alive in India and if he was Margaret's father it would have been appropriate for his family to take responsibility for Margaret's upbringing. This still leaves the question as to who was really taking responsibility for this arrangement and who was funding it. Rowland Cockerell's presence in the household in the 1871 census raises questions as to what part he played. The long and potentially hazardous voyages to and from India were usually only taken with very strong motivation for doing so – simply visiting relatives was not common. The special motivation of spending time with a natural daughter would make more sense of Rowland's visit. Notably it is Rowland rather than Francis who has risked so much to visit the teenage Margaret. If Rowland was indeed Margaret's natural father, perhaps it had been agreed within the wider family that the 'official line' was that Francis was Margaret's father to avoid unnecessary and awkward questions.

Nothing is conclusive, but why do we never see any record of Francis being present during Margaret's upbringing if he was her real father? If Margaret was Francis's daughter, did he even tell his second wife about this child from his first marriage? As far as we know Francis and his second wife continued to live in India, so perhaps they simply left all responsibility for Margaret to Francis's relatives in England. Much later, Francis did return from India, dying on 29th August 1887 at Glencairn House, Crieff, Perthshire, Scotland. The probate record dated 27 October 1887, which records his personal estate as the considerable sum of £10,585, states his residence as 2 Eaton Place, Brighton, Sussex.

In summary, the above speculation may be entirely misplaced, and all may be as per the official birth, marriage, and death records, pointing to Francis as Margaret's actual father, but other evidence doesn't naturally support this, and there remain some intriguing unanswered questions regarding Rowland Vyner Cockerell's involvement. We revisit this later when looking specifically at Rowland himself.

Having now looked at Samuel Pepys Cockerell & Anne's 11 children in brief sketches, and staying with this Fifth Generation, we turn to the children of Elizabeth Cockerell and her husband John Belli, Warren Hastings' personal or private secretary in India. For the reasons outlined earlier, the children of the third surviving sibling, Charles Cockerell, are not investigated any further.

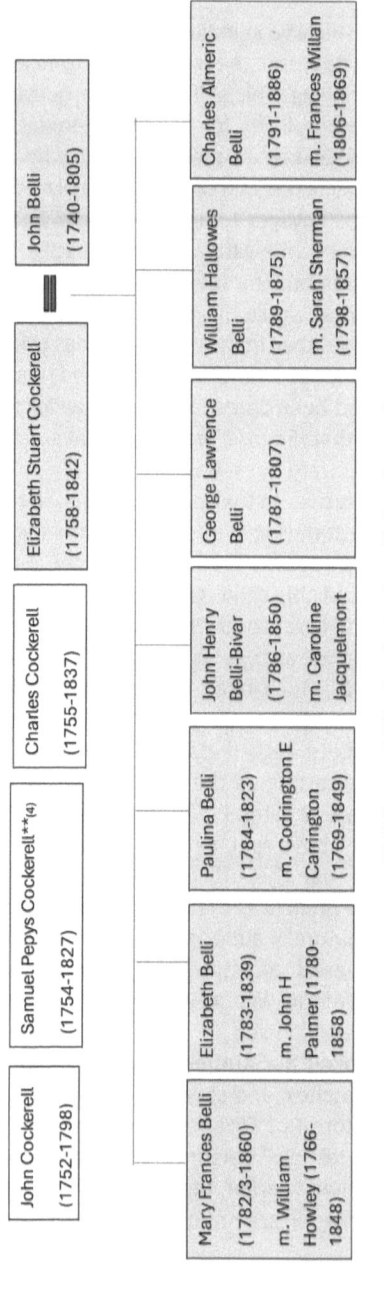

Children of Elizabeth Cockerell & John Belli

Mary Frances Howley (1782/3-1860)

Mary Frances Howley (Nee Belli) By Margaret Carpenter
(1793-1872) Signed 'Marg. Carpenter/April 1826'

Her date of birth is still to be established definitively, but in the 1851 census, as a widow and now head of the household at 7 Eaton Square, she is recorded as being aged 68, so she was born either late in 1782 or early 1783, the latter being the year given in the portrait details below. The same census record gives her place of birth as

Calcutta, British India, seemingly the same birthplace as her sister Elizabeth, born in 1783. On 29th August 1805, just a few weeks before the Battle of Trafalgar, Mary married William Howley (1766-1848) who would later become Archbishop of Canterbury, holding office between 1828 and 1848.

As with her sisters (covered shortly), we are fortunate to have a contemporary portrait of Mary. The artist was Margaret Carpenter, perhaps best known for her 1836 life-size National Portrait Gallery painting of Ada Lovelace, a mathematician and early pioneer in computer programming. Margaret Carpenter had spent some time in Thomas Lawrence's studio and was influenced by his work. While not directly copying his style, she achieved a similar attractive result.

In the early hours of June 20th 1837, while she slept, Victoria became queen. The sun had already risen when she was awoken by her mother who informed her that the Archbishop of Canterbury [William Howley, on the right] *and the Lord Chamberlain of the Household wished to see her. Obediently, Victoria got out of bed. It was the last time she ever had to obey anyone. For as she walked into a draughty room at Kensington Palace, her visitors fell to their knees.*
The great reign had begun.
https://queensconsortofengland.blogspot.com/2020/06/ the-accession-of-queen-victoria.html

Painted in 1826, significantly later than her sisters' portraits at the turn of the century (see below), dress and headwear fashion had moved on. The dress exhibits the more reserved and modest elements which became common in the following decades, as late-Georgian louche transitioned into Victorian restraint. Perhaps this more modest choice of dress was also influenced because her husband Wiiliam Howley was at that time Bishop of London and just two years later would become Archbishop of Canterbury. In 1837 he would share the formal duty of informing the young Princess Victoria that she was now Queen (see painting below). With further historic significance, Mary and William were responsible for the rebuilding of Lambeth Palace.

As noted earlier there are numerous letters written by men in our narrative, which add a significant dimension to their individual characters. Regrettably, available female first-hand evidence is meagre, although one of Sarah Siddons's illuminating personal letters to Samuel Pepys Cockerell was quoted earlier. We can at least further redress the balance slightly here, with a letter written by Mary Frances Howley from Lambeth Palace in 1840 to a Jane Porter who, it would appear, was requesting support from the Archbishop for a particular book in which Jane has an interest. In reply, Mary notes that His Grace (*her husband the Archbishop of Canterbury*) had previously acknowledged receipt of a copy of the first volume of the work in question by Count Krasinski, '*and paid him handsomely*'. Mary's letter continues politely but assertively in resisting what is clearly increasing pressure from Jane Porter. Mary comments, ' *I am therefore sorry the subject is pressed as it is, for at this season it is hardly possible to find time to read with full attention such a work; and when the state of our own Country is considered, and the deep interest every one must take in the passing events and the times, I fear it will be difficult to call general attention to Count Krasinski's work*'.

Mary's reference to '*the state of our own Country*' implies the book in question relates to a foreign country, and this is apparently Poland. Mary's expression of general concern about '*passing events and the times*' probably refers to the continuing unstable social environment and unrest in England.

The first three pages of Mary's 1840 letter to Jane Porter,
concerning a book by Count Krasinski

[*Count Zygmunt Krasinski (1812-1859) was a Polish romantic poet.*
An ardent patriot and Slavophile, he lived much of his life abroad.
His works, often set in classical antiquity, include an allegory of the
tragic history of Poland entitled Iridion (1835, tr. 1927).]

When her husband William died in 1848 Mary would have had
to vacate Lambeth Palace. The next information we have is in the
1851 census which provides more details about her and her
relatives. Having moved from Lambeth Palace to 7 Eaton Square,
Mary is listed as the head of household, aged 68, and described
as the widow of the late Archbishop of Canterbury,

Listed with Mary in fashionable Eaton Square, in the heart of
the rapidly expanding West End of London, are four other family
members. Their identities and family relationships are not
immediately obvious and invite further investigation and
clarification. As context, census details formally record as 'visitor'
those present on the day of the census but whose residence is
elsewhere. These four family members, however, are not listed as
'visitors' and are therefore recorded as living with Mary at the time.

The following rather lengthy passage of text unravels what is a
particularly intricate web of family relationships, and the reader
may wish to simply skim through it. However, it is recorded here
not only to record these family relationships but also as the
perfect example of the propensity for contemporary wealthy and

high-status families to intermarry within a very narrow circle, and form powerful, mutually supportive, networks.

The first of the four family members recorded in the census at 7 Eaton Square is Constance Beaumont, aged 16, and described both as a granddaughter (of Mary) and a 'Baronet's daughter', born in Addington, Surrey. The second is Paulina Beaumont, married and aged 22, also a granddaughter of Mary and described as 'Baronet's Wife', born in Calcutta, British India. The third family member listed is George H Beaumont, aged '3w' (3 weeks), a great grandson of Mary, described as 'Baronet's son', born in the Parish of St. George, Middlesex. This is the parish location of 7 Eaton Square, so he was probably born at that address with the various family members present. Focus on the family's Beaumont connections follows shortly. The census also evidences that there were 3 male and 11 female servants, including a nurse, presumably employed for a few months around the time of the baby George's birth.

The fourth family member listed is Mary F H Kingsmill, aged 9, a granddaughter of Mary Howley, born at Lambeth Palace in 1841. She is the daughter of Mary Frances's daughter Anne Jane Howley (1808-1871) who had married William Kingsmill in 1837. [*It was noted very early in the book that the maiden name of Samuel Pepys's mother-in-law was Kingsmill – not a common name – so there may be some connection.*] Another of William Howley and Mary Frances's daughters was Harriet Elizabeth Howley (1812-1837) who married John Adolphus Wright on 12th October 1832 in Addington, Surrey. The stories of these two daughters, Mary Kingsmill and Harriet Wright, are not pursued here, as it is focus on the third daughter Mary Ann Howley (1806-1835) which provides the link with the Beaumont family.

On 16th June 1825 Mary Ann Howley married George Howland Willoughby Beaumont, so this explains the surname of three of the 1851 census entries at Lambeth Palace, and he must be the G H W Beaumont witnessing, as her brother-in-law, Harriet Howley's marriage to John Adolphus Wright in 1832. The official marriage record for Mary Ann Howley and George Beaumont has further family interest and ties. The ceremony was conducted by the bride's father William Howley, at that time noted as being Lord Bishop of London (before his later elevation to Archbishop of

Canterbury) and formally witnessed and signed by him using his official title as 'W. London'.

We can now home in on the Beaumonts. Mary Ann's husband George Howland Willoughby Beaumont (1799-1845) was the cousin of Sir George Howland Beaumont, 7th Baronet (1753-1827), whose portraits by two of the leading contemporary artists are below.

By Sir Thomas Lawrence RA   By John Hoppner RA

The Hoppner portrait, painted in 1803, was exhibited at the 1809 Royal Academy Exhibition (Catalogue number 54). This 1809 exhibition throws up several other Cockerell connections and these are picked up much later in Chapter 10. Also in the 1809 exhibition was a portrait of George's mother the Dowager Lady Beaumont by William Owen RA, now in the National Gallery of Victoria, Melbourne, Australia.

The Beaumonts were keen patrons of the arts and, like their relatives the Cockerells, commissioned portraits from leading artists, often sharing their patronage by using more than just one favoured artist. Sir George Howland Beaumont, 7th Baronet (6 November 1753 – 7 February 1827) was a significant British art patron and amateur painter. He played a crucial part in the creation of London's National Gallery by making the first bequest of paintings. Beaumont welcomed John Constable to his home at Coleorton Hall to see his collection. In 1823, '*Constable spent five or six weeks at Coleorton hall much to the displeasure of his wife, Maria, who thought the visit was much too long. Sir George was a lifelong supporter of John Constable and source of friendly and good advice which was very helpful, particularly when John was a student in the Royal Academy schools'. [https://www. flatfordandconstable.org.uk/wp-content/uploads/2016/10/ People-Who-Influenced-Constable-1-1.pdf]*

This is further evidence of the strong interest by the wider Cockerell family in the arts, and not just an interest but active participation and patronage. And there is yet a further link between the Beaumonts, their family seat Coleorton Hall, and the Pepys and Pepys Cockerell families. A later relative Frederick Pepys Cockerell (1833-1878) was a prominent artist and architect. On the architectural side, the Oxford Dictionary of National Biography notes that, '*his earliest success was in raising and making additions to Coleorton Hall, the seat of Sir George Beaumont'*.   The Beaumonts were second cousins, this commission for Frederick Pepys Cockerell being another example of wider Cockerell family connections proving mutually helpful.

On the death of the 7th Baronet (portraits above), without a male heir, his cousin George Howland Willoughby Beaumont, Mary Ann's husband, had inherited the title, becoming the 8th Baronet of Stoughton Grange. Mary Ann and George's son George Howland Beaumont would later become the 9th Baronet in 1845 when Mary Ann's husband, the 8th Baronet, died.

Crucially in tying down the 1851 census entries, the daughter of Mary Ann and George Howland Willoughby Beaumont was Constance Mary Beaumont, born on 25th July 1834, tallying with every detail in the census. Very sadly, Constance's mother Mary Ann died on 15th February 1835, when Constance was only 6 months old. This also makes sense of Constance, now aged 16, being housed with female relatives in the home of her grandmother Mary Frances Howley in 1851, because by then she had been orphaned, her father, the 8th Baronet, having died in 1845, when Constance was only 10.

On 6th July 1852 Constance Beaumont, aged 17, married William Unwin Heygate, MP, JP, Doctor of Laws, and landowner, aged 27, at the Parish Church of Cole Orton in Leicestershire. The marriage service was conducted by yet another relative, Charles Almeric Belli (covered later). Constance's brother G H Beaumont, the 9th Baronet, signed as one of the witnesses. Prior to the wedding, a document of

26th June 1852 evidences that *'the consent of Frances Mary Howley** the guardian of the person of the said Constance Mary Beaumont, lawfully appointed (her father being dead) hath been obtained to such marriage'.* [** The names Mary and Frances have been incorrectly transposed but are correctly cited by Mary Frances herself in an accompanying document.]

Again, this neatly ties in with Constance living at 7 Eaton Square with her grandmother Mary Frances Howley in 1851 the year before the marriage. Mary had presumably been looking after Constance since her father's death in 1845, and probably since her mother's death in February 1835. Two years after the marriage, William and Constance had a son, William Howley Beaumont Heygate, baptised on 14th June 1854, and the abode of the family is given as still being 7 Eaton Square, which is perhaps a little odd as it would be expected that by this time the not-so-newly-weds would be established in a new home. Perhaps Constance's young age, about 19, meant that the security of living with relations was still prudent and comforting. However, seven years later the 1861 census for Brent Pelham, Hertfordshire, records William Heygate, aged 36, and Constance, aged 26, living at Brent Pelham Hall, with their first-born son, William Howley Heygate, now aged 6, a second son Reginald Heygate, aged 3, and a daughter Mary F Heygate , aged just 2 months.

Having now broadly understood Constance's story and why she was at 7 Eaton Square in the 1851 census, this leaves two individuals from the 7 Eaton Square 1851 census to identify and place in the family tree. These are Paulina Beaumont and George H Beaumont, who is only 3 weeks old, described as a Baronet's son, and great grandson of Mary Frances Howley. He is possibly Paulina's son, and therefore our last identification target is Paulina Beaumont, shown as aged 22 in 1851 and born in Calcutta, British India.

Things now reach new levels of intergenerational complexity but again provide an excellent example of the upper middle classes keeping marriages and relationships within tight family circles in the late 18th and early 19th centuries. Paulina is described as wife of a Baronet and cited in the census as another granddaughter of Mary Frances Howley. After much searching, it turns out that Paulina's Baronet husband is Constance's brother George Howland Beaumont, the 9th Baronet, so Paulina is a granddaughter through marriage rather than being a direct blood granddaughter. However, there is also a close blood relationship because intricate family ties are further tightened by the fact that Paulina's father turns out to be a brother of Mary Frances Howley (nee Belli), namely William Hallowes Belli (1790-1875) who married Sarah Sherman (1798-1857) in Calcutta on 29th October 1818. This ties in geographically with Paulina Belli (1828/9-1870) having been born in Calcutta. Paulina is therefore not only Frances's granddaughter by marriage but also her niece. Overall, an intricate and tangled web of family relationships, an example of marriages between cousins and between other closely related individuals, particularly in high status families, being common during this period.

Returning to the 1851 census for 7 Eaton Square for the last time, Paulina being described as a Baronet's wife ties in with the fact that she had married George Howland Beaumont (9th Baronet since 1845) on 4th June 1850 the year before the census was taken. The child described as Mary Frances Howley's great grandson is undoubtedly the first child from George and Paulina's marriage. He was born on 10th March 1851, just over 9 months since the marriage, and in the same month as the 1851 census taken on 30th March, confirming the census entry for his age as 3 weeks. Named George Howland William Beaumont (1851-1914) he became the 10th Baronet when his father died. He married Lillie Ellen Craster on 24th February 1880.

Finally, coming full circle to where we started this section – challenging for both the reader and the author – we refocus on Mary Frances Howley (nee Belli) within this Fifth Generation. Mary died on 13th August 1860, having had a particularly eventful life, from her birth in Calcutta, voyage to England, marriage to William Howley (then Bishop of London and shortly afterwards Archbishop of Canterbury), through to seeing her children, grandchildren, and great grandchildren thrive, no doubt affording her great pride and happiness. We also know from the lengthy passage above that she was never lonely either at Lambeth Palace or 7 Eaton Square. She died a wealthy woman, her probate record evidencing assets of just under £60,000, an enormous sum in 1860.

Elizabeth Horsley Palmer (1783-1839)

Born on 2nd September 1783, Elizabeth was the second daughter of John Belli and Elizabeth Stuart Cockerell. On 16th November

1810 she married John Horsley Palmer (1779-1858), an extremely wealthy and prominent banker, who also had commercial trading interests in the Far East.

We are fortunate in having a glorious studio portrait of Elizabeth Horsley Palmer by Sir Thomas Lawrence. The painting is in his typical early nineteenth century flattering style and backdrop, including rich red drapery and loosely defined glimpses of an imaginary landscape.

Elizabeth Horsley Palmer by Sir Thomas Lawrence

A brief profile of her husband sheds light on the level of society in which Elizabeth led much of her life. During his service as a Director of the Bank of England from 1811 to 1857, John served as Deputy Governor from 1828 to 1830, and Governor from 1830 to 1833. He was a member of the Political Economy Club and published several esoteric financial papers, such as *The Causes and Consequences of the Pressure Upon the Money-market*.

This period coincided with ongoing national introspection over the whole question of slavery and its central role in Britain's imperial expansion and wealth. Two centuries later, following the investigation by the Centre for the Study of the Legacies of British Slave-ownership at UCL, the Bank of England issued a public apology in June 2020 for the slave trade involvement of John Horsley Palmer and other Bank employees.

Of lighter interest, on 5th August 1794, together with an elder brother, John participated in the first ever recorded school cricket match, playing for Charterhouse School, and representing the City of London. Their opponents were Westminster School, representing the City of Westminster. For the record, Charterhouse were soundly beaten.

Elizabeth and John had 3 sons and 4 daughters, whose life stories have their own interest but are not pursued here. In 1820 John purchased Hurlingham House, some details of which have already been given. Although it was let out to the brother of the Duke of Wellington for a short time, it was the Horsley Palmer's principal family home, and Elizabeth died there on 22nd June 1839. She was only 55. John lived on as a widower for a few years before furthering strengthening the Cockerell family links by marrying Elizabeth's cousin Jane Louisa Cockerell, as outlined earlier. John Horsley Palmer died aged 78 and was buried at Kensal Green Cemetery. Jane Louisa continued to live at Hurlingham House after John's death.

Paulina Carrington (1784-1823)

As with her elder sisters, we are fortunate in having an extremely attractive and professionally executed portrait of Paulina. Painted once again Sir Thomas Lawrence, it is similar in style and costume to that of her sister Elizabeth, and typically late Georgian in its sensuality, as a further contrast with the somewhat later, and far more demure, portrait of her sister Mary Frances.

Paulina Carrington by Sir Thomas Lawrence RA

One anonymous commentator notes that, '*Society portraitists of the time, such as ... Thomas Lawrence, who excelled at painting fabrics, often favoured the neoclassical look over high fashion as it rendered the painting more timeless and engendered a certain nobility in the sitter*'.

Born the year after her sister Elizabeth in the official records, some sources assert that Paulina's birthplace was, like her other sister Mary Frances, in Kolkata (Calcutta) in Bengal, India. This is entirely plausible, even probable, but no official records have been located.

Paulina married Sir Codrington Edmund Carrington, the marriage licence being dated 1st August 1801. He is recorded as 21 years old, and Paulina is just 16, the licence confirming that she is marrying with the consent of her father John Belli. Her husband's age of 21 cited in the marriage licence is a quirk of the marriage licence recording system where the age of 21 is merely a default given for all those at least that age. *(In marriage certificates the equivalent default expression is '[of] full age'.)* Codrington's date of birth, definitively recorded as October 22nd 1769, makes him 31 at the time of their marriage, 15 years older than his young bride. He had been called to the bar at the Middle Temple on 10th February 1792, aged 22, and went to India that same year. He only returned to England in 1799 on account of ill health, having spent 7 years as a lawyer in Calcutta. It seems likely that he and Paulina met in India.

As with his wife's portrait, his is also by Thomas Lawrence, and it is perhaps appropriate that both their portraits currently hang in the Victoria & Albert Museum, although sadly in different galleries, at odds with their intimate relationship in life.

Back in England, Codrington was given the task of preparing the code of laws for the island of Ceylon (now Sri Lanka) and, not long after that, was appointed Chief Justice of the Supreme Court there. His knighthood was conferred on him shortly before the outward voyage. The assumption must be that he took up this appointment shortly after his marriage, but it is not clear whether Paulina accompanied

Sir Codrington Edmund Carrington by Sir Thomas Lawrence RA

him to Ceylon. He once again suffered ill health and returned to England in 1806. Perhaps it is significant that the birth of their first child, Elizabeth Maria, was that same year, and many others followed in rapid succession. Movements to and from Ceylon probably explain why official documents relating to him and Paulina are sparse during this period.

He died in 1839, and although he had remarried after Paulina's early death in 1823, his last Will and Testament document focuses on children from his marriage to Paulina. This document provides some helpful information. Firstly, that at the time it was drawn up in 1849, there were 8 daughters and 2 sons still alive from his marriage to Paulina, and these are specifically named. Other documentary evidence suggests that Paulina gave birth to 14 children but, if so, any not named in the Will must be presumed to have died before 1849. Furthermore, the terms of the Will aim to support any grandchildren of Paulina and Codrington, and there is no mention of any such grandchildren, so any sons or daughters of Paulina and her husband not named in the will would appear not to have left any such children of their own at the date of this Will. It seems most likely therefore that any children over and above the ten named in the Will had died at an early age.

Secondly, daughters are named ahead of sons, and all are treated equally. Also, the married daughters are fully given their fair share, which was not always common practice.

Thirdly, administration was granted to Henry Carrington and not jointly to him and Codrington's widow Mary, his second wife. There is certainly a specific statement that Mary could, on application, be granted administrative powers, but it would appear she has not come forward and is content for her stepson Henry to execute the administrative powers. She was only 46 at this time, and would live to age 95, so her standing aside seems unlikely to have been for health reasons.

Fourthly, the children of his second marriage, to Mary Capel (see below), are neither named nor mentioned. In leaving his residual estate to his second wife he is presumably confident that she will in turn ensure that her children are cared for and be specified in her own will.

Overall, Paulina and Codrington clearly had a long-lasting intimate relationship. Having given birth to at least the ten surviving children – some sources cite fourteen – Paulina died aged 38 in 1823, the same year as the birth of the last of the known children. It may be that she died in childbirth or of complications resulting from the birth. Her adult life had been spent in an almost perpetual state of pregnancy.

As noted above, after Paulina's death Sir Codrington Edmund Carrington married a second time, to Mary Ann Capel (1803-1898), and their marriage produced at least one child, Julia Capel Carrington, but this family's life story is outside our scope.

To return briefly to the portraits of Paulina and Codrington by Thomas Lawrence, the V&A Museum records that Paulina's portrait was :-

Bequeathed by Miss L. M. Carrington to the museum in 1874, along with the portrait of Sir Codrington Edmund Carrington, museum number 1359-1874. Laura Carrington was a younger daughter of Sir Codrington Edmund Carrington.'

The V&A notes also provide further information as follows :-

This portrait by Sir Thomas Lawrence of Paulina, Lady Carrington, is thought to date to around 1806. Much of what is known about the sitter comes from the copy of a manuscript supplied to the museum in 1921 by her granddaughter, Countess Evelyn Martinengo Cesaresco. This tells us that Paulina was the youngest daughter of John Belli, 'of a noble Italian family but born in England'. Belli was private secretary to the first Governor-General of India, Warren Hastings. The sitter's mother was of equally aristocratic heritage, 'from the Spanish family of Bivar which claimed descent from the Cid and the sister of Pepys, the diarist, ancestress of all the Pepys Cockerells'. Paulina married in 1801 Sir Codrington Edmund Carrington (1769-1849) who was Chief Justice of Ceylon (1800-1806) but [Paulina] was said to have died young in 1823 [which is confirmed by official records, which give her date of death as 9th August 1823].

The museum also holds a related portrait of the sitter's husband, Sir Codrington Edmund Carrington (museum number 1359-1874), also by Lawrence (see Kenneth Garlick, Sir Thomas Lawrence: A Complete Catalogue of the Oil Paintings, Oxford and London, 1989, no. 170). Originally it was thought that both paintings were commissioned at the same date, probably 1801-2, as companion pieces to celebrate the couple's marriage. Countess Cesaresco claimed that 'The Lawrence pictures of Paulina & probably also of Sir C. E. Carrington were done by commission of Mrs Belli [born Elizabeth Stuart Cockerell] [mother of Paulina] probably just before or after her daughter's marriage'. However, Garlick states that the portrait of Lady Carrington appears 'stylistically... to be somewhat later than [Sir Codrington] and it may have been painted after Sir Codrington's return from Ceylon in 1806' (Garlick, 1989, no.171).

John Henry Belli-Bivar (1786-1850)

After welcoming their three daughters, Mary, Elizabeth, and Paulina, into the world, John and Elizabeth Belli (Samuel Pepys's great great niece) had their first son in 1786. Naming him John after his father, as was common, he used the double surname Belli-Bivar the latter Bivar part honouring his paternal grandmother. He followed a military career, rising to the rank of Lieutenant Colonel in her Majesty's *[Victoria's]* 16th Regiment of Lancers.

John died on 12th April 1850 in Paris. His last Will and Testament give several clues to his life story and his relationships with other family members. The text of the Will gives us his wife's name, Caroline, with various secondary sources giving her maiden name as Jacquemont, Jacquemain or Jacquemard. The more convincing evidence is for Jacquemont. The Will also tells us that John had two daughters, Henrietta Caroline and Eugenie Elizabeth, and two sons, Henry Stuart Belli Bivar and Charles Stuart Belli Bivar, and a few brief details of these four siblings are noted here. Once more, as with so many of the wider family, the two sons, both in the military, have strong links with India.

<u>Henrietta (1815-1881)</u> was married on 28th September 1848 to Joseph Louis Ferrari. Again, there is some variation in the references regarding spelling of the surname.

<u>Eugenie (1818-1855)</u> was married in 1850 (presumably just after her father's death) to Felix Adolphe Juge, who died around 1864. We have a record of the text of Eugenie's Will, from which it is clear she didn't marry the Viscount mentioned in her father's will. Perhaps it was a form of arranged marriage that she resisted, and after her father's death she felt free to marry as she chose. Her will is recorded in the documents of the Prerogative Court of Canterbury.

<u>Henry (1823-1893)</u> married Emily Jane Kelso (1830-1868) on 6th August 1849 at Assam, West Bengal, India. He is cited in the British Army Lists as reaching the rank of Lieutenant Colonel, matching his father and brother (see below)

<u>Charles (1828-1874)</u> married Matilda Emma Hunter and they had daughters Ethel Matilda and Agnes, who married a Major Willis on 12th August 1882. When Charles died he left a modest estate of just under £1,500. Like his father, he followed a military career and similarly reached the rank of Lieutenant-Colonel, his regiment being the 1st Regiment of Her Majesty's Madras Light Cavalry, being then described as afterwards living at Brighton and then Paris.

William Hallowes Belli (1789-1875)

William Hallowes Belli, who has already featured briefly in the section above (focusing on his sister Mary Frances Belli), was born in Southampton on 9 October 1789, the son of John Belli and Elizabeth Stuart Cockerell. He was a senior merchant in the Honourable East India Company, and married Sarah Sherman on 29 October 1818 in St John's Cathedral, Calcutta. Sarah, the daughter of John Standiver Sherman, had been born in Madras on 31st December1798. William and Sarah had 14 children, with 11 of them surviving into adulthood, and one, Paulina, married William's great nephew George Beaumont, as previously outlined.

W. H. Belli, Esq. (1789-1875)
15 February 1861

After returning to England, he appears in the 1851 census living at 9 Prince's Gate, Kensington, with his wife Sarah, two sons, two daughters, and six servants. He gave as his profession 'Retired E. I. *[East India]* Co. Civil Service.' A decade later, in the 1861 census, he is described as a widower living at 1 Queen's Gate Terrace, Kensington, with his son, daughter, grandson, and seven servants. The photograph below was taken in 1861, when he was 71 years old.

His entry in the 1871 census has not been identified, so his residence then is uncertain, but four years later he died on 29 July 1875 at 'Courtlands,' his home at Beulah Hill, Upper Norwood, South London. He left an estate valued at £4,000.

A short obituary in the Norwood News (7 August 1875) provides valuable information and insight into the character of this three times great nephew of Samuel Pepys.

> *'For several months past the deceased has been confined to his house, primarily from an acute attack of bronchitis, until other complications supervened, and he passed away almost painlessly in the full enjoyment of every faculty. Those only who had the privilege of Mr Belli's friendship knew what sterling worth, what nobility of character, lay beneath his genial face, and those who knew him the best will miss him the most. Mr Belli's intellectual faculties were in keeping with the nobility of his mind, he was both a classical and an oriental scholar, and his conversational powers and immense innate knowledge of men and manners made him a universal favourite. Dr Hetley and Dr Wise were most assiduous in their attentions to the very last, the latter, as an old and intimate Indian friend and colleague. Requiescat in pace.'*

Charles Almeric Belli (1791-1886)

Born in Bath on 8th December 1791, Charles is another family member with cultural associations. He is also one of the wealthiest; when he died on 6th January 1886, he left the enormous personal estate of £233,356, the equivalent today of many millions of pounds. Given that he was a vicar, and that his brother, a successful merchant, left only about £4,000, the source of this fortune is unclear.

Charles Almeric was vicar of South Weald in Essex, and surely it cannot simply be a coincidence that his cousin, Henry Cockerell (1801-1880), was vicar at North Weald, Essex. As well as being the Vicar of South Weald in Essex, Charles was Precentor of St. Paul's, Bentley, a nearby settlement, but neither of these posts would have generated anything approaching the substantial amounts evident in his estate. He married Frances Willan on 14th November 1827, but there is no information available to indicate she was rich or a wealthy heiress. When she died in 1869 at South Weald her personal estate was just under £8,000 which, although substantial, does nothing to explain her husband's eventual large fortune, but perhaps she did indeed bring an enormous fortune into the marriage which would then effectively and legally become his property.

Another possible explanation could be that his elder brother William, who had been a successful senior merchant in the East Indies, may have bequeathed Charles a large inheritance aside from the relatively modest 'personal estate' cited in William's probate record. Without positive evidence of this or other possible sources of Charles's £233,356, no conclusions can be drawn. Unfortunately, the details of his Will were not found in the limited research of public records.

Charles's wealth and some of the uses he put it to are, however, commented on in notes relating to the church of which he was Vicar, St. Peter's in South Weald.

Essex is generally a county of small churches, especially in the south, so it can be a surprise to come across such substantial buildings as this one, set impressively in its otherwise quiet little village. The overall impression is one of length, the chancel emerging beyond the low south aisle like a train overtaking another one, and this is accentuated by the sheer bulk of the west tower. The lower stages of the tower reveal its late medieval origins, but otherwise the church was entirely rebuilt by that maverick architect SS Teulon in the 1860s at the expense of Charles Almeric Belli, the wealthy rector of South Weald who also paid for the construction of the chapel of ease at Bentley a few years later. The fairytale castle top of the tower is Teulon's, the nave, aisle and chancel entirely his, although he reused a Norman doorway from the original church.

Not surprisingly, you step into a space which is all of a piece, dark and shadowy and suggestive of Belli's High Church enthusiasm. The south aisle looks eastward to a pleasing ironwork screen to the design of George Gilbert Scott, but the lack of a clerestory reinforces the length of the nave and chancel beside it. As at Bentley, the stone carving was by Thomas Earp, although the sanctuary seems to have been reordered after Belli's death, the east window being his memorial and the sanctuary furnishings installed to the design of EC Lee who Belli had employed for his church at Bentley.

Simon Knott, January 2022

He commissioned and funded one of the bells at St. Paul's, Bentley, the inscription on which reads :-

> *MEARS & STAINBANK, FOUNDERS, LONDON, 1879.*
> *TO THE GLORY OF GOD*
> *AND FOR THE JOY OF HIS PEOPLE*
> *ME-THE REVEREND CHARLES ALMERIC BELLI*
> *CAUSED TO BE MADE DEC 19TH A.D.1879.*

Charles also appears to have been a patron of the arts, as so many of the wider Cockerell family were, and the British Museum holds over seventy items relating to him, presumably donated.

In the 1851 census Charles is living at the Vicarage, South Weald in Essex. Aged 59, he is living with his wife Frances, cited as aged 33, who was born in Brighton. This age must simply be incorrectly recorded because his marriage to Frances Willan had been 24 years earlier in 1827. They have 6 servants in this 1851 census.

In the 1861 census they are still living at the Vicarage, with his age given as 69 which tallies with him being 59 in the previous 1851 census, but his wife Frances's age is given as 55. Both Frances entries give her place of birth as Brighton, and the age 55 given in the 1861 census does tally with Frances Willan having been born in 1806. The age of 33 shown in the 1851 census is probably simply an error. In the 1871 census Charles is still at the Vicarage, but now described as a widower, his wife having died in 1869. No records have been found of Charles and Frances having any children.

Fifth Generation Summary

The narratives for this generation evidence large numbers of children born and surviving into adulthood. Interconnections between family members from different branches feature strongly, with a common thread of 'Pepys' awareness acting as a unifying factor, not least in the naming of children. Another recurring theme is the extraordinary frequency of links with India. These familiar patterns continue into the Sixth generation. The natural increase in numbers of family members in successive generations dictates that a less comprehensive coverage of the Sixth generation is inevitable, and a much more selective approach is adopted.

CHAPTER EIGHT

Sixth Generation – Contributions to Victorian Culture

Only a selected few of the many Sixth generation family members are explored in any detail. The individuals featured are all descended from Samuel Pepys Cockerell (1754-1827), and this branch of the wider family tree contains all the subsequent successive heirs of the diarist Samuel Pepys. As well as perpetuating the Pepys connection, several of those featured have worthy stand-alone claims for inclusion through their own achievements or interesting life stories. A few had national impact.

The family's ownership of Samuel Pepys's historic artefacts, letters and other documents had been passed down through the previous generations and those individuals now entrusted with the core items of this collection are naturally included below, this sequence of individuals being followed right through to the 21st century. The succession of Samuel Pepys's heirs has been indicated in the various family tree graphics interspersed at key points in the text, and this succession is summarised in Chapter 11.

Typically born in the early decades of the 19th century the family members of this Sixth generation would live through the later years of the Georgian era and the early period of Queen Victoria's long reign. The accelerating pace of change in many aspects of British life continued to be strongly influenced by rapid advances in industry, scientific discoveries, travel, and engineering, but equally there were cultural shifts, with Georgian laissez-faire gradually evolving into more rigid behavioural codes. Not the least of these latter changes was a greater focus on family values, both formal and sentimental, with Victoria and Albert's well publicised adoption of these values being a key factor influencing attitudes and behaviours in the wider society. Associated with this, the home environment acquired far more significance, accompanied by massively increased access to

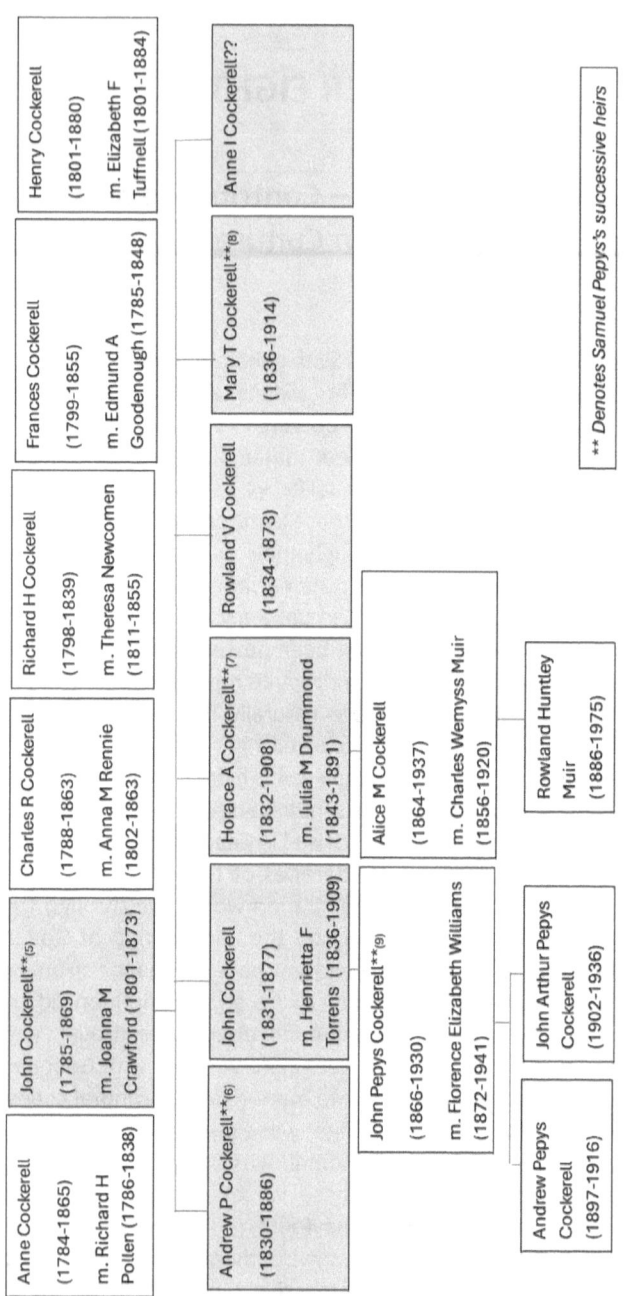

Children of John Cockerell & Joanna Mary Crawford

Anne Cockerell (1784-1865) m. Richard H Pollen (1786-1838)

John Cockerell(**(5)) (1785-1869) m. Joanna M Crawford (1801-1873)

Charles R Cockerell (1788-1863) m. Anna M Rennie (1802-1863)

Richard H Cockerell (1798-1839) m. Theresa Newcomen (1811-1855)

Frances Cockerell (1799-1855) m. Edmund A Goodenough (1785-1848)

Henry Cockerell (1801-1880) m. Elizabeth F Tuffnell (1801-1884)

Andrew P Cockerell(**(6)) (1830-1886)

John Cockerell (1831-1877) m. Henrietta F Torrens (1836-1909)

Horace A Cockerell(**(7)) (1832-1908) m. Julia M Drummond (1843-1891)

Rowland V Cockerell (1834-1873)

Mary T Cockerell(**(8)) (1836-1914)

Anne I Cockerell??

John Pepys Cockerell(**(9)) (1866-1930) m. Florence Elizabeth Williams (1872-1941)

Alice M Cockerell (1864-1937) m. Charles Wemyss Muir (1856-1920)

Rowland Huntley Muir (1886-1975)

Andrew Pepys Cockerell (1897-1916)

John Arthur Pepys Cockerell (1902-1936)

*** Denotes Samuel Pepys's successive heirs*

222

mass-produced domestic paraphernalia, both functional and decorative. The decorative arts would be a field in which several family members of this Sixth generation played a significant role.

Children of John Cockerell & Joanna Mary Crawford

Andrew Pepys Cockerell (1830-1886)

If Andrew was the first-born-son, as the records indicate, it was slightly unusual for him not to have been given his father's name, John. Perhaps there had been an earlier first-born, given the name John, but who had died in infancy. In any event Andrew's younger brother was subsequently named John. Andrew's father John had inherited responsibility for Samuel Pepys's remaining legacy of artefacts and documents. When his father died, Andrew in turn, as the eldest son surviving to adulthood, took responsibility as Samuel Pepys's next heir. With each passing generation, the chances of the family's collection of artefacts and documents remaining intact naturally declined, with some of the legacy artefacts no doubt distributed amongst other relatives, spreading the memory of Samuel Pepys amongst the wider family in a very tangible way. Nevertheless, the private Pepys documents which the family possessed and continued to safeguard were largely kept together as a coherent collection until the 1920s, as were several family portraits.

Born on 4th July 1830 at Putney, Andrew would die in his fifties on 9th June 1886 in Manchester Square, Marylebone. There is no record of him ever marrying or having children. On his death, or perhaps slightly earlier, it appears from later evidence that the collection of documents passed to Andrew's nephew, John Pepys Cockerell (1866-1930), the son of Andrew's younger brother John who had sadly predeceased Andrew in 1877. Following the family tradition, this nephew was given his father's name John, with the middle name Pepys once again incorporated, and the Pepys memorabilia became known as the Pepys Cockerell Collection.

There is limited information about Andrew's life, but we know a certain amount from the censuses. In 1841, aged 10, he was at school, together with his brothers John, aged 9, and Horace, aged

8, at number 7 Sussex Square in Brighton. The school was run by Benjamin Guest, aged 50, described as Classicals Master, and his wife Elizabeth, aged 40. Living with Benjamin and Elizabeth were their four daughters and one son. Also resident were a governess and three male assistants, all in their mid-twenties, and seven teachers, six of whom were female. All 28 school pupils at this address were male, ranging in age from 7 to 14.

From the census, it is apparent that on another side of Sussex Square there was a similar school for female pupils. It appears to have been a very respectable location, as the Russia Vice Consul also lived in the Square. Brighton was known for its Royal connections, healthy climate and sea air, and most of the pupils were almost certainly from wealthy families. It is not clear whether these were boarding schools with sleeping and eating facilities, or simply day schools, but the latter seems more likely because although servants were itemised there is no specific mention of cooks or kitchen maids.

Three years later, in 1844, Andrew Pepys Cockerell ma. (major), appears in the records of Eton School, listed as being in the Sixth Form, and the eldest of the brothers attending the school. He is shown as having later become Lieutenant in the Gloucestershire Militia and Aide de Camp to the Lord Lieutenant of Ireland.

Andrew next appears in the 1851 census as a visitor at the Norfolk Hotel, Kings Road in Brighton, together with a fellow student from Christchurch College, Oxford. The reason for their stay is not known and looking back at the names in the 1841 census they were not fellow pupils at the Brighton school at that time. Maybe they were simply having a break from their Oxford studies at this fashionable seaside town, which appears to have been a particular magnet for several Cockerell family members. Brighton was a popular out-of-London location through the late 18th century and much of the 19th, assisted by Royal patronage of the resort and development of the Brighton Pavilion.

We know that Andrew's father John Cockerell, died in 1869, and the 1871 census tells us that Andrew, now aged 40, is living with his mother Joanna, aged 70, and his sister Mary, aged 34, at 9 Adelaide Crescent in Brighton. Joanna is described as a fundholder, i.e. living by her own means rather than having an occupation, and Andrew, under the census heading of rank, profession or occupation, is simply described as being son and owner with no occupation given.

In 1875, the London City Directories of that year record Andrew living at 45, Hertford Street, Mayfair. These directories often give an occupation or profession and indicate that Hertford Street housed a substantial number of medical professionals. Neighbours at numbers 42, 44 and 46 were physicians, number 43 housed a surgeon, with several other physicians further along the street. The electoral register of 1877 shows him still living there.

Four years later, the 1881 census provides evidence of a significant change in Andrew's circumstances. In the 1871 census he had still been living with his mother and sister in Brighton, with no occupation specified, but in 1881, aged 51, he is living as the head of the household at 11, Mandeville Place, Marylebone. His occupation is given as 'Household of H.R.H. P. Wales', so as well as moving from Brighton to London he has acquired a role in the household of the Prince of Wales (later Edward VII). Living with him were a young footman, as well as three servants, two male and one female.

Fortunately, the Oxford University Alumni records provide more details, including his role in the royal household.

> **Cockerell**, *Andrew Pepys, IS. John, of Putney, Surrey, arm. CHRIST CHURCH, matric. 15 June, 1848, aged 17; student 1848-65, B.A. 1852, M.A. 1855, groom of the bedchamber-in-waiting to the Prince of Wales, died unmarried 9 Jun, 1886. See Foster's Baronetage, RUSHOUT.*

> [The reference to RUSHOUT must link to his great uncle Sir Charles Cockerell having married into the Rushout family, but researching the connection is outside scope here.]

By the time of Andrew's death in 1886, it appears that his sister Mary Theresa Cockerell was also living with him. Certainly, when his will was proved, the probate entry dated 10th July 1886 records that she was living at 11, Mandeville Place, information which proves useful in tracing the provenance of the Cockerell double portrait (see Chapter 10). It also provides further contextual information about Andrew, including confirmation of his move from Hertford Street to Mandeville Place.

> **COCKERELL Andrew Pepys (*Personal Estate £72,082 16s. 10d.* *Resworn February 1887 £71,651 12s. 1d.*)**
>
> *10 July. The Will with a Codicil of Andrew Pepys Cockerell formerly of 45 Hertford-street Mayfair but late of 11 Mandeville-place Manchester-square both in the County of **Middlesex** Esquire who died 9 June 1886 at 11 Mandeville-place was proved at the **Principal Registry** by Mary Theresa Cockerell of 11 Mandeville-place Spinster the Sister the sole Executrix.*

His wealth was substantial, his quoted Personal Estate being the equivalent today of several million pounds, almost certainly inherited as the senior member of family in this generation and next in the sequence of Samuel Pepys heirs. His sister Mary continued to live at 11, Mandeville Place after his death and her story is outlined shortly. However, keeping to chronological order of birth, set out next are brief details of her other brothers John, Horace, and Rowland.

John Cockerell (1831-1877)

John was born in Putney on 12th June 1831. He appears, aged 9, in the 1841 census records for the school at Brighton where his brothers Andrew and Horace were also listed.

John enlisted in the army on 20th September 1848. The army officer service records show his regiment as the 20th Hussars and his rank as cornet, the lowest commissioned officer rank. The cornet officer traditionally carried the regiment's colours, the current equivalent rank being second lieutenant. We don't have a photograph of John from this time but given below is an excellent contemporary image of just such a British Hussars cornet officer. Winston Churchill also held this rank in 1895 in his early military service.

John married Henrietta Frances Torrens on 9th January 1862, but it was not her first marriage, as the record shows her status as 'widowed'. The marriage was another conducted by Henry

Cockerell, John's uncle, witnessed by his sister Mary Theresa Cockerell, with John, having been promoted, now described as a Captain. On December 20th that year church records evidence the baptism of their first child, Joan Constance, in the parish of Brighthelmeston (generally simplified to Brighton, as it was in the marriage document). In the baptism document John and Henrietta's 'abode' is given as 2 Holland Road, and John's army rank is again cited as Captain, with his

Cornet Henry Wilkin, 11th Hussars (British Army, 1855)

regiment given as the 28th Hussars. This latter reference to the 28th Hussars is very legibly entered in the record, and possibly the earlier reference to the 20th Hussars is simply a misreading of a poorly written record, even though another record (see below) repeats this. The rank of Captain is two above his entry rank of cornet in 1848.

One of the main conflicts in this period was the Crimean War, but there is no record of his involvement there. We do, however, know a considerable amount about his active service in India in the 1850s because, very fortunately, there is a record of the auction sale of some of his medals which also gives valuable details of the background to their award.

[https://www.noonans.co.uk/auctions/archive/lot-archive/results/108943/] Extracted 24/11/2023.

LOT № 75
2 MARCH 2005
HAMMER PRICE:
£1,300
DESCRIPTION
The Indian Mutiny medal to Captain John Cockerel, Hodson's Horse
Indian Mutiny 1857-59, no clasp (Lieut. I. Cockerell, 1st Regt. Hodson's Horse) nearly very fine £500-600

SPECIAL COLLECTION

This lot was sold as part of a special collection, The Brian Ritchie Collection of H.E.I.C. and British India Medals.
FOOTNOTE

John Cockerell, the son of John Cockerell, D.L., J.P., of Malmesbury, Wiltshire, and Putney, and his wife Joanna Mary, eldest daughter of Brigadier-General Catlin Craufurd, 91st Highlanders, was born on 12 June 1831. His grandfather, Samuel Pepys Cockerell was Surveyor to the H.E.I.Co.'s Home Service, and designed Sezincote House, a unique example of the architecture of Akbar, and the only Moghul building that has survived in Western Europe, as a private commission for his brother, Sir Charles Cockerell, 1st Bart., who amassed a considerable fortune in India and later entered Parliament. Considering that the majority of John Cockerell's kinsmen attended the Civil College at Haileybury, it may be assumed that he was either 'too idle or too stupid' for the Civil Service and was nominated like other rejects to the cavalry, for which nothing so vulgar as training was required. Appointed Cornet on 20 September 1848, he embarked for India in the Indus that same day, and arrived at Fort William on 10 November following. Posted to the 4th Bengal Light Cavalry at Cawnpore on 16 December 1848, he was promoted Lieutenant on 1 August 1849.

At the outbreak of the Mutiny Cockerell must have learnt with horror and rage the news of the murder of his cousin, Henry Edmund Cockerell, of the Bengal Civil Service. One night in mid June 1857, Henry, who had chosen to remain at his isolated post in the Banda district longer than was wise, decided there was nothing more he could do to enforce the Company's authority over the surrounding country. He ordered his syce to saddle his horse, and set out to seek the protection of the Nawab of Banda. But on reaching the Nawab's palace, he was treacherously pulled from his horse and hacked to pieces by the Nawab's retainers.

On 15 December 1857, John Cockerell, whose regiment was showing signs of disaffection and was ultimately disbanded, was attached to Hodson's Horse. His 'Record of Services' states: 'Served with Hodson's Horse in the Indian Mutiny of 1857. Present at the action of Khoolagunge and re-capture of Futteghur'. His career with Hodson's Horse, however, was short lived, for on 23 January 1858 he was placed at the disposal of the Government of the Central Provinces for employment with the Police Cavalry and, having been granted the local rank of Captain, was appointed Commandant of the Divisional Battalion at Benares in April 1858. On 12 January 1860 he became Captain in the 2nd Bengal European Light Cavalry (afterwards the 20th Hussars), and on 19 April 1864 exchanged into H.M.'s 8th Foot, from which he promptly sold out. Cockerell married Henrietta, daughter of Henry Torrens B.C.S., and died at Brighton on 27 May 1877, outliving his younger brother Rowland Vyner Cockerell, B.C.S., who died by falling into a crevasse near Simla in 1873.

Refs: Hodson Index (NAM); IOL L/MIL/10/67; IOL L/ MIL/10/45; IOL L/MIL/10/65: IOL L/MIL/10/98; WO 76/550; WO 76/130 f. 76.

Notable from the above are the violent deaths of John's younger brother Rowland Vyner Cockerell and of his cousin Henry Edmund Cockerell, but for now we continue to focus on John himself. In the 1871 census John, aged 39, is recorded as the head of the household at 15 Onslow Gardens, Brompton, Chelsea, and described as a retired army officer. His wife Henrietta, aged 34, is with him as are their 5 children, Joan (8), Mary (7), Ethel (5), John (4), and Margaret (1), the eldest four being described as scholars. Henrietta is noted as having been born in India but had clearly settled in England well before her marriage. Her eldest and youngest children were born in Brighton, a town which clearly plays a major part in the Cockerell family's lives as we have seen above when exploring Andrew Pepys Cockerell's life and others. Mary, the second child, was born in Canterbury and the other two children, Ethel and John, in London. Also living with the family were 5 female servants – a nurse, undernurse, nursemaid, housemaid, and cook. The nursemaid was born in Switzerland, the others in England.

While perusing the 1871 census records, as remarked in an earlier chapter, it was noticed that the immediate neighbours at 16 Onslow Gardens included the intriguing entry for Anne Thackeray, aged 33, described as 'Authoress', still a rarity at that time. It took only minimal research to establish that Anne was the daughter of William Makepeace Thackeray, the more famous early 19th century writer, his books including the novel 'Vanity Fair', with Indian connotations.

Anne Thackeray herself became an established writer. In the census, Anne's status was given as sister-in-law of the head of the household, Leslie Stephen, described as 'Editor and journalist'. He had married Anne's sister Harriet, the eldest daughter of William Makepeace Thackeray. Harriet, aged 30, included in the census as Leslie's wife, is listed together with their daughter Laura. Also listed are Amy and Ann Thackeray, aged 7 and 5 respectively, described as 'visitors', and born in India. This may be linked to the fact that Leslie and Harriet's daughter Laura is noted as then being only 3 months old, so would have held a fascination for Amy and Anne who were presumably close relatives. It is possible that baby Laura may have had a difficult birth and first few months, and that this was the first time it had been deemed appropriate for Amy and Anne to visit, not least because their presence would put more pressure on running the household. Having visitors also carried the risk of bringing infections into an otherwise reasonably self-contained environment.

Another literary connection resulted after Harriet sadly died at a young age. The widowed Leslie Stephen married Julia Prinsep Duckworth and the couple had two daughters who would later become leading figures in the early 20th century Bloomsbury Group, namely Virginia Woolf the writer and Vanessa Bell the artist. Julia's aunt was Julia Margaret Cameron (1815-1879), the famous early photographic pioneer in the field of soft-focus portraiture. This medium provided the perfect transition from fine-art oil painting portraits which the Cockerells had commissioned with such enthusiasm.

Finally, before resuming John Cockerell's life story, it is worth noting that William Makepeace Thackeray's cultural network, influence, and personal support was instrumental in securing an important element in the career progression of one of our key Pepys' relatives, namely John Hungerford Pollen, covered below. As well as the Thackerays and Cockerells being neighbours at 15 and 16 Onslow Gardens, there were clearly also active friendships and mutual cultural links with the closely related Pollen family.

John Cockerell died two weeks before his 46th birthday on 27th May 1877 in Brighton and he was buried on 31st May at neighbouring Hove. Henrietta lived on for many years and is recorded as a witness at her daughter Joan's wedding on 9th April 1890. John and Henrietta's son, John Pepys Cockerell (1866-1930), who became the next Samuel Pepys heir, was also a witness at this happy occasion at St Paul's Church, Knightsbridge.

Horace Abel Cockerell (1832-1908)

Born on 18th July 1832, Horace appears in the Eton School List for 1844, for the Upper School, Fourth Form, and is shown as Cockerell mi (i.e. Minor), corroborating his elder brother Andrew being at the school. The list is updated long after pupils had left and includes brief details of what happened to them in terms of career, honours etc. Horace is denoted as 'Civil Service, Bengal'. Also listed is their other brother Rowland Vyner Cockerell min., and he is in the Lower School Second Form. His later career is also shown as 'Civil Service, Bengal'.

In the 1851 census Horace, aged 18, appears as a student at the East India College. At that time there were nearly a hundred such students; governing British India required large numbers of administrators. The East India Company College, or East India College, was an educational establishment situated at Hailey, Hertfordshire, nineteen miles north of London, founded in 1806 to train "writers" (administrators) for the East India Company. It provided general and vocational education for young gentlemen of sixteen to eighteen years old, who were nominated by the Company's directors to writerships in its overseas civil service. The college's counterpart establishment for the training of officers for the company's Presidency armies was Addiscombe Military Seminary, Surrey. The East India Company was later nationalised, and the East India College closed in 1858, becoming a public school with continuing ties to the former college.

Horace is shown in the 1851 census as having been born in Putney, Surrey. The census entry directly above Horace's is for another student, Andrew B Barnard, also aged 18. There are members of a Barnard family appearing elsewhere in the investigation of the wider Pepys Cockerell family, and Horace's maternal grandmother was Anne E Barnard raising the likelihood that this Andrew Barnard, training alongside Horace Cockerell, was a relative.

Several census entries in the college lists show individuals who were born in the East Indies. It would appear likely that these were children of East India Company staff working in India at the time of the births, whose parents then returned to England, but wished their children to follow the same career path. A variation on this scenario saw parents remaining in India, sending their children back to be educated in England.

Horace married Julia Mary Drummond (1843-1891) in 1863, and they had six daughters, the eldest being Alice Mary Cockerell (1864-1937). When Horace died in 1908 his probate record reads :-

> **COCKERELL** Horace Abel of 27 Beaufort-gardens Middlesex C.S.I. died 23 April 1908 Probate **London** 4 July to Charles Wemyss Muir colonel His Majesty's army and Crauford Alexander Gordon Clark lieutenant colonel His Majesty's army. Effects £16218 12s. 2d.

The first of the two individuals to whom probate was granted is Charles Wemyss Muir who had married Horace and Julia's eldest daughter Alice. Three years after Horace's death, the 1911 census shows Charles and Alice, and their children, staying at the Golden Lion Hotel in the recently established seaside resort of 'New Hunstanton', Norfolk. (See the text for Rowland Vyner Cockerell below for the likely significance of this.)

The first name of the other probate grantee, Craufurd, reflects links with the Craufurd or Crawford family, members of which have already appeared several times in the investigation. Indeed, Horace's mother's maiden name was Crawford.

Rowland Vyner Cockerell (1834-1873)

Rowland has already appeared when exploring the life story of his uncle Henry Cockerell, the eleventh and last child of Samuel Pepys Cockerell and his wife Anne. Rowland's early death, its unusual circumstances, and the nature of his relationships with other family members raised some questions in that exploration, ultimately not definitively resolved. It was hoped that these gaps could perhaps be clarified by focusing directly on him and any evidence available about him and his life. However, while a few more details and source records have been identified, elements of mystery persist.

He was born in the Parish of St. James, Paddington on 10th December 1834, and baptised on 26th March 1835 at St. James' church. As noted above he was in the Fourth form in the Upper School at Eton in the 1847 school lists. On the same page in that list is another pupil Alfred Guy L'Estrange. The L'Estranges lived at Hunstanton Hall in Norfolk and developed the seaside resort of New Hunstanton in the second half of the nineteenth century. The centrepiece of this major development was the Golden Lion Hotel, completed in 1846 and originally called the New Inn. Initially standing alone in an isolated raised location overlooking the sea, about a mile from Old Hunstanton, it marked the beginning of the new town.

We have just noted above that Rowland's niece Alice Cockerell, her husband Charles Wemyss Muir, and their children were staying at the Golden Lion Hotel in New Hunstanton at the time of the 1911 census. Given that Alice's father Horace Cockerell and his other brother Andrew were also, like Rowland, at Eton at much the same time as Alfred Guy L'Estrange, this family stay at the L'Estranges' Golden Lion Hotel appears more than mere coincidence.

After Eton, Rowland went to Radley College, and the following extract headed 'New boys at Radley 1849' from the College records is helpful in adding more detail of his death falling off a precipice near Simla in India.

Cockerell, Rowland Vyner. Born 1835. Aged 14 on admission. The son of John Cockerell, D.L., J.P. Appointed one of the first eight prefects in 1851. He left Radley in 1851, and attended the East India College, Haileybury, from 1853-55. Joined the East India Company Service in

1856. He was killed by his pony shying and falling over a
precipice with him near Simla, India, on 9th October, 1873.
L. [the L denoting that he joined in the Lent term in January]

[https://victorianweb.org/history/education/radley/
newboys1849.html]

He was buried at the Kanlog Cemetery. The description of his death in this College entry, if taken at face value, seems to quash any question of him having committed suicide, a possibility raised earlier in the text. However, this official version of the circumstances of his death may simply be worded this way, i.e. putting the blame for his death on the pony, to avoid unnecessary family embarrassment or shame. The unusual set of circumstances previously outlined, together with the reported extraordinary manner of his death, means that the possibility of suicide cannot be ruled out, but it should be stressed that this remains speculative.

The following is an extract from the website [https://shimlawalks.com/kenlog-cemetery-in-shimla/]ofKanlogCemetery:-

Left Hand Side
14 : Ellen Julia, w/o (illegible)
15 : Rowland Vyner Cockerell, Born 11 Dec 1843 Died Oct 9
1873
16 : Richard Watson, PAG Dir of GER. England PDDGMP
Age 54 years Died 18 Mar 1937.

The year of Rowland's birth is given as 1843, but this is incorrect and should read 1834. The Radley College record above is also incorrect, asserting 1835. These items of apparent misinformation are symptomatic of the fog shrouding key episodes in Rowland's short, but eventful, and ultimately tragic life. By comparison, his sister Mary's life appears more sedate, but she plays an important role in the guardianship of at least part of the Pepys Cockerell Collection.

Mary Theresa Cockerell (1837-1914)

Mary had a long life, but never married, and inherited both money and Pepys Cockerell family artefacts partly because several close relatives predeceased her. Among these inherited artefacts was the double portrait of Mary's grandmother (Anne Pepys Cockerell) and aunt (Anne Cockerell). As outlined in Chapter 10, this painting was exhibited in 1809 at the Royal Academy and there is reliable evidence that in 1907 it is in the possession of 'Miss Cockerell' at 11 Mandeville Place, an address already encountered above, and one which Mary inhabited from 1891 or earlier, and retained for the rest of her life.

Although no record of the date of her birth has been identified, records show that she was baptised at St. James' Church, Paddington on 4th July 1836. The next identified record is in the 1861 census showing Mary, aged 24, living with her parents at 9, Adelaide Crescent, Brighton. Thirty years later in the 1891 census, now aged 54, she is head of the household at 11 Mandeville Place, Marylebone, London, and living on her own means. The only others living with her are six servants, whose roles are cook, ladies' maid, nurse, under housemaid, butler, and footboy. She can clearly afford lavish support, and female company, the cook (53) and ladies' maid (50) being of a similar age. Perhaps the presence of a nurse also indicates some health problems.

In 1911, Mary is shown as head of a household in Littlehampton, Sussex, with a visitor and two servants. Given that we know, from two pieces of evidence, that she retained her London address, 11, Mandeville Place, right through to her death, there is a strong possibility that the Littlehampton residence near the coast is for health reasons. Mary died on 11th July 1914, just before the start of the Great War, perhaps a minor blessing because some of her younger male relatives were to perish in that disastrous tragedy.

> **COCKERELL** *Mary Theresa of 11 Mandeville Place Manchester Square* **Middlesex** *spinster died 11 July 1914 Probate* **London** *6 October to John Pepys Cockerell esquire Mary Francis Pemberton (wife of Arthur Ralph Pemberton) and Harry Chester esquire. Effects £102864 5s. 5d.*

Her probate record above shows the enormous value of her estate, the equivalent of around £15m today. It appears that she benefited from inheriting accumulated wealth from several of her close relatives. One of those to whom probate was granted was John Pepys Cockerell (1866-1930), who next takes over guardianship of the remaining Samuel Pepys memorabilia and Pepys Cockerell Collection. His life story is picked up later.

Children of Anne (nee Cockerell) & Richard Pollen

Richard Hungerford Pollen (1815-1881)

Richard was Anne and Richard's eldest son, born on 19th October 1815, in Paddington. To give some context, his birth was just four months after the Battle of Waterloo, which for the foreseeable future ended any serious threat to Britain's security from external threats. Internal political and socio-economic pressures would, however, cause barely less hardship and anxiety for the general population. The Pollen family members, with wealth, status, and social connections, were largely immune from such concerns.

As the first-born son and principal heir, Richard lived at the family's home, Rodbourne House, for most of his life and, after his father's death, continued there with his wife Charlotte, their children, and his widowed mother Anne. He was a Justice of the Peace and, aged 22 at Queen Victoria's accession, appears to have followed a typical privileged upper middle-class life through the early decades of her long reign. Given the expectations of him as the eldest son and heir he probably had little choice but to take responsibility for the family, their property, social standing, wealth, and reputation.

Richard married Charlotte Elizabeth Godley on 5th June 1845 in Carrigellan, Leitrim, Ireland. The Godley family was a notable one, broadly matching the status of the Pollens. Killegar House in Carigellan was the Godley's ancestral home, and one of Charlotte's close relatives, Arthur Godley, 1st Baron Kilbracken (1847-1932) was Permanent Under-Secretary of State for India, in yet another substantial family connection with the sub-continent.

Much of the next three paragraphs cover similar details previously given in the context of his mother's life, but given here from Richard's perspective, with some additional information. The 1851 and 1861 censuses for Rodbourne House give some

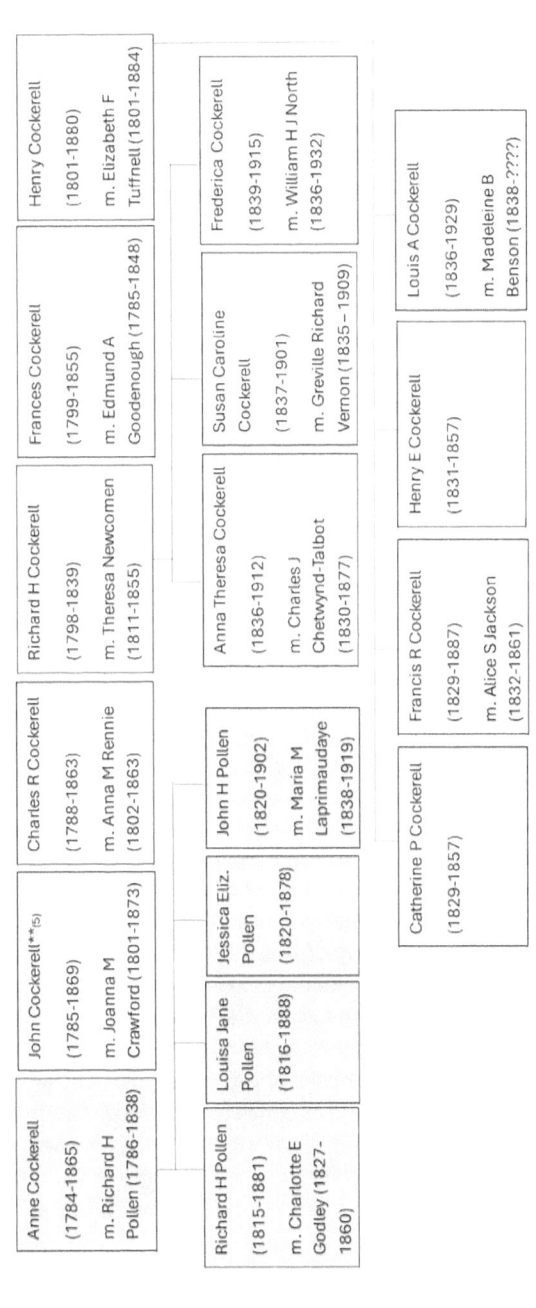

Anne Cockerell
(1784-1865)
m. Richard H Pollen (1786-1838)

John Cockerell(**(5))
(1785-1869)
m. Joanna M Crawford (1801-1873)

Charles R Cockerell
(1788-1863)
m. Anna M Rennie (1802-1863)

Richard H Cockerell
(1798-1839)
m. Theresa Newcomen (1811-1855)

Frances Cockerell
(1799-1855)
m. Edmund A Goodenough (1785-1848)

Henry Cockerell
(1801-1880)
m. Elizabeth F Tuffnell (1801-1884)

Richard H Pollen
(1815-1881)
m. Charlotte E Godley (1827-1860)

Louisa Jane Pollen
(1816-1888)

Jessica Eliz. Pollen
(1820-1878)

John H Pollen
(1820-1902)
m. Maria M Laprimaudaye (1838-1919)

Anna Theresa Cockerell
(1836-1912)
m. Charles J Chetwynd-Talbot (1830-1877)

Susan Caroline Cockerell
(1837-1901)
m. Greville Richard Vernon (1835 – 1909)

Frederica Cockerell
(1839-1915)
m. William H J North (1836-1932)

Catherine P Cockerell
(1829-1857)

Francis R Cockerell
(1829-1887)
m. Alice S Jackson (1832-1861)

Henry E Cockerell
(1831-1857)

Louis A Cockerell
(1836-1929)
m. Madeleine B Benson (1838-????)

** *Denotes Samuel Pepys's successive heirs*

Children of Anne (nee Cockerell) & Richard Pollen

indication of the family's lifestyle, and underline the substantial responsibilities Richard inherited. In the 1851 census his widowed mother Anne (nee Cockerell), aged 66, is still head of the household. He is aged 35, living with his wife Charlotte, aged 24, and their children Richard (4), Mary (3), Katherine (1), and Laura (just 12 days old). Richard's sister Jessie, aged 31, is still living at home. A cousin, Annabella Goodenough, aged 25, is described as a visitor, probably there to help with looking after the young children around the time of the baby Laura's birth.

In the 1861 census for Rodbourne House, Richard is a widower, his wife Charlotte, who was aged 24 in the 1851 census, having tragically died. The Probate record gives her date of death as 22nd February 1860 at Gloucester Place, Middlesex, and she was buried six days later. Her effects were valued at £1,200. Richard's eldest son, in traditional fashion also named Richard, was now aged 14 and described as a scholar, as were all the children. The other 3 children who, ten years earlier had appeared in the 1851 census, are now 13, 11, and 10 years old and have been joined by four more, namely Constance (8), Anne (7), Helen (6), and Charles (3). Given the frequency of Charlotte's pregnancies, perhaps her death was linked to another one, some two years after Charles had been born. Complications during pregnancy, and childbirth itself, were common contemporary health risks.

The 1861 census evidences that all the children had been born at Rodbourne, except Richard the eldest, born in Paddington. Richard's mother Anne, now 76, is still living at Rodbourne, as are her daughters Louisa, aged 44, and Jessica, now 41. Also recorded there are Frederick Goodenough (33) and Lucy Goodenough (34), Richard's cousins. There are 4 male and 10 female servants. Anne, who had been head of the household in 1851, is now described as Widow of Landed Property, with Richard the head of the household and described as J.P. of Wiltshire, living off landed property. His ultimate responsibility for this substantial household, house and land would fill his time and dominate his focus. Perhaps unsurprisingly, there is no record of any other activities of note.

Twenty years later there is an unexpected entry in the 1881 census. Richard, now 65, has inherited the Baronetcy, but at the time the census is taken he is living as a 'Boarder' at the Turkish Baths, College Place, in the Parish of St. Augustine's in Bristol.

What is also slightly surprising is that he is noted as 'Married' rather than the status of 'Widower' in 1861. On this latter point, there is no record of Richard remarrying after his wife Charlotte's death in 1860, and unless evidence is discovered, the default assumption must be that the entry 'Married' is simply an error. Perhaps the person taking the census record at the Baths may simply have asked a critically-ill Richard whether he was married and, in his severely weakened state (see below), he simply answered yes because he had indeed, in the past, been married. In any event, the paramount focus would appear to have been his seriously failing health.

The Turkish Baths in Bristol represented the flagship in a chain of such establishments run by Charles Bartholomew, aged 51 in the 1881 census. His occupation is given as Bath Proprietor, married to Emma, aged 48.

https://archives.bristol.gov.uk/records/43207/32/2/15

Although the Turkish Baths also operated purely for bathing and hygiene purposes, the reason for Richard boarding there is almost certainly for treatment of one or more health conditions. If so, any such treatment ultimately failed because, just a week after the census was taken, he sadly died at the Baths on 8th April 1881, as evidenced by the following Probate entry.

POLLEN Sir Richard Hungerford Bart. *(Personal Estate £4,586 6s. 11d)*

*15 July. The Will with four Codicils of Sir Richard Hungerford Pollen late of Rodbourne near Chippenham in the County of **Wilts** Baronet who died 8 April 1881 at the Turkish Baths College-place in the City of Bristol was proved at the **Principal Registry** by Sir Richard Hungerford Pollen of Rodbourne Baronet the Son the sole Executor.*

Such Turkish Baths were frequented by a wide spectrum of society, and ages, and by both sexes. Among the other fourteen 'boarders' itemised alongside Richard, ten of whom were female, occupations included housemaid, schoolmaster, Inland Revenue Officer, Wesleyan Minister, Lady's Maid, and Professor of Music. The ages of these other 14 individuals ranged from 24 to 61.

The building itself was extensive. Those described as 'boarders' spent the night of the census there as part of their residence at the Baths, but such establishments were also used daily by the public for both hygiene and health reasons. While undergoing regimes of ill-health treatment extending over days or weeks, boarders were no doubt housed in varying degrees of luxury related to their financial resources, and able to have visits from family members and friends.

As an aside, the Professor of Music boarding at the Turkish Baths at the same time as Richard was John Horth Deane, born in 1824, and a composer of religious music. A few bars extracted from one of his works, 'Lord with glowing heart I'd praise thee', are shown below.

Sorrento, 87.87 D

John H. Deane (1824-1881)

https://musescore.com/user/33012693/scores/5738439

Given that he and Richard were of similar age, with highly respectable and educated backgrounds, both probably in ill-health and trying hydrotherapies of one sort or another at the Turkish Baths, it is likely that they would have formed some level of friendship and support for each other. If so, Richard's death in April 1881 would have been a blow to the musician, indicating the limited efficacy of any treatments they were receiving. John Deane's own death followed just two weeks later, on 22nd April.

John Hungerford Pollen (1820-1902)

Five years after the arrival of their first-born son, Anne (nee Cockerell) and Richard Pollen welcomed a second son, John Hungerford Pollen, born on 19th November 1820, the year of George III's death and accession of the Prince Regent as George IV. John's childhood spanned the two short reigns of George IV and William IV, and he was just 16 at Queen Victoria's accession. While he marginally outlived the queen, therefore living briefly into the Edwardian era, his adulthood was effectively entirely a Victorian one. Appropriately, his significant contribution to the arts was influential in shaping Victorian tastes.

As outlined above, his elder brother Richard was heir to the Pollen family property and in due course a baronetcy, together with all the attaching responsibilities. As the second son, John would have more freedom to steer his own course in life, and he did so with impressive dynamism, talent, and determination. These qualities were engaged to excellent advantage, leading to appointments in senior positions with wide public recognition.

Many of his papers and documents are held in the Bodleian Library in Oxford, a city on which he had some considerable artistic influence, and the library's website has an excellent summary of his life, cited here in full. Yet again there are strong connections with India.

John Hungerford Pollen was born on 19 November 1820, the second son of Richard Pollen (1786–1838) and his wife Anne Cockerell (1784–1865). Pollen was educated at Eton College and Christ Church, Oxford. He became a fellow of Merton College after taking his BA in 1842 and was (at various points) dean, bursar, and garden master. Pollen became a Senior Proctor of the University of Oxford in 1851.

In 1846, Pollen was ordained as a priest by the Bishop of Oxford, Dr Samuel Wilberforce. The following year, he became pro-vicar at St Saviour Church in Leeds during an interregnum. During his time there, the use of auricular confession sparked a controversy which ended up with Pollen and his colleagues being banned from holding the Christmas Eve service in 1850. Whilst his colleagues converted to Catholicism, Pollen argued his case with the Bishop and was reinstated. In 1851, he published NARRATIVE OF FIVE YEARS AT ST. SAVIOUR'S, LEEDS, defending Tractarianism and the use of Catholic practices within the Church of England. This was a prelude to Pollen's own conversion and he was received into the Roman Catholic Church in Rouen on 20 October 1852. By converting to Catholicism, Pollen forfeited his fellowship at Merton and his other university offices.

Pollen's elder brother, (Richard) Hungerford Pollen (1815-1881), became a Catholic the following year. Both brothers were consequently disinherited by their uncle Sir John Walter Pollen, 2nd Baronet of Redenham (1784-1863). Whilst Hungerford still inherited the baronetcy, Sir John's will made membership of the Church of England a condition for the inheritance of his estate: after the death of Sir John's widow in 1877, Redenham was inherited by Hungerford's son, Richard Hungerford Pollen (1846-1918).

Pollen, now without career or inheritance prospects, travelled to Rome where he met the writer William Makepeace Thackeray. He also became acquainted with the Reverend Charles John La Primaudaye (1805-1858) and his wife Anne Francesca Hubbard (1811-1854), who were also recent converts to the Catholic Church. In 1854, Pollen became engaged to Charles's daughter, Maria Margaret La Primaudaye (1838-1919). They were married on 18 September 1855 in the church of Woodchester monastery, near Stroud, Gloucestershire. In November 1854, through his connection with the La Primaudayes, Pollen received an offer from John Henry Newman (1801-1890) to become professor of fine arts at Newman's new university in Dublin and design the university church.

In 1857, Pollen moved to London, where he became acquainted with members of the Pre-Raphaelite Brotherhood, including Dante Gabriel Rossetti, William Morris, Edward Burne-Jones, William Holman Hunt, and John Ruskin. Through Ruskin, Pollen was commissioned in 1858 to design the carvings for the façade of the new University Museum of Natural History in Oxford. Ruskin also commissioned Pollen to work alongside Rossetti, Burne-Jones, and William Morris on the mural decoration of the Oxford Union library depicting scenes from Arthurian myth. Among many other commissions in the 1860s and 1870s, Pollen also designed interiors at Blickling Hall, Aylsham for William Kerr, eighth Marquess of Lothian, and designed the fresco decoration at Alton Towers for the Earl of Shrewsbury. He worked with the architect Benjamin Woodward in Ireland, designing rooms for James Anthony Lawson's new house, Clontra, near Dublin and a picture gallery for the Marchioness of Ormonde at Kilkenny Castle.

Pollen was appointed one of the jurors for the International Exhibition held in London in 1862. The following year, at the suggestion of William Makepeace Thackeray, he was appointed by Sir Henry Cole as Assistant Keeper of the South Kensington Museum (now the Victoria and Albert Museum), which had opened in 1857. As Assistant Keeper, Pollen produced catalogues of furniture, sculpture, and metalwork. He also taught in the Government School of Design and submitted entries to the ENCYCLOPÆDIA BRITANNICA. Pollen was a juror for the International Exhibition in Dublin (1865) and also for the Exposition Universelle in Paris (1867), where he was awarded a gold medal for the first part of his 'Universal catalogue of books on art'.

The Pollens found that a good Catholic primary education could be obtained more cheaply abroad and so, in 1871, Maria Pollen took their ten children to live in Münster, Westfalia (due to work demands, Pollen could *only spend holidays there with them). The family moved permanently back to England in 1875 and the boys went on to study at Newman's new Oratory School in Edgbaston, Birmingham. The Pollens divided their time between London and Newbuildings, the house in Sussex rented from the poet and writer Wilfrid Scawen Blunt (1840–1922) and his wife, Anne Isabella Noel Blunt [née King], suo jure Baroness Wentworth (1837–1917). Blunt was a longstanding friend of the La Primaudaye family, having first made their acquaintance as a child in Italy in 1852. The Pollens rented Newbuildings until 1889, when relations between the two families irretrievably broke down (after Blunt's daughter Judith Anne Dorothea (1873–1957) accused Pollen's sixth son, Arthur Joseph Hungerford Pollen (1866-1937) of over-familiarity).*

In 1876, Pollen resigned his post at the South Kensington Museum when he was invited to become private secretary to Lord Ripon (George Frederick Samuel Robinson, 1st Marquess of Ripon, 1827-1909), a fellow Catholic convert. Ripon was made Viceroy of India in 1880. Though Pollen remained in London for most of this period, he visited India towards the end of the Viceroyalty in 1884. Whilst in India, Pollen commissioned exhibits for the Colonial and Indian Exhibition of 1886 and also advised the Maharaja of Kuch Behar [Cooch Behar] on the decoration of his palaces. Pollen's artistic commissions and exhibition work continued into the 1890s and he lived to see the laying of the foundation stone of the new Victoria and Albert Museum in 1899. John Hungerford Pollen died in 1902, shortly after his 82nd birthday. Maria Margaret Pollen, who was likewise interested in the decorative arts and had become an expert in the history of lace, published SEVEN CENTURIES OF LACE *in 1908.*

The Pollens' children were:

1. *Anne Gertrude Mary Pollen (1856-1934)*
2. *Lucy Mary Pollen (b. and d.1857)*
3. *John Hungerford Pollen (1858-1925)*

4. *Walter Michael Hungerford Pollen (1859-1889)*
5. *Anthony Cecil Hungerford Pollen (1860-1940)*
6. *Francis Gabriel Hungerford Pollen (1862-1944)*
7. *George Charles Hungerford Pollen (1863-1930)*
8. *Margaret ('Daisy') Winifred Pollen (1864-1937)*
9. *Arthur Joseph Hungerford Pollen (1866-1937)*
10. *Stephen Hungerford Pollen (1868-1935)*
11. *Clement Hungerford Pollen (1869-1934)*
12. *Benjamin Hungerford Pollen (b. and d.1876)*

Pollen's eldest son and namesake, John, became a Jesuit priest and historian. His brothers Anthony and George also entered the priesthood: Anthony became a noted composer and George became a Fellow of the Geological Society. The Pollens' eldest child, Anne, entered the Convent of the Sacred Heart, Roehampton, in 1881 and became a nun. She published a memoir of her father in 1912 and a biography of Mother Mabel Digby in 1914.

Pollen's second son, Walter, became a soldier and was aide-de-camp to Lord Ripon between 1883 and 1884. Walter was part of the Survey of India Department between 1884 and 1887, though he was invalided out due to fever. He returned to the east in 1888 and became Survey Officer to the Lushai Expedition in early 1889, but died of fever in Chittagong in March that year. Pollen's seventh son, Stephen, also became a soldier and served as aide-de-camp to two successive Viceroys in India (Lord Lansdowne and Lord Elgin) before serving in the South African campaign. Francis became a naval officer who fought in the Sudan between 1884 and 1885. He became part of the Naval Brigade in the Gordon Relief Expedition in Burma in 1886. Both Francis and Stephen retired in 1902, but returned to service during the First World War.

The Pollens' youngest surviving child, Clement, settled in British Columbia, Canada and was involved in the construction of the Kootenay Central Railroad. He was at some point secretary to Sir Ambrose Shea during his time as Governor of the Bahamas. During the First World War,

Clement served in The Kootenay Regiment, Canadian Forces and became a Lieutenant-Colonel.

Arthur struck out a different career to his siblings, training as a barrister and becoming a businessman, inventor, and journalist. His son, Arthur Joseph Lawrence Pollen (1899–1968), a sculptor, married Daphne Baring (1904–1986), the daughter of Cecil Baring, third Baron Revelstoke. Daphne was also an artist: like Arthur, she had studied at the Slade School of Fine Art. Their daughter Lucy Margaret Pollen (1932-2014) married the architect and Liberal Party politician Philip Vincent Belloc Jebb (1927-1995), a grandson of Hilaire Belloc (1870-1953), in 1955.

Extract from the Bodleian Libraries website.

Collection: Archive of John Hungerford Pollen and the Pollen Family | Bodleian Archives & Manuscripts (ox.ac.uk)

Photograph of the family of John Hungerford Pollen (with beard, standing centre), unknown photographer, Archive of John Hungerford Pollen and the Pollen Family, Oxford, Bodleian Libraries, MS. 17906 Photogr. 3.

When John died on 2nd December 1902 he was living at 11 Pembridge Crescent, Middlesex in the West End of London, and probate, with effects valued at £10,286, was granted to his son Arthur Hungerford Pollen on 3rd March 1903.

As can be seen from the substantial Bodleian Library biographical summary above, his wife, together with several of their children and subsequent generations continued to be heavily involved in the arts, inspired by his example. Within the Pollen family there are also strong religious and military strands, and one notable additional narrative is set out below.

John's son **Arthur Hungerford Pollen (1866-1937)** didn't follow a military career, but his most notable legacy, emerging in the middle years of his life, was his influence on naval matters, strongly resonating with Samuel Pepys, his 17th century relative. Arthur's career was largely legal, industrial, and science based, but he was deeply inquisitive and enterprising in a variety of other fields. One keen mechanical interest led to him inventing and identifying improvements in naval weaponry and range-finding. The timing of this interest, sparked by a chance meeting with a Goodenough and Cockerell family relative, coincided with the looming threat of war at the turn of the 20th century. After initial interest from the Admiralty his work was largely ignored and sidelined, arguably compromising the British Navy in the period leading up to the First World War. If his recommendations and technology had been implemented and refined, the single serious Anglo-German naval engagement during the war, the inconclusive Battle of Jutland in 1915, may have had a significantly different outcome. He did, however, receive some belated recognition and substantial financial recompense, and his work was subsequently adapted and used by several other navies.

At the tail end of the war Arthur vented his frustration, albeit in a typically measured fashion befitting his legal and scientific background, with a forensic study, *The Navy in Battle*, first published in late November 1918. Its general theme was a critique of the deficiencies of the Royal Navy's fighting capacity, and in parallel it set out a far more specific analysis of the use of gunnery in the Battle of Jutland as well as criticism of both the wider strategic and tactical decision-making by the Admiralty. Even setting aside a natural tendency towards self-justification in this polemic publication, his main criticisms are supported by contemporary evidence, not least exposure of the Admiralty's overconfidence and overreliance on mere weight of firepower, rather than matching this with the accuracy of delivery.

Changes certainly followed but, in any event, wider and more fundamental factors were at play. Britain's 'ruling of the waves' which had persisted from the Battle of Trafalgar in 1805 through the whole of the nineteenth century and well into the next, was increasingly being challenged by other nations. Britain's leading role in the Industrial Revolution was being emulated by others, shipbuilding being just one example of Britain being caught up and, in some other fields such as industrial chemistry, overtaken. Arthur was inventive, imaginative, and visionary. He was of somewhat similar character and temperament to a more famous industrial engineer and developer of innovative solutions to military challenges, their two lives overlapping for 50 years. This broadly contemporary figure was Barnes Wallis with his pioneering work on early airship design during and just after the First World War, and the 'Dam Busters bouncing bomb' in the Second.

Arthur Pollen's life story is briefly sketched. The 1891 census shows him still living with his parents at 11 Pembridge Crescent, now aged 24 and a 'Student of Law'. His father, John Hungerford Pollen, by this time, as outlined above, a renowned Pre-Raphaelite and Arts & Crafts acolyte and much more, was then aged 70 and his occupation given as Painter and Architect. By the time of this census Arthur had completed his school education at the Birmingham Oratory School, and had gained a BA from Trinity College Oxford, in 1888. Two years after the census, now aged 26, he became a Lincoln's Inn Barrister. In the 1895 General Election he stood unsuccessfully as the Liberal candidate for Walthamstow, his 4,523 votes being beaten by the 6,876 of his opponent Edmund Byrne. When Byrne resigned two years later, Arthur declined to stand at the by-election. He was admitted into the Freedom of the City of London on 7th June 1899 and, through this, so was his son John Anthony Lawrence Pollen. This Freedom was linked to the "Company of Coach Makers and Coach Harness Makers". Qualification for the Freedom passed down the generations.

Arthur would no doubt have been very aware of, and perhaps inspired by, his relative James Graham Goodenough (1830-1875), who had been an expert on naval gunnery, and whose story is related later. By chance, while Arthur was in Malta in 1900 he was invited by another 'Pepys' relative, William Goodenough, who had just been promoted to Commander, to watch a naval gunnery practice nearby. *[Fifteen years later, in the Great War, William was to command the Second Light Cruiser Squadron at the Battle of Jutland from the bridge of his flagship, the light cruiser 'Southampton', and would later rise to be Admiral Sir William Goodenough.]* Witnessing this naval practice, Arthur Pollen was struck by the abysmal gunnery accuracy, which was so poor that even at ranges of less than a mile the big guns could not reliably hit their targets. This was the trigger for Arthur to put his inventive mind to improving this crucial deficiency. Two years earlier, his wide range of interests and talents had led to him being made managing-director of Linotype & Machinery Co. Ltd., and he was rapidly forming an understanding of manufacturing and engineering possibilities.

A further motivation for exploring improvements to the accuracy of naval gunnery was provided by Britain's leading scientist, Lord Kelvin, being on the Linotype Board. He proposed using an analogue computer to solve the equations representing the relative motions of the ships, the time delay in the flight of shells, and calculation of their required trajectory, in turn determining the direction and elevation of the guns. Kelvin's brother had done some pioneering work on a tidal differential analyser which helped in designing the suggested analogue computer. Crucially, the inputs to any such computer needed to be highly accurate data on the target's position and relative motion, and it was Arthur Pollen who developed a plotting unit to collect this data, also adding a gyroscope to allow for the yaw of the firing ship. This approach required significant ground-breaking engineering work and Arthur used Linotype company resources, including design elements delivered by Harold Isherwood.

Initial trials in 1905 and 1906 simply emphasised the scale of the technical and practical challenges and Arthur Pollen realised that further development had to be more than just a distraction from Linotype's core business. In 1909 he set up the Argo Company and in 1911 bought a holding in the York firm Thomas Cooke & Sons, who were already manufacturing components for his equipment.

In the 1911 census Arthur, aged 44, is living with his wife Maud Beatrice, 33, at Walton on the Hill, Surrey. It evidences that they have been married for 12 years and have had 3 children, one of whom, a daughter, sadly died at just 4 years old. Arthur's occupation is given as Director of Companies in Engineering trades. At home and living with them they have a French cook & housekeeper and a gardener. The two surviving children are not there on the night of the census, presumably either away on holiday or more likely at boarding school.

While Arthur was demonstrating his system to the Navy, he liaised with a promising gunnery lieutenant Frederic Dreyer, who was given a key role as assistant to the Director of Naval Ordnance and Torpedoes. Over time, Dreyer developed his own system

which differed significantly from Arthur Pollen's, each system having its strengths and weaknesses. Dreyer, however, operating within the naval establishment unlike the outsider Arthur Pollen, had a key Admiralty role in deciding which system elements to use. He always chose his own.

When the Great War broke out, relations between Arthur and the Admiralty had completely broken down and he was removed from the Admiralty's list of recognised naval contractors. Instead of pursuing a lost cause, Arthur accepted a post as a feature writer for *Land and*

Arthur Hungerford Pollen

Water, and turned this into a full-time occupation, helped by good relations with individual naval officers who had been involved with, and impressed by, his Argo system. As well as publishing *The Navy in Battle* at the end of 1918, Arthur also became a public speaker about naval affairs.

Once the Great War was over and there was time for reflection, Arthur Pollen's Argo system received some belated recognition. The Dreyer system had used aspects of the Pollen design and £30,000 compensation was paid to Pollen in 1926 based on a theoretical number of his Argo units that could have been fitted in Royal Navy ships. Commentators debated, without resolution, the relative shares of blame attributable for poor naval gunnery performance at the Battle of Jutland between the deficiencies of the Dreyer system and the questionable tactics of Vice-Admiral David Beatty, the commander of the British battlecruiser.

Irrespective of partisan positions, Pollen was a highly influential figure in naval matters but also had run-ins with the Admiralty, reminiscent of his 17th century relative Samuel Pepys, with whom he also shared the trait of enthusiasm for continually aiming for technical and operational improvements.

Arthur lived latterly at 238 St. James Court, Westminster and died on 28th January 1937. Probate was granted to his widow Maud Beatrice Pollen, his effects being valued at £12,430. Alphabetically listed immediately next in the National Probate Calendar (Index of Wills and Administrations) for 1937 is the entry for Margaret Winifred Pollen "*of Teresa's Cottage Gillingham Dorsetshire spinster died 10th May 1937 at 238 St. James Court Westminster Probate London 24 June to Francis Gabriel Hungerford Pollen retired captain R.N. and John Francis Hungerford Pollen lieutenant-commander R.N. Effects £340*". Three years older than him, Margaret is the younger of Arthur's two sisters, with Francis Gabriel and John Francis being two of Arthur's seven brothers, respectively 5 and 8 years older than him. As the probate record confirms, Margaret never married and was living at the same address as Arthur at her death.

As well as having high-profile Goodenough naval relatives (of which more shortly), Arthur's interest in naval matters was surely and almost inevitably further influenced by having two naval officers as brothers. The probate records indicate strong ongoing family links persisting. The 1871 census for 11 Pembridge Crescent, their parents' home, as well as recording the 10 young siblings (Arthur for example was then only 4 years old), shows their uncle Clement Laprimaudaye, his mother Maria's brother, living there. Clement is aged 27, and his occupation is given as Lieut. R.N. The children, and especially the eight young males, were no doubt inspired by this role model in their household, further contributing to Arthur's later interest in naval matters. His two brothers, in becoming naval officers themselves, as evidenced above, were clearly even more directly influenced by their uncle Clement. He had already had one other family influence because the youngest of Arthur's siblings was christened Clement. In the 1891 census, aged 21, this youngest sibling is entered as Secretary to the Governor of Bahamas, perhaps an early example of working from home, as he is still then living at 11 Pembridge Crescent.

To conclude this consideration of Arthur Pollen's life, as well as being related he has other connections with the 17th century diarist Samuel Pepys. Both have historic and naval significance. In addition, Samuel's extensive and historically important Pepys Library and the equally extensive archive of Arthur Pollen's papers – even the summary catalogue of the Pollen Archive runs to well over a hundred pages – are both housed at Cambridge University.

The several Royal Navy connections outlined above, when added to others in the wider Pepys-Cockerell family, emphasise the preponderance of naval careers and influences passed down through the generations.

Children of Charles Robert Cockerell and Anna Maria Rennie

John Rennie Cockerell (1830-1897)

John was Charles and Anna's first child, born on August 8th 1830. He remained single for most of his life, eventually marrying Louisa Elizabeth Rennie, on May 19th May 1883 at the Parish Church in

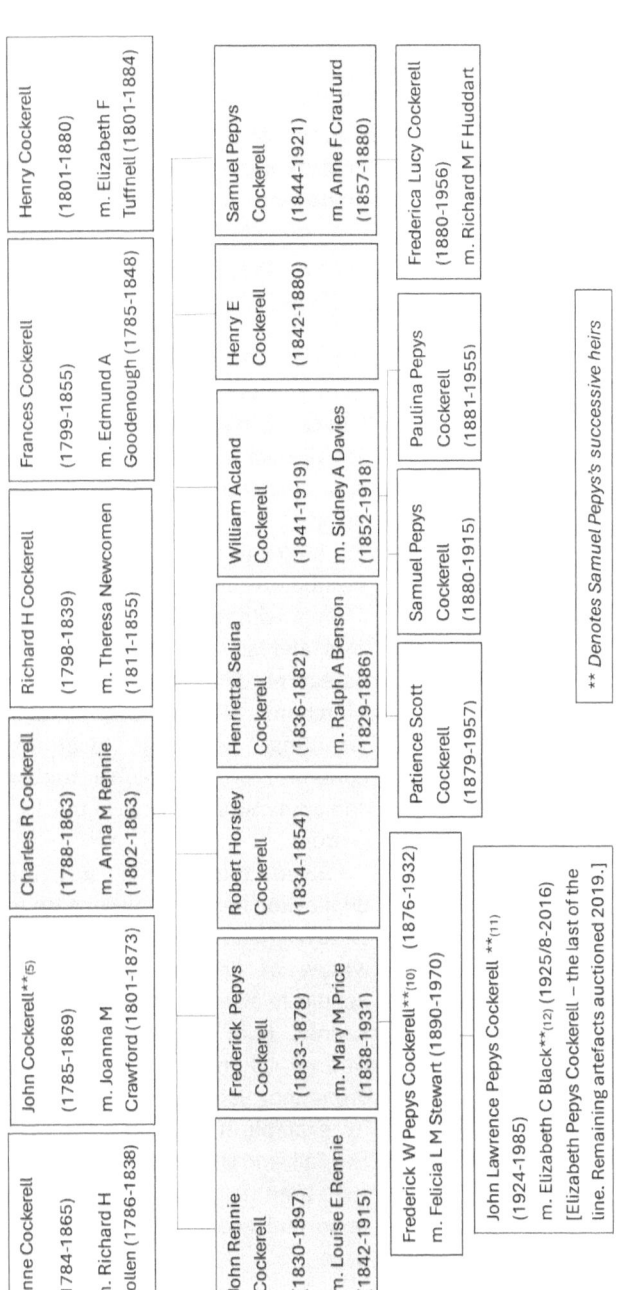

Children of Charles Robert Cockerell & Anna Maria (nee Rennie)

Anne Cockerell
(1784-1865)
m. Richard H
Polten (1786-1838)

John Cockerell**(5)
(1785-1869)
m. Joanna M
Crawford (1801-1873)

Charles R Cockerell
(1788-1863)
m. Anna M Rennie
(1802-1863)

Richard H Cockerell
(1798-1839)
m. Theresa Newcomen
(1811-1855)

Frances Cockerell
(1799-1855)
m. Edmund A
Goodenough (1785-1848)

Henry Cockerell
(1801-1880)
m. Elizabeth F
Tuffnell (1801-1884)

John Rennie
Cockerell
(1830-1897)
m. Louise E Rennie
(1842-1915)

Frederick Pepys
Cockerell
(1833-1878)
m. Mary M Price
(1838-1931)

Robert Horsley
Cockerell
(1834-1854)

Henrietta Selina
Cockerell
(1836-1882)
m. Ralph A Benson
(1829-1886)

William Acland
Cockerell
(1841-1919)
m. Sidney A Davies
(1852-1918)

Henry E
Cockerell
(1842-1880)

Samuel Pepys
Cockerell
(1844-1921)
m. Anne F Craufurd
(1857-1880)

Frederick W Pepys Cockerell**(10) (1876-1932)
m. Felicia L M Stewart (1890-1970)

Patience Scott
Cockerell
(1879-1957)

Samuel Pepys
Cockerell
(1880-1915)

Paulina Pepys
Cockerell
(1881-1955)

Frederica Lucy Cockerell
(1880-1956)
m. Richard M F Huddart

John Lawrence Pepys Cockerell **(11)
(1924-1985)
m. Elizabeth C Black**(12) (1925/8-2016)
[Elizabeth Pepys Cockerell – the last of the
line. Remaining artefacts auctioned 2019.]

*** Denotes Samuel Pepys's successive heirs*

253

Paddington. On the marriage certificate John, living at 5 Cavendish Square, is cited as a bachelor with his rank or profession described as 'Indian Civil Service retired'. Even allowing for India being so important to Britain in the late eighteenth and nineteenth centuries, the number of Cockerell family connections with the subcontinent is extraordinary. John's marriage partner was Louisa Elizabeth Rennie, aged 41, the widow of William Hepburn Rennie C.M.G. (Companion of the order of St. Michael and St. George), who was Lieutenant-Governor of the island of St. Vincent. At the time of the marriage Louisa is living at 36 Westbourne Terrace in Paddington, an area with many Cockerell family links, and her father is cited as John Coysgarne Sim, described as a Merchant. These connections, including far-flung locations, epitomise Britain's global trading and administrative focus in the 19th century.

George Rennie 1801-1860

Louisa Elizabeth Sim, 10th May 1861

Given the Rennie surname duplication here, it is no surprise to discover that John has married the widow of one of his mother's Rennie relatives, William Hepburn Rennie. Both he and his father George Rennie had highly prominent colonial roles, George, for example having presided over the Falkland Islands as Governor at the time it was becoming an important economic and strategic base.

Fortunately, we have an early photograph of John Rennie Cockerell's wife Louise Elizabeth Sim (her maiden name before she married twice, first to William Hepburn Rennie and then to John Cockerell).

John's marriage to Louisa was conducted by a family relative, the Reverend Louis Arthur Cockerell vicar of North Weald, a character already mentioned earlier and profiled later in the text. John's career in the Indian Civil Service has not left any record of outstanding actions or achievements, and it appears that he was simply part of that great network of administrators which underpinned the governing of British India.

When John died on June 30th 1897, the probate record, dated July 22nd 1897, provides a little more information, including the substantial probate value of his effects :-

COCKERELL *John Rennie of 26 Westbourne-terrace Middlesex esquire died 30 June 1897 Probate* **London** *22 July to William Acland Cockerell esquire and Sir Richard Temple Rennie knight Effects £14393 13s. 10d.*

Frederick Pepys Cockerell (1833-1878)

Frederick Pepys Cockerell

Frederick, the second son of Charles and Anna, was born in March 1833 at 87 Eaton Square, and in 1841 he was living with the family at Golders Hill, Hendon. He followed his father's impressive architectural career with his own. The substantial text entry in the Oxford Dictionary of National Biography (ODNB) gives a good summary of the impact he had, and emphasises that although primarily an architect, he was also an artist, his first entry in the Royal Academy exhibitions being in 1854, with 23 other entries exhibited between then and 1877.

On the architectural side, the ODNB notes that, *'his earliest success was in raising and making additions to Coleorton Hall, the seat of Sir George Beaumont'*. The Beaumonts, already introduced above, were closely related, this commission being another example of wider Cockerell family connections proving mutually helpful. A London building of note was Frederick's Freemasons' Hall of 1861 in Great Queen Street. This was the year after he had been elected an Associate of the Royal Institute of British Architects. He came extremely close to winning the commission for the Albert Memorial. The ODNB comments that *'Cockerell's competition designs for the National Gallery were commended and much admired, and that for the Albert Memorial was selected by the judges, but the queen preferred a Gothic design, and that of Sir G. G. Scott was finally accepted'*.

Frederick married a widow, Mary Mulock Price, on 20th July 1867 at the Parish Church of St. James in Westminster. They were married, as with so many Cockerell family weddings, by a relative, in this case Revd. Henry Cockerell.

Of Frederick's death, the ODNB notes that *'Cockerell died suddenly, in Paris, on 4 Nov. 1878, on which day he had been invited to a dinner party at the house of M. Viollet le Duc, the architect. He left a widow and six children, at the time residing at 18 Manchester Square, London'*.

Frederick provides a key link in tracing the history of family ownership of the double portrait of his grandmother Anne Cockerell and her daughter Anne, his aunt. The painting ends up in the possession of Frederick's son Frederick William Pepys Cockerell (1876-1932) and his wife Felicia L M Stewart (1890-1970), before passing to his grandson John Lawrence Pepys Cockerell (1924-1985) and wife Elizabeth (d. 2016). Chapter 10 deals with the double portrait and its story, and Chapter 11 covers the Pepys Cockerell Collection of which the double portrait and other inheritances form a part.

Robert Horsley Cockerell (1834-1854)

Robert was Charles and Anna's third son, born on 22nd November 1834, and baptised in the Parish of St. George, Hanover Square, in the West End of London. In the 1841 census he is recorded as living at Golders Hill, Hendon, Middlesex, with his parents and siblings. His middle name Horsley came from his relative John Horsley Palmer, featured above.

At the time of the 1851 census, Robert is a 16-year-old Gentleman Cadet in the Royal Artillery, based at Woolwich Arsenal Cadet Barracks, and within three years has become a Lieutenant, deployed in the Crimean War. Sadly, he was killed on 20th September 1854 at the Battle of Alma. His death at such a young age, just 19, must have been a bitter blow to his parents, siblings, and many close relatives. He was just one of several family members involved in 19th century global conflicts.

Henrietta Selina Cockerell (1836-1882)

Henrietta was Charles and Anna's fourth child, born at the family's address in Eaton Square. On 7th August 1860, at St. James Westminster, at another service conducted by Henry Cockerell, she married Ralph Augustus Benson Esquire, a barrister. The name Beaumont was mentioned under Frederick Pepys Cockerell above, and one of Henrietta's sons was given Beaumont as a middle name.

Intriguingly, in the 1871 census, Henrietta is described as the head of the household at an address in Hastings, with no mention of her husband. She is 34, entered as married, and described in the census as 'Wife of Metropolitan Magistrate'. Living with Henrietta in Hastings are their four young children, three boys and one girl. Two of the children, aged 6 and 4 were born in Dover and two, aged 7 and 5, born in St. George's Hanover Square in London, so alternate births in the two locations, and all four children described as scholars.

Rather than implying anything wrong with Ralph and Henrietta's marriage, living largely apart in London and Hastings appears to fit with their priorities, Ralph having to work in the capital as a barrister and magistrate, and Henrietta living with the children at school on the south coast. At this time there were several large schools in coastal towns, probably both for economic and health reasons. London was far from a healthy environment, especially for children. Henrietta, residing in Hastings, and looking after the children, is helped by two live-in servants.

Ralph and Henrietta lived latterly at Lutwyche Hall, Much Wenlock, Shropshire, as evidenced by the 1881 census, further evidencing a secure marriage, and three of the children are living with them, as well as seven servants. The gardener and family live in a separate dwelling on site. Henrietta died there on 23rd August 1882 aged only 46. As noted in the Historic England image and description below, Henrietta's brother Frederick Pepys Cockerell was involved in Lutwyche Hall's remodelling.

Lutwyche Hall: the entrance front as remodelled
in the mid-19th century by F.P. Cockerell.
Image: Historic England

William Acland Cockerell (1840-1919)

William was born on 27th November 1840 and baptised on 2nd April 1841 at Hendon. In the 1851 census he is 10 years old and a 'scholar at home', living at 63 Golders Hill in Hendon, with his parents Charles and Anna and his four siblings. Educated at Westminster School he was appointed a Junior Clerk in the Foreign Office in 1860 and was attached temporarily to the Embassy at Berlin. Promoted to Assistant Clerk in 1877, he was in attendance on the Siamese Special Embassy to London in 1880 and attended on His Imperial Majesty the German Emperor during his visit to England in August 1889, eventually being promoted to Senior Clerk in 1896. This tallies with the 1861 census with the 20-year-old William still living with the family, now at 13 Chester Terrace in St. Pancras, and his occupation given as Foreign Office Clerk. He is still given this generic description, now aged 50, in the 1891 census. He has by this time married Sidney Ada Davies on 5th June 1877, and is living with her, aged 38, and their three children, at 20 Glos'ter Place, in the parish of St. Marylebone. They have 6 servants.

In common with many others in the wider Pepys-Cockerell family, they named their son Samuel Pepys, keeping their famous 17th century relative very much in focus. Further emphasising this focus, one of their daughters has been given the names Paulina Pepys, deliberately resurrecting the link with Samuel Pepys's sister Paulina Pepys from whom the whole blood line directly descends.

In 1901 William is described as Chief of a department in the Foreign Office, and in the 1911 census he is described as Senior Clerk Foreign Office Retired. This document also notes that his wife Sidney Ada was born on the Island of Madeira, a Portuguese territory. In the first such record we have among the family, William appears in an early London phone directory of 1906, assigned 'Western' exchange number 2475.

Very sadly the Great War was to claim their son, Samuel Pepys Cockerell (1880-1915). Educated at Eton and Cambridge he had been, like his father, initially a Junior Clerk in the Foreign Office, but then a Lieutenant in the Royal Flying Corps in

Samuel Pepys Cockerell (1880-1915) Son of William Acland Cockerell and Sidney Ada Cockerell

the First World War. He died aged 34 on 20th March 1915 in the Middle East and is buried in the Ismailia War Memorial Cemetery.

As for so many parents losing sons in the Great War, William and Sidney would have been devastated by Samuel's death. William himself died on 12 April 1919. In the Probate record his address is given as 24 Old Court Mansions, High Street Kensington, and his effects valued at the relatively modest amount of £5,809. Probate was granted to Patience Scott Cockerell and Paulina Pepys Cockerell spinsters *[William's daughters, Samuel's sisters]* and Frederick Crawfurd Goodenough esquire *[a cousin]*. Neither Paulina nor Patience ever married, Paulina dying in hospital in Plymouth in 1955, and Patience in a nursing home in Minehead in 1957.

Henry E Cockerell (c. 1842-1860)

Establishing any firm details of Henry's life presents a significant challenge. One secondary source gives the middle name of Wellesley, but this is questionable and not confirmed by any official records. The 1851 census, showing Charles, Anna and their children, has an entry for a Henry Cockerell, aged 9, but the middle initial on that census looks clearly to be an 'E' rather than a 'W'. However, if the name Wellesley is correct, it perhaps reflects the Cockerells' Indian links three or four decades earlier with the Duke of Wellington and his brother, both of whose surnames were Wellesley. Henry does not appear with the family in the 1861 census, but he would then have been 19 and, if alive, presumably pursuing whatever career he had chosen. In any event, secondary sources claim that Henry died on 8th August 1860 in Bangalore, Madras, India which, if correct and if he had spent much of his short adult life in India, may explain the lack of official British records.

Samuel Pepys Cockerell (1844-1921)

The last of Charles and Anna's seven children, he was yet another distant nephew of 17th century Samuel Pepys who was given the name Samuel Pepys Cockerell, underpinning repeated resurrection of 'Samuel Pepys' through multiple generations. He was the uncle of the Samuel Pepys Cockerell who died in the Great War, as noted above. Born in Hampstead on 19th December 1844, he lived through till after the war, dying on 12th March 1921. A scholar at home at Golders Hill, Hendon in the 1851 census, ten years later in the 1861 census he is a Queen's Scholar, aged 16, at Westminster School. Samuel went on to gain an MA from Merton College, Oxford, and pursued a career as an artist and sculptor.

On the 13th August 1878, Samuel married another member of the Craufurd, or Crawford, family which features prominently in the overall narrative. His fiancé, from the Parish of Lyndhurst in the New Forest, Hampshire, was Anne Frances Craufurd, the daughter of Henry William Craufurd Captain R.N.. Henry had died in 1859 not long after Anne's birth, and there is no record of any other children.

The Craufurds and Goodenoughs were close Cockerell relatives, Samuel having a Goodenough uncle and a Craufurd aunt, evidencing more entangled family connections, frequently the case when tracing the wider Pepys Cockerell family tree. We are fortunate in having some very early photographs from the 1860s of Samuel's future wife 'Annie', one of which shows her with 'Harry', of similar age or perhaps slightly older, and possibly a brother or cousin.

Samuel and Anne's marriage was conducted by one of the Cockerell family, but the initials are indistinct. The witnesses include Lucy Goodenough and William Acland Cockerell as well as the bride's Craufurd relatives. In 1879, the year after their marriage, Samuel and Anne had a daughter, Frederica Lucy Cockerell, and her baptism is recorded on June 18th that year.

Devastatingly, on September 11th 1880, the year after giving birth to Frederica, Anne died. An ornate sculptural memorial was commissioned and created in their local church, as shown below. Given her husband Samuel's profession as artist and sculptor, he may well have been the designer and/or creator.

In 1881, the census shows Samuel as head of the household, aged 36, and a widower. Living with him at 13 Argyll Road, Kensington are his unmarried aunt Lucy Goodenough, aged 55, who had witnessed his marriage less than 3 years earlier, and his one-year-old daughter Frederica Lucy Cockerell, born in Marylebone. Presumably, Frederica's middle name Lucy had been deliberately chosen by Samuel in honour of his aunt. They have 5 female servants. Samuel is described as 'Artist painter sculptor', and his aunt Lucy is living on 'income from dividends'.

Twenty years later in 1901 Samuel, Lucy, and Frederica, now 21, are still living together, but have moved to 35 Phillimore Gardens, Kensington. Samuel is described as 'artist sculptor', and Lucy is described as 'living on own means'. Frederica is still single. They continue to have 5 female servants, and there is also a 53-year-old visitor, Minnie Foxen staying with them at the time of this 1901 census. Born in Penzance, Cornwall she, like Lucy, and of similar age, is living on her own means.

When Samuel Pepys Cockerell died, in 1921, he was still at 35 Phillimore Gardens and probate is granted to Arthur Goodenough Craufurd, Captain R.N., with Samuel's effects having a probate value of £19,920.

Frederica Lucy Cockerell married Richard Huddart, an architect, in 1908 and her probate record of early 1957, after her death, gives some details of her husband and where they lived :-

HUDDART *Frederica Lucy of The Copse Pennington Lymington* **Hampshire** *(wife of Richard Melvil Fane Huddart) died 15 December 1956 Probate* **London** *12 February to the said Richard Melvil Fane Huddart retired architect and Edward William Huddart solicitor. Effects £18720 1s. 10d.*

Children of Richard Howe Cockerell and Theresa Newcomen

Anna Theresa Cockerell (1836-1912)

Yet another family member born in India, she entered the world in Calcutta on 20th September 1836 into a moderately wealthy family environment. Anna would later, through a sequence of deaths and marriages in a short period of time, achieve noble social status. Her father Richard Howe Cockerell died aged 41 in 1839, and her mother Theresa, having remarried an Earl, thereby becoming Countess of Eglinton and Winton, also died young in 1853.

Theresa had come from a high-status family, her father being Sir Thomas William Gleadowe-Newcomen, 2nd Baronet of Carrickglass, 2nd Viscount Newcomen, and her mother was Harriet Holland, Sir Thomas's mistress. When Theresa died it was at Eglington Castle in Scotland. Sadly, Sir Thomas, Anna's grandfather, committed suicide in 1825, well before Anna was born. Such unfortunate family history was typically quietly hidden, and Anna may never have known about her grandfather's suicide.

As shown by the marriage certificate below, dated 15th February 1855, two years after her mother's death, Anna Theresa Cockerell made a socially, and financially, very advantageous marriage to Charles John Chetwynd-Talbot (1830-1877).

Richard Howe Cockerell's wife Theresa, Anna Cockerell's mother Image of Theresa as Countess of Eglinton and Winton, after her second marriage

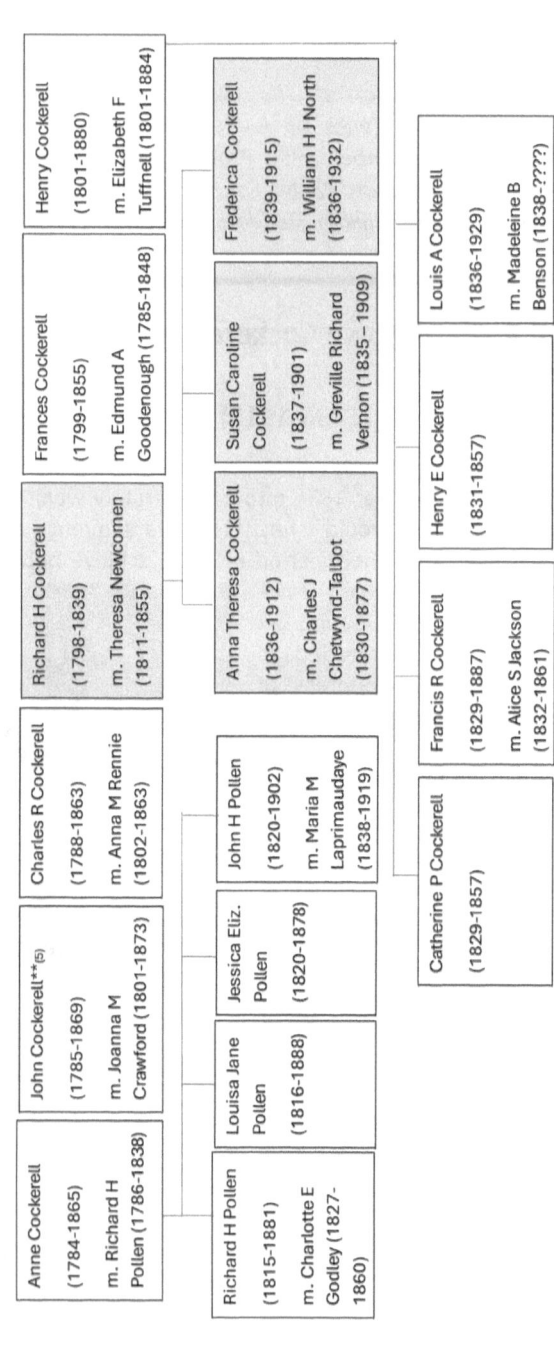

Children of Richard Howe Cockerell & Theresa Newcomen

Anne Cockerell (1784-1865) m. Richard H Pollen (1786-1838)

John Cockerell**(5) (1785-1869) m. Joanna M Crawford (1801-1873)

Charles R Cockerell (1788-1863) m. Anna M Rennie (1802-1863)

Richard H Cockerell (1798-1839) m. Theresa Newcomen (1811-1855)

Frances Cockerell (1799-1855) m. Edmund A Goodenough (1785-1848)

Henry Cockerell (1801-1880) m. Elizabeth F Tuffnell (1801-1884)

Richard H Pollen (1815-1881) m. Charlotte E Godley (1827-1860)

Louisa Jane Pollen (1816-1888)

Jessica Eliz. Pollen (1820-1878)

John H Pollen (1820-1902) m. Maria M Laprimaudaye (1838-1919)

Catherine P Cockerell (1829-1857)

Francis R Cockerell (1829-1887) m. Alice S Jackson (1832-1861)

Henry E Cockerell (1831-1857)

Louis A Cockerell (1836-1929) m. Madeleine B Benson (1838-????)

Anna Theresa Cockerell (1836-1912) m. Charles J Chetwynd-Talbot (1830-1877)

Susan Caroline Cockerell (1837-1901) m. Greville Richard Vernon (1835 – 1909)

Frederica Cockerell (1839-1915) m. William H J North (1836-1932)

** Denotes *Samuel Pepys's successive heirs*

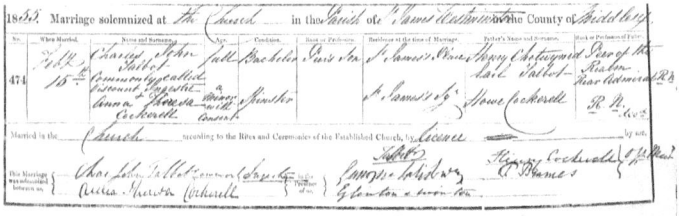

The details on the certificate show that the ceremony was yet another one conducted by Henry Cockerell. The marriage strengthened Anna's naval connections, adding to those of her father Richard Howe Cockerell, a naval captain and commander. The marriage certificate records that her father-in-law Henry John Chetwynd-Talbot (1803-68), 3rd Earl Talbot and 18th Earl of Shrewsbury, was not only a Peer of the Realm but also a Rear Admiral in the Royal Navy. He had entered the Royal Navy in 1817 and was promoted to Captain for his actions at the Battle of Navarino in 1827, where he commanded the H. M. S. Philomel. He was promoted to Rear-Admiral in 1854, and to both Vice-Admiral and then Admiral in 1865. When he died in 1868 his son Charles, Anna's husband, became Earl of Shrewsbury, Anna therefore becoming Countess of Shrewsbury. By that time Charles and Anna had produced three daughters and one son. Their main ancestral residence was Alton Towers in Staffordshire.

Charles Chetwynd Talbot, Earl of Shrewsbury, and Anna,
daughter of Richard and Theresa Cockerell

The timing of the 1871 census is particularly fortuitous for us in tracing the social strata in which Charles and Anna spent their lives, as it coincides very closely with the royal marriage of one of Queen Victoria's daughters, Louise, on 21st March 1871, and at which they were prominent guests.

Along with several other high-profile guests, Charles and Anna were still being housed at Belvoir Castle as part of the ongoing lavish celebrations when the 1871 census was taken 10 days after the royal wedding. The relevant census entries for Charles and

Anna Theresa describe them as Earl and Countess of Shrewsbury, with her place of birth cited as 'India Calcutta'. Links with India, given its major source of Britain's imperial wealth, were certainly no barrier to elevation in the British social hierarchy. Anna's husband Charles died in 1877 but, as Dowager Countess of Shrewsbury, she continued to move in elevated social circles and was a guest at the Coronation of Edward VII in 1902.

Princess Louise's wedding, 1871

Sitter: Anna Theresa, Countess of Shrewsbury (1836-1912)
Occasion: The Coronation of King Edward VII, 9 August 1902.
Location: The Lafayette Studio, 179, New Bond Street, London.
Biog: Eldest daughter of Captain Richard Howe Cockerell R.N. ;
m. (1855) 19th Earl of Shrewsbury.
Date: 11 August 1902.

Anna died a decade later in 1912 in the early part of George V's reign, two years before the outbreak of the Great War so, like her cousin Mary Theresa Cockerell, she was spared experiencing the deaths of some of her young relatives. Given her status, it is no surprise to see the scale of the fortune in her probate record :-

> ***Dowager Countess of SHREWSBURY*** *and **TALBOT** right honourable Anna Theresa of 37 Lowndes-square **Middlesex** widow died 29 July 1912 Probate **London** 20 November to the right honourable Charles Henry John earl of Shrewsbury and Talbot K.C.V.O. and Alfred Charles Duncombe esquire. Effects £99746*

Susan Caroline Cockerell (1837-1901)

Susan was Anna Theresa's younger sister, born on 5th December 1837 in Calcutta, West Bengal, a year after Anna. Like Anna, Susan

was well positioned through her family's status and connections to secure an advantageous marriage. On 13th April 1858 in Dublin, Ireland, she married the Honourable Greville Richard Vernon (1835-1909), a Liberal Unionist politician in Scotland. He was the Member of Parliament for South Ayrshire from 1886 to 1892, and was the youngest son of Robert Vernon, 1st Baron Lyveden. The couple had 6 sons and 3 daughters, born between 1859 and 1879. Two of the sons were born in London, but all the others in Scotland, mainly in Ayrshire.

Greville Richard Vernon, Susan Cockerell's husband

Aged 63, Susan is recorded in the English 1901 census living at 18 Chesham Place, Chelsea with her husband, a son, and a daughter, but all her entries in previous censuses were in Scotland and it was there that she died later in 1901.

Frederica Cockerell (1839-1915)

The youngest daughter of Richard Howe Cockerell and Theresa, Frederica was born in Calcutta, India. She emulated her older sisters by marrying into the nobility. In January 1858 she married William Henry James North, later the 11th Lord North. The North's ancestral home was Wroxton Abbey, near Banbury, Oxfordshire. In another family link, it was from an earlier Lord North that her great uncle Colonel John Cockerell had purchased the Sezincote estate in neighbouring Gloucestershire, in 1795.

As we have seen with many other family members, while having access to a large country house, a London residence was also the norm, and almost obligatory. In the 1861 census the family are at 16 Arlington Street, and in the 1871 census, Frederica North is listed at 39 Brompton Road, Kensington, with a large household including her son and four daughters, together with 9 servants. In 1881, they have moved several doors along Brompton Road to number 51.

Children of Edward Goodenough and Frances Cockerell

James Graham Goodenough (1830-1875)

James is another Cockerell relative choosing to follow a naval career. Again, it seems that Samuel Pepys's fame inspired several descendants in their career choice, being both a source of pride and a spur to emulate his achievements in naval affairs. James has the distinction of having Goodenough Island, Papua New Guinea, in the Solomon Sea, named in his honour when it was discovered in 1874 by one of his naval colleagues, Captain John Moresby.

Eventually rising to the rank of Commodore, James had a lengthy and eventful career in the Royal Navy, as evidenced by his substantive entry in the Dictionary of National Biography. Of particular interest are his involvement in the Crimean War, including bringing 1200 Russian prisoners back to Britain, and his reputation as a highly scientifically trained and astute gunnery officer,

James Graham Goodenough

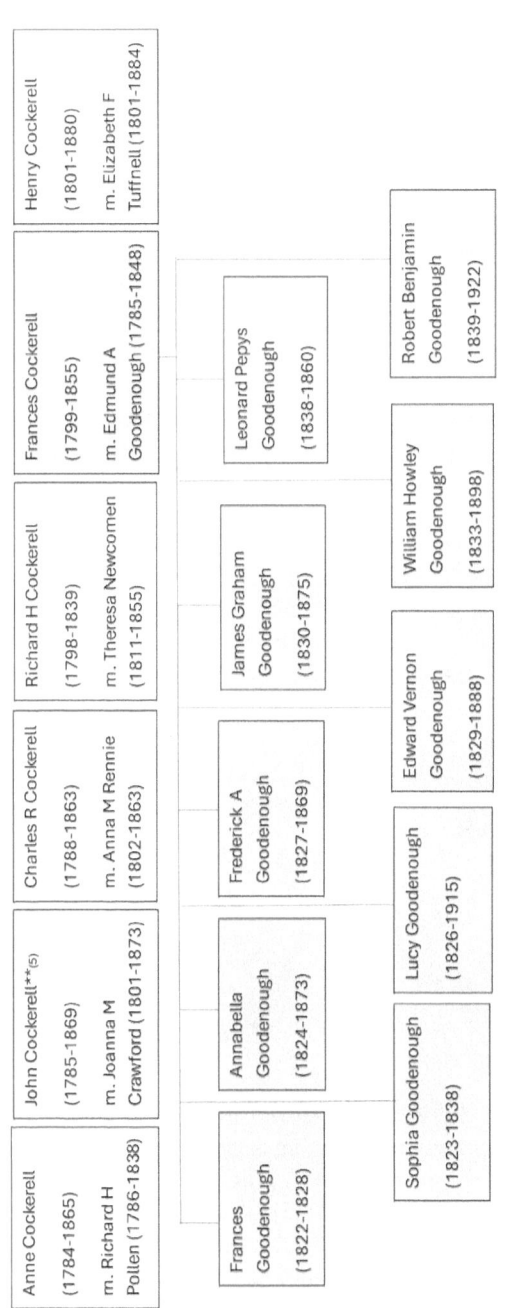

Anne Cockerell (1784-1865) m. Richard H Pollen (1786-1838)

John Cockerell(**(5)) (1785-1869) m. Joanna M Crawford (1801-1873)

Charles R Cockerell (1788-1863) m. Anna M Rennie (1802-1863)

Richard H Cockerell (1798-1839) m. Theresa Newcomen (1811-1855)

Frances Cockerell (1799-1855) m. Edmund A Goodenough (1785-1848)

Henry Cockerell (1801-1880) m. Elizabeth F Tuffnell (1801-1884)

Frances Goodenough (1822-1828)

Sophia Goodenough (1823-1838)

Annabella Goodenough (1824-1873)

Lucy Goodenough (1826-1915)

Frederick A Goodenough (1827-1869)

Edward Vernon Goodenough (1829-1888)

James Graham Goodenough (1830-1875)

William Howley Goodenough (1833-1898)

Leonard Pepys Goodenough (1838-1860)

Robert Benjamin Goodenough (1839-1922)

** Denotes Samuel Pepys's successive heirs

Children of Edmund Goodenough & Frances Cockerell

269

being sent to observe the latest advances in guns and their capabilities during the American Civil War in the 1860s.

This specialist gunnery aspect of his naval career links very neatly with the subsequent exploration of gunnery innovations and techniques carried out by his relative, and Pepys Cockerell descendant, Arthur Pollen, three decades later in the years immediately prior to the First World War. As already indicated, Arthur's interest had been first inspired by a chance encounter in Malta in 1900, with James Graham Goodenough's son, William Edmund Goodenough, later an Admiral. Attempts by these relatives to improve the Royal Navy's effectiveness chime strongly with the efforts of his 17th century relative Samuel Pepys in radically restructuring naval administration and fighting efficiency.

Mirroring a few individual family members in previous generations, James suffered a violent and highly unusual death. While on service in the Pacific in 1875, he took a party from his ship onto one of the Santa Cruz Islands, part of the wider Solomon Islands, and engaged in what seemed initially to be amicable dialogue with native islanders. However, for some reason the natives suddenly became aggressive and shot James in the side

Memorial Prize for Gunnery (Instituted in 1878)
featuring James Graham Goodenough
[NB The designer of the reverse side of the medal, on the right, is
James's relative Frederick Pepys Cockerell. Although too small to
see clearly on the image above, 'F P Cockerell D.' is inscribed just
below the crouching figure on the right.]

with an arrow, closely followed by a volley of arrows towards his men. Five more were hit and the whole party immediately fled back to their ship. Although their relatively modest physical injuries were clearly not sufficient in themselves to prove fatal, they were worried about the arrows possibly having been poisoned and promptly set sail for Sydney, Australia, to secure any necessary medical attention. Whether or not poisoned, three of the six injured, including James, contracted tetanus and sadly died on the voyage. The above images of the Memorial Prize for Gunnery record his date of death, 1875, and the location of the events leading to it, namely Santa Cruz.

William Howley Goodenough (1833-1898)

Sir William Howley Goodenough
Dressed in his Lt.-General Uniform

Lt. Gen. Sir William Howley Goodenough, to give him his full eventual title, was born on 5th April 1833 in Wells, Somerset, with his two forenames having historic family significance. His mother's cousin Mary Frances Belli (nee Cockerell) was married to William Howley, the Archbishop of Canterbury at the time of Queen Victoria's accession to the throne. Christening him William Howley is another example of honouring and leveraging the names of a famous family member, just as the forenames Samuel and Pepys were used over four generations of the family, viz. Samuel Pepys Cockerell (1754-1827), Samuel Pepys Cockerell (1794-1869), Samuel Pepys Cockerell (1844-1921), and Samuel

Pepys Cockerell (1880-1915). These were clearly deliberate acts of memorialising historic figures of whom the family were understandably particularly proud.

In 1873 William married the 21-year-old Countess Anna Kinsky Von Wchinitz und Tettau, in Vienna. She had been born in Austria on 23rd August 1852. They had three daughters, in 1878, 1880, and 1890. Anna survived her husband William for over 40 years, dying during the Second World War in London on 11th November 1941.

Lady Anna Goodenough (nee Countess Kinsky)
with her two of her daughters, the Misses Goodenoughs

William had a long and distinguished military career, including service in India (1857-8) at the time of the Indian Mutiny, being involved in the siege and capture of Lucknow as well as in the attack and capture of Fort Birwah. He was severely wounded and mentioned in despatches. In 1882 he was in command of the Royal Artillery at the Battle of Tel el-Kebir, again being mentioned in despatches. This battle was the decisive engagement of the Anglo-Egyptian War, with the British victorious. The rear book cover has an image of the battle.

The timing of William's death, occurring at the peak of his military career as commanding officer of the British Army in Southern Africa, was significant, although the circumstances are not clear. The second Boer War started in 1899, a year after William's death. He had devised the plans and strategies for coping with any resurgent Boer uprisings, highlighting the extreme challenges of securing a large area with limited military numbers. His untimely death left his successor facing a dangerous and precarious situation, crystallised very shortly afterwards when the vulnerable nature of Britain's military position was exposed. It was only by deploying massively disproportionate numbers of British troops over a lengthy period that the much smaller Boer forces were eventually overcome, the British suffering substantial deaths and casualties in the process.

Children of Henry Cockerell and Elizabeth Tuffnell

Catherine Paulina Cockerell (1828-1857)

Henry and Elizabeth's first child was christened Catherine Paulina, but usually referred to as Paulina, resonating with Samuel Pepys's sister Paulina Pepys, from whom they were all directly descended. No official birth records have been found, but she was born sometime between April 1828 and April 1829, as her age is given as 22 in the 1851 census, which gives her place of birth as Massing, Essex. Given that her brother Francis (see below) was born on 23rd August 1829, we can reasonably deduce that she was born in 1828.

In 1851, aged 22, she is living with her maternal grandfather John Jolliffe Tufnell, widower, at Great Waltham, Essex. She is described as an annuitant, i.e. has a regular unearned income, but the reason for her living there rather than with her own parents at North Weald is unclear.

The records of her death, on Tuesday 25th November 1857, note that she was unmarried and was buried at Fulmer, Buckinghamshire, on 1st December that year. Why her burial was there rather than in Essex, the county of her birth and where she spent most of her life, are unknown. The low value of her estate when probate administration was granted in 1859 may indicate that she never accumulated any significant assets during her

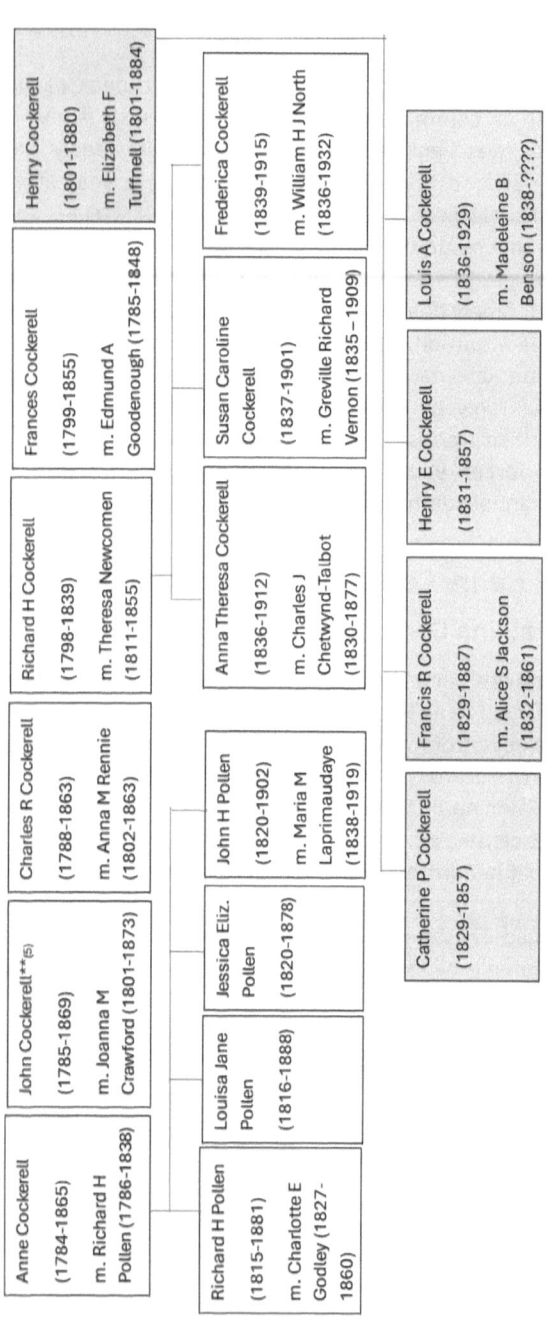

Anne Cockerell
(1784-1865)
m. Richard H
Pollen (1786-1838)

John Cockerell**(5)
(1785-1869)
m. Joanna M
Crawford (1801-1873)

Charles R Cockerell
(1788-1863)
m. Anna M Rennie
(1802-1863)

Richard H Cockerell
(1798-1839)
m. Theresa Newcomen
(1811-1855)

Frances Cockerell
(1799-1855)
m. Edmund A
Goodenough (1785-1848)

Henry Cockerell
(1801-1880)
m. Elizabeth F
Tuffnell (1801-1884)

Richard H Pollen
(1815-1881)
m. Charlotte E
Godley (1827-1860)

Louisa Jane
Pollen
(1816-1888)

Jessica Eliz.
Pollen
(1820-1878)

John H Pollen
(1820-1902)
m. Maria M
Laprimaudaye
(1838-1919)

Anna Theresa Cockerell
(1836-1912)
m. Charles J
Chetwynd-Talbot
(1830-1877)

Susan Caroline
Cockerell
(1837-1901)
m. Greville Richard
Vernon (1835 – 1909)

Frederica Cockerell
(1839-1915)
m. William H J North
(1836-1932)

Catherine P Cockerell
(1829-1857)

Francis R Cockerell
(1829-1887)
m. Alice S Jackson
(1832-1861)

Henry E Cockerell
(1831-1857)

Louis A Cockerell
(1836-1929)
m. Madeleine B
Benson (1838-????)

** Denotes Samuel Pepys's successive heirs

Children of Henry Cockerell and Elizabeth Tufnell

274

short life. It appears that she had been granted an annuity early in her life, perhaps created and held in trust.

The limited evidence, taken together, may indicate some physical or mental condition or disability, with her parents putting in place financial security to enable relatives to look after her, supported by a steady annuity income covering associated expenses. If correct, her place of death may well have been a specialist care institution. Her early death aged just 28 would fit with this speculation. In official records of Administration for 1859, this was granted to her father Reverend Henry Cockerell.

> **COCKERELL Catherine Paulina.** *18 June. Letters of Administration of the Personal estate and effects of Catherine Paulina Cockerell late of Iver in the County of* **Buckingham** *Spinster deceased who died 26 November 1856 at Iver aforesaid were granted at the* **Principal Registry** *to the Reverend Henry Cockerell of North Weald Bassett in the County of Essex Clerk the Father of the said Deceased he having been first sworn.* **Effects under £100.**

Francis Richard Cockerell (1829-1887)

Born at North Weald Bassett, Essex, on 23rd August 1829, and baptised there on 12th October, the next record of Francis is at school in Brentwood in the 1841 census with his younger brother Henry. Like several of the male Cockerell family members, he went to India, joining the Bengal Civil Service in 1850, and was appointed Commissioner of Revenue and Circuit, Rajshahye and Cooch Divisions.

Reiterating some of the information set out earlier in a slightly different context, he married Alice Shakespeare Jackson on 24th June 1853 in Calcutta, West Bengal, Alice having been born at Patna in Bengal in 1831. Francis and Alice had one child, Margaret Madeline Cockerell, born on 4th September 1857 in Calcutta. She and her mother Alice next appear back in England in the 1861 census for Upton with Chalvey, Buckinghamshire, living with Welby and Elizabeth Jackson, Alice's parents. Alice is aged 29, and her daughter Margaret Madeline is listed as Madeline Cockerell aged 3. It is not clear why or when Alice and her daughter returned to

England, but it was not unusual for wives and children to return to England, often because of the challenging climatic and other conditions in India, with children more likely to thrive in England.

Judging by the next recorded event it is possible that Alice's health may have been a further stimulus, because only two

Margaret Madeline Cockerell, 1860s

months after the 1861 census she died on 5th June that year, aged either 29 or 30. Her death was at Axbridge, Somerset, but it is not known why she was there. Certainly, the Cockerells had an ancestral home in Somerset and perhaps she was visiting relatives in the area. Her daughter Margaret was left effectively orphaned, with her mother dead and her father in India, and she next appears in the 1871 census, aged 13, and described as 'Civilian's daughter', presumably referring to her father's Bengal Civil Service status. She is living with her father's family in North Weald Bassett, Essex, and her relationship with the

head of the household is Granddaughter. Her grandfather Henry Cockerell is the Vicar of the Parish, and recorded as head of the household, aged 69. His wife Elizabeth is aged 70, and the other family member present is their unmarried son Louis Arthur Cockerell, aged 34, described as 'Clergyman'. As flagged up earlier, an unexpected census entry in the household is Rowland Vyner Cockerell, aged 36, unmarried, and described as a 'Visitor' at the time of this census. Rowland's occupation is given as East India Civil Service. Rowland's presence at North Weald Bassett at this time and his relationship with Margaret has already been considered twice, from different perspectives, and the questions raised previously remain unanswered.

Francis Cockerell appears to have remained in India after his wife and Margaret returned to England. Although his wife Alice died in 1861, leaving his supposed daughter without either parent present during her childhood, there is no record of him returning to England till Margaret is much older and, in the meantime in

1863, he remarried in India to Evelyn Thompson. There is no record of Francis and Evelyn returning to England while Margaret was in her formative years and approaching adulthood. Neither Francis nor Evelyn appears in the English 1871 census, and they were almost certainly still in India.

Francis and Evelyn do eventually return from India, although we have no record of exactly when, or even whether they returned at the same time. Evelyn died in Brighton on 21st March 1881, which would explain why she doesn't appear in the 1881 census taken ten days later. However, Francis was still alive in 1881, dying in Scotland in 1887, but doesn't appear in the 1881 census. Perhaps Evelyn returned from India before Francis, and one possible trigger for his return to Britain is her death in 1881. In any event, we are left with the probability that Francis never saw Margaret, his daughter according to official records, until at least the very last years of his life, if at all. This seems most unnatural and again raises questions about why it is his cousin Rowland, rather than Francis himself, who returns to England for a period around 1871 and stays with Margaret before returning to India and dying soon afterwards in highly unusual circumstances, as described previously.

Francis died at Glencairn House, Crieff, Perthshire, aged 58, on Monday 29th August 1887, and was buried in the Extra Mural Cemetery, Brighton, Sussex on 3rd September. His Will, dated 21st August 1885, with codicil dated 6th July 1887, was proved on 27th October 1887 by Alexander McLaurin Monteath of Weybridge, Surrey, the sole executor. The Will, which may have shed light on the parts of his life and relationships which remain unclear, has not been seen.

Whoever her biological father was, Margaret Madeline Cockerell later married Keith Ellis Tarling and lived a long life, the couple latterly living in a residential street in Oxford. After her death, probate was granted to her husband, described as a schoolmaster, and to Sir John Montresor Jackson, a baronet. The latter appears a little surprising given the modest social status of Margaret and her husband. While Jackson is a reasonably common surname, it does, of course, raise questions about possible connections with family ties between the Jacksons and Cockerells in the early 18th century, and with Samuel Pepys's nephew and immediate heir John Jackson.

Henry Edmund Cockerell (1831-1857)

Henry was born on 1st May 1831 in North Weald, Essex. In the 1841 census he appears, recorded as aged 10, as does his elder brother Francis (11), as a pupil at school in the 'Hamlet of Brentwood'.

Henry was appointed to the East India Company Civil Service in 1852 as evidenced in official records. When the Indian Mutiny broke out, Henry was drawn into the associated actions. Henry's gruesome death has already been described when trying to piece together the unusual family relationships reflected in mid-century census entries for his father's parish, North Weald, and the account is repeated here as a reminder:-

> *At the outbreak of the Mutiny, one night in mid-June 1857, Henry, who had chosen to remain at his isolated post in the Banda district longer than was wise, decided there was nothing more he could do to enforce the Company's authority over the surrounding country. He ordered his syce to saddle his horse and set out to seek the protection of the Nawab of Banda. But on reaching the Nawab's palace, he was treacherously pulled from his horse and hacked to pieces by the Nawab's retainers.*

He was only 26 years old. His death is recorded as being on 15th June 1857, but it is not clear where he was buried. Perhaps his body, even if it was retrievable, was so badly mutilated that a normal burial was not physically possible. There is no record of Henry marrying or having children during his tragically short life.

Louis Arthur Cockerell (1836-1929)

Born at North Weald, Essex, on 20th November 1836, Louis's first probable identified record is in the 1841 census at Great Waltham, the entry for a 5-year-old Louis/Lewis Cockerell being indistinct. In the 1851 census, aged 14, he is certainly a student at the all-male St. Peter's College, Radley, Abingdon, Oxfordshire.

Ten years later the 1861 census for North Weald records him back living with his parents Henry and Elizabeth, at the Vicarage, being described as Clergyman's son, unmarried, with his age given as 26 (perhaps incorrectly, as it would be expected to be 24 based on his date of birth). A further ten years later, with his age correctly given as 34, the 1871 census records him still living with his parents, unmarried, but now described as 'Clergyman'. The 1881 census again records him at the Vicarage, North Weald, but now Head of the household, still unmarried, and described as the Vicar of North Weald. His father Henry had died in 1880 and Louis has taken over as Vicar.

There are two other family members cited in this 1881 census. One is Elizabeth Fanny Cockerell, now widowed, aged 80, and described as Louis's stepmother. This is a little odd, as there is no record of Henry, Louis's father, having had a previous marriage to that with Elizabeth Fanny Tufnell. The other person listed is Margaret Adeline (Madeline?) Cockerell featured above, aged 23, described as Louis's niece, and unmarried, so there is an unusual diversity of ages and family relationships in this vicarage setting. The household is supported by one male and three female servants.

On 31st January 1882, Louis married Madeleine Barbara Benson at Easthope, Shropshire. Given the patterns of intermarriages between families, Madeleine may well be the sister of Ralph Benson who married Louis's cousin Henrietta Selina Cockerell as described earlier, but this has not been confirmed. The 1891 census has Louis, now 54, as Head of the household and Vicar of North Weald, living with his wife Madelenie (a slightly different spelling), aged 53. By the time of the 1901 census, they have moved to 106, Banbury Road, Oxford. Louis, now 64, is described as Clergyman (Ch. of England). Madeline (yet another spelling variant) is now 63 and her place of birth cited as Belgium (British Subject). The final record we have is the probate details after Louis's death, aged 92, evidencing a moderately wealthy financial legacy. The reason for the re-sworn uplift in value is not known.

> **COCKERELL** *the reverend Louis Arthur of 106 Banbury-road* **Oxford** *clerk died 4 March 1929 Probate* **Oxford** *11 June to William Griffith Richards wine merchant and Barclays Bank Limited. Effects £14594 19s. 2d. Resworn £20124 19s. 9d.*

CHAPTER NINE

Beyond the Sixth Generation

The Sixth Generation had spanned a lengthy historic period, broadly the whole of the Victorian age and into the 20th century. In commenting on later generations two things are forced on the structure of the text. Firstly, setting out even brief historic contexts which keep in step with each of these later generations is virtually impossible, and secondly, the sheer numbers of offspring make an even more highly selective approach inevitable. This last section therefore adopts a far less comprehensive approach, focusing on just a few individuals.

John Pepys Cockerell (1866/7-1930)

John was the son of John Cockerell (1831-1877) and Frances Torrens. As another direct Samuel Pepys heir he is a key figure, facilitating a two-volume publication in 1926 of a large quantity of the 17th century diarist Samuel Pepys's private correspondence, not previously publicly accessible. A further similar follow-up publication of 1929 provided additional letters. This historically important private correspondence, part of the so-called Pepys Cockerell Collection, had passed down the Cockerell family line from the time that John Cockerell had married Frances Jackson in the mid-18th century. The accessibility of this contemporary correspondence has enabled comparisons with entries in Pepys's Diary, sometimes corroborating the factual accuracy of the Diary, sometimes challenging its details, but more often simply enriching the value, relevance, depth, and breadth of historical understanding that the Diary provides.

John is a particularly significant figure for this book's narrative. Putting all the evidence together it is during his tenure of responsibilities as one of Samuel Pepys's heirs that much of the physical inheritances pass out of the Pepys Cockerell family's tight control. Most notably, Samuel Pepys's private correspondence, a key element of the so-called Pepys Cockerell Collection, was made public, with John co-operating in the publication of three volumes of letter covering the periods 1679-1700 & 1700-1703 (published in 1926) and 1662-1679 (published in 1929). Various paintings and prints also entered the public domain around this time, noted as being "in the possession of J. Pepys Cockerell Esq.".

In the 1901 census John Pepys Cockerell and his family are living in London, and he is described as the Land Agent to the Duke of Devonshire, whose main property was the magnificent Chatsworth House. This tallies with John and his family later living at Chatsworth Edensor, Derbyshire, recorded in the 1911 census, and still described as a Land Agent, a prestigious position. There were six servants listed in the household. John had two sons, both of whom sadly died young and whose life stories are briefly sketched below.

Andrew Pepys Cockerell (1897-1916)

John's eldest son Andrew Pepys Cockerell (1897-1916) was tragically killed in the Battle of the Somme on 15th August 1916 at Mametz, in Picardie. The brief entry in the Kings Royal Rifle Corp army records, giving the date of his demise, is shown below, together with the black-edged correspondence sent to his father, then in Sussex.

Much later, there was a formal burial at the Dantzig Alley British Cemetery, Mametz, Departement de la Somme, Picardie, France.

John Arthur Pepys Cockerell (1902-1936)

The younger of the two brothers, John was only 14 when his elder brother Andrew was killed at the Somme. Although it was just one of hundreds of thousands of war deaths, news of which was suffered by families across Britain, Germany, and many other countries, it was no less a devastating personal blow for John and his parents.

We have only a few details of John's life, but there is a shipping record of 15th August 1929 evidencing him and his parents leaving

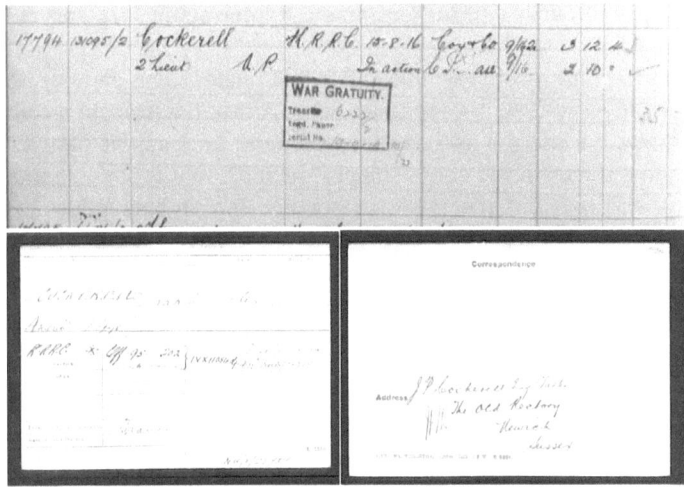

Southampton bound for Genoa, with the ship ultimately going on to Java, Indonesia. A month later another shipping record from September 17th 1929 shows him and his parents arriving back in Southampton on a ship travelling from Batavia, Indonesia. Not surprisingly they are travelling First Class. It may simply be coincidence, but Batavia has strong connections with the

Cockerell family's historic commercial interests in Java and the Far East.

The only record identified after that relates to his early death on 30th May 1936 in Cape Town, South Africa. The probate record shows his address as 12 Lennox Gardens, Chelsea, his parents' home shown in the above shipping records, so it is possible that he was only in Cape Town temporarily. The probate value was over £43,000, no doubt mostly inherited when his father died in 1930. His mother Florence lived on until 1941, having endured the deaths of her husband and their two sons.

One result of all these early male deaths, and the end of this family branch, was the passing of what remained in the Pepys Cockerell Collection of Samuel Pepys memorabilia, including documents, to a different, but closely related, branch of the Cockerell family. The evidence would suggest that John Pepys Cockerell (1866/7-1930) was relinquishing responsibility from around 1925, when allowing publication of Pepys's private correspondence. With his elder son dead, and the younger known to have been in South Africa for part of his life and perhaps not expected to be permanently resident in England, it appears that the individual to whom John entrusted the remaining Pepys memorabilia was a cousin of the same generation, Frederick William Pepys Cockerell (1876-1932) next briefly covered.

Frederick William Pepys Cockerell (1876-1932)

Grandson of Charles Robert Cockerell (1788-1863), and son of Frederick Pepys Cockerell (1833-1878), the 1891 census lists him as a 14-year-old scholar at Winchester College. In the 1911 census he is described as single and a Barrister at Law, living in Mayfair & Knightsbridge with his widowed mother, his married Army Captain brother, Lawrence Pepys Cockerell, and Lawrence's wife Florence Octavia.

An electoral register of 1920 shows Frederick and his mother living at 20 Albert Hall Mansions, Kensington Gore. Shortly after this, he would marry in his mid-40s to Felicia Louisa Marie Stewart on Valentine's Day 1922. An electoral register entry for 1922 shows Frederick and Felicia Louise Marie Cockerell living at 36

Kensington Square. They had one son, John Lawrence Pepys Cockerell (1924-1985), who in due course would inherit what remained of the Pepys Cockerell Collection, and a daughter, Mary Georgina Felicia Pepys, born at 57 Princes Gate on 22nd February 1926.

After Frederick's death in 1932, the next record of interest is a shipping record, showing the widowed Felicia, aged 48, with her son John Lawrence, 14, and daughter Mary Georgina, 13, arriving on 28th April 1939 at Southampton on a ship which had sailed from Durban, South Africa. Their address is given as 8, Westbourne Park Road, London, so they had presumably simply been on a visit. The Cockerells had long had relatives in South Africa, and the ship had sailed from Durban, but the family's port of embarkation was given as Madeira so whether they had travelled as far as South Africa is not certain. Equally unclear is whether this (possibly curtailed) trip and their return had anything to do with the volatile international situation in 1939, with war breaking out just a few months later.

The special census taken at the outbreak of the Second World War in 1939 shows Frederick's widow Felicia residing at Holt Castle, Holt Heath, Worcestershire, presumably having deliberately relocated out of London, as so many did at this dangerous time. She was living on 'Independent Means' and was a 'Women's Voluntary Service rep. for Holt'. Her daughter Mary Georgina Cockerell is shown in the same record as 'at school', and there are ten servants listed. Both John and Mary, Felicia's children, survived the war. Records show that Mary died on 31st October 2012, and John's story is briefly given below as he is the penultimate crucial link in the narrative.

John Lawrence Pepys Cockerell (1924-1985)

Son of Frederick W P Cockerell and Felicia, and born on June 18th 1924, John was the latest in a long line of Pepys Cockerells to have ownership of the remaining elements of the so-called Pepys Cockerell Collection. Amongst these documents and artefacts, several paintings of Cockerell and Pepys Cockerell family ancestors came into his possession. These eventually passed into the ownership of his second wife after his death in 1985.

In 1943, during the Second World War he was in the King's Royal Rifle Corp, and after the war the 1950 electoral register shows him living at The Brook House, Aldermaston, Berkshire. In 1955 he married Patricia Hill, daughter of Lord and Lady Sandys, but they had no children in their extremely short married life, Patricia sadly dying in 1957. Shipping records show that he then travelled between England and Nigeria in 1958 and 1959.

In 1966, he remarried, to an American, Elizabeth Charteris Black (1925/8-2016), and her story, the final one covered, is very briefly given next. After John's death in November 1985, Elizabeth lived for another thirty years. The subsequent probate record shows John's assets as just over £55,000 and noted that he died in St George's Nursing Home, St George's Square, London.

Elizabeth Charteris Pepys Cockerell (1925/8 –2016)

Her date of birth has not been definitively established. According to one source, Elizabeth was born on 19th December 1925 in Franklin, Ohio, USA. Another source asserts 1928 as her year of birth, based on her age on a US Federal Census of 1940. Unless more evidence is found, her birth year must be considered uncertain.

What is more certain is the date of her death, 4th April 2016. Elizabeth was the last of this branch of the Pepys Cockerells and, with no obvious successors, much of what remained of the Pepys Cockerell Collection and other artefacts were sold off at auction in 2019 as individual lots and consequently dispersed rather randomly. Two of the auction lots have particular significance for our narrative.

One lot was a portrait of Colonel John Cockerell, who featured prominently in the early text above and had purchased the house and estate at Sezincote in the late 18th century. Another auction lot was the double portrait, already referenced in the text, of Anne, the wife of Samuel Pepys Cockerell (the architect of the Mughal style remodelling of Sezincote), and their daughter Anne. The story of this double portrait follows in the next, and penultimate, chapter.

CHAPTER TEN

The Pepys Cockerell Double Portrait
(1809-2025)

Mystery & Discovery

Sold at auction in the early 21st century this painting's origins had become obscured by the passage of time, with an uncertain attribution of artist, and the pattern of previous ownership also unclear. However, because of its quality and the labels on the back of the frame speculating on two famous contemporary artists, it justified further investigation. Research focused first on the 21st century evidence, before reverting to its early 19th century origins. Its chronology was then built from there back up to the present.

Elizabeth Pepys Cockerell, the last member of that branch of the family, died in 2016. She had no children or obvious close relatives for whom the Cockerell and Pepys Cockerell items she owned had any special meaning or significance. In 2019, many items from her estate were therefore auctioned, and one of the lots was the Cockerell double portrait. Other paintings in this auction included three generations of 18th century John Cockerells, the last of these being a portrait of Colonel John Cockerell (1752-1798) who purchased the Sezincote estate in Gloucestershire in 1795.

For many of these paintings the artists were supposedly identified by attached rear labels, all in the same handwriting. It is far from clear whose hand this was, but perhaps this was a family member with at least some knowledge of their history, even if based only on memories or reported verbal accounts. Focusing on the double portrait, there was an attribution to Sir Thomas Lawrence in the writing style matching the others. However, it was apparent that the painting had been reframed at least once, with indications that this had last been done by Reeves and Sons Ltd of Kensington in the mid-20th century. Another label on the rear of the frame, with a red border and stylistically also mid-20th century, claimed that the painting was 'by Hoppner'. Oddly, despite this conflict of attributions, the handwritings for each claim match. A further twist is that auction details claimed yet a third possible attribution, namely to Margaret Carpenter or an artist in her studio.

Various labels on the reverse of the frame

This presented a considerable challenge. With only amateur appreciation of stylistic clues and estimates of approximate costume dates there was limited prospect of identifying the artist with any certainty. Thomas Lawrence seemed the most likely of the three attributions, given that he was known to be the painter of a small number of other Cockerell family portraits held in major galleries in the UK and America. Samuel Pepys Cockerell (1754-1827), whose wife and daughter were the subjects of the painting, had also been one of the first to welcome the young prodigy Lawrence on his arrival in London. As described in earlier chapters, Samuel Pepys Cockerell and Thomas Lawrence also shared a close common friend, the actress Sarah Siddons. The painting's costumes indicated a date somewhere in the period 1800-1810, and Lawrence was very active at this time.

Trying searches of Lawrence's known works on the internet was always a long shot and, not surprisingly, proved fruitless. Given my own feeling that the painting was of considerable quality both in composition and execution, and that the three competing attributions were of leading artists, another long shot felt worthwhile. This involved contacting the producers of the

BBC programme 'Fake or Fortune', to see if this artistic mystery would be of interest, still at this point with a very uncertain Sir Thomas Lawrence link. Although there was sufficient interest for them to pursue it with further questions and clarifications, and indeed a further follow up a couple of months later, it was not ultimately chosen as one of the cases for broadcast. A different approach was needed.

Having previously used the National Portrait Gallery (NPG) online resources several times when researching material for previous books, an obvious next step seemed to be to make a formal approach for their assistance. This proved an eye-opener in terms of what is held in their archive. Expert assistance from NPG staff was much appreciated, and although requiring planning, advance booking, and open-ended time commitments, physical searches were permitted through a multitude of box files catalogued both by artist and by sitter. Because Lawrence was such a prolific portraitist it took two or three hours going through all his NPG images. Disappointingly, this drew a blank – no sign of the Cockerell double-portrait, or any connections. However, absence of evidence couldn't rule Lawrence out. Similar searches focusing on John Hoppner and Margaret Carpenter as potential artists similarly failed, but again they couldn't be ruled out.

Having focused on searches 'by artist', the next focus was searching 'by sitter', using Cockerell as the obvious target. After carefully searching through the several boxes of Cockerell portrait images, the very last image in the very last box fortunately delivered spectacularly, with a black and white copy image of the double portrait, together with crucial information about the artist and the painting's ownership in the early-to-mid-20th century. This image at the NPG was their copy of the original record held by the Courtauld Institute. The NPG stamp indicated that they took the copy of the Courtauld record in 1957, evidencing that the Courtauld record existed at least at that time and probably many years earlier. (See images below.)

The record was invaluable as it named the artist as Sir William Beechey. While this still needed to be cross-checked, and ideally independently corroborated, the record also helpfully evidenced that the portrait was, at the time of the record, part of the Pepys Cockerell Collection. In addition it recorded the precise size of the

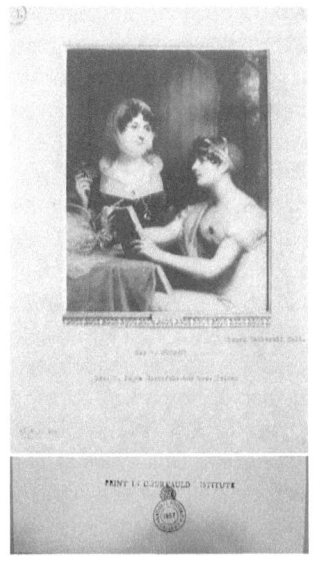

painting (41 x 33 inches), exactly matching the size of the painting under investigation. The frame in the recorded Courtauld image differs from that now being researched, and this tallies with the stamps and labels on the reverse of the painting evidencing a reframing, seemingly in the mid-20th century and presumably after the original Courtauld recording.

A visit to the Courtauld Institute involved negotiating a different archive system but, after assistance from their staff, the image was eventually located. It was hoped that this Courtauld original record would be accompanied by additional information. Unfortunately, although the staff were extremely helpful, this was not the case, and neither was there any information as to exactly when the image record was created. However, the key information had by now been established. As well as the frame being different when the Courtauld took their photographic record, the other change was the frame plaque.

The most likely scenario is that the Courtauld had obtained their photographic record prior to the Second World War and that, like many other valuable paintings in London, the double portrait, along with others in the Pepys Cockerell Collection, was removed from its frame and put into safe (i.e. bomb and fire-proof) and compact storage. If so, after the war when the painting was reframed, the name of the artist (which had been clear on the pre-war frame plaque – see image above) had possibly been forgotten or not recorded, hence the hypothesising about attribution. The sitters, however, would still have been known to the family, as owners of the painting, and are accurately represented both on the new frame plaque, and the handwritten rear frame labels. While the new frame plaque simply refers to the younger sitter as Anne's "daughter", the rear frame labels do explicitly and correctly also refer to her later married name of Mrs Pollen, just as the Courtauld frame plaque does. In fact, strictly speaking, the new frame plaque more accurately reflects the sitters' identities because at the time of the painting's execution the younger sitter was still single, only becoming 'Mrs Pollen' after marrying Richard Pollen several years later.

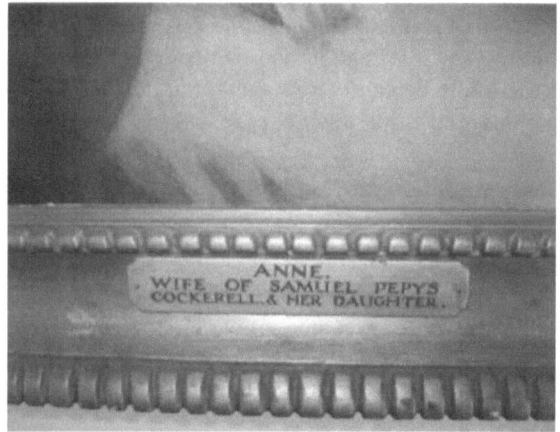

With the artist apparently positively identified from the NPG and Courtauld archives, the next step was to focus on information about Sir William Beechey to try to cross-check whether there was a record of the painting in any catalogue or review of his work. While there is no definitive catalogue of his work, a copy of Beechey's biography by W. Roberts, published in 1907, was obtained. In its Preface, Roberts acknowledges that his book doesn't represent a definitive catalogue of all Beechey's work, but it does come reasonably close. He notes that, '*My own preference would have been a Catalogue Raisonne of Beechey's work, and it is in this form that my material was first arranged; but it would not have fallen in with the general scheme of the series in which this volume appears. So my Catalogue Raisonne may be conveniently postponed and an exhaustive Index serve here in its stead*'. He is being modest, given the content of this biography. His Index lists all Beechey's known exhibited works, and the main text describes many of the most notable. I have found no record of Roberts' intended definitive catalogue ever being subsequently published.

Robert's book delivered much more information than could reasonably have been expected or hoped for. As well as confirming that Beechey was indeed the artist of the double portrait, it also outlines the painting's history, critical acclaim, and several other background details. Those guessing at attribution in the mid to late 20th century had presumably not considered Beechey as a possible artist or had simply not done any follow-up research.

One key piece of information extracted from the Roberts biography is that the painting was displayed at the Royal Academy in its 1809 Exhibition. These annual exhibitions featured works submitted by most of the leading contemporary artists, and typically the submissions were the artists' works completed in the previous 12 months. The double portrait received very positive critical comment, deemed to be one of Beechey's best paintings.

The painting is not only featured in the biography's Preface, but commands nearly a full page of description and commentary in the main text. An extract is given here :-

"This one of the most pleasing pictures which this artist has ever produced. There is a peculiar softness, a kind of feminine grace and elegance in the composition which, without any effort or seeming labour, fixes our attention and justifies our fullest admiration. The background, the opening perspective, the decorations of the work table, the employment of the

*two ladies, the agreeable complacency of the countenance,
their feminine industry – in a word, every part of the
composition, drawing, colour and general effect, does high
honour to the taste of Sir William Beechey … we venture to
assert that Sir William Beechey succeeds better in the female
figure than any painter of the day"* (The Messenger, May
1809). *Another paper describes this as the best of Beechey's
exhibits of the year. It should be pointed out that Mr Graves
describes this as a picture of Mrs. And Miss Cockerell.*

[Roberts, 1907, p112]

Very helpfully, the biography contributes significantly in terms of
tracing the provenance and filling in the painting's history and
location at the time of the biography. We are told that in 1907 it
was in the ownership of Miss Cockerell at 11, Mandeville Place in
the West End. This tallies perfectly with Mary Theresa Cockerell in
the Cockerell family tree and with the expected journey that the
painting would have taken in passing from generation to
generation, both before 1907 and its predicted subsequent route,
ending up with Elizabeth Pepys Cockerell in the early 21st century.

Having established Sir William Beechey as the artist, and only
then reviewing his most well-known portraits, it comes as no
surprise that in the National Portrait Gallery, as well as his
unfinished portrait of Admiral Nelson, these include the dramatic
life-size painting of Sarah Siddons, with her close connections to
the Cockerells.　Another Beechey portrait was that of Lord
Cornwallis, to whom Colonel John Cockerell had directly reported
as his Quarter Master General in India. Beechey had also painted
Samuel Pepys Cockerell (1754-1827), so perhaps he had always
been a prime candidate as artist of the Cockerell double portrait –
but only recognised with post-research hindsight.

A closer examination of the 1809 Exhibition at which
the painting was first shown provides more information and
context.

The 1809 Royal Academy Exhibition

The exhibition featured most of the major artists operating at the
time. Sir William Beechey was well represented, as were J M W

Turner, John Hoppner, James Northcote, Benjamin West, Philip J De Loutherbourg, John Constable, Martin A Shee, Paul Sandby, and Henry Bone. Some of these artists were approaching the end of their careers, while others were only recently emerging. The veteran Paul Sandby, for example, sadly died later that same year, while it would be several years before John Constable was to produce his most famous works, such as *The Hay Wain* (1821) and *Dedham Vale* (1828).

When looking at the contemporary commentary of the exhibits (or 'performances' as they were then termed) one of Turner's four exhibits was heavily criticised whereas at least two of Beechey's eight were highly praised, including the Cockerell double portrait.

LIST of the EXHIBITORS, 1809, with their Places of Abode.

☞ The Figures at the End of the Exhibitors' Names, refer to the corresponding Numbers in the Catalogue, specifying the respective Performances.

A

Acres, E. 30, Russell court, Covent garden—506, 718
Agbo, A. 8, Gerrard street, Soho—252, 482
Askin, H. 3, Bartlett's buildings, Holborn—844, 849
Alexander, D.—884
Allason, T. 10, Bentinck street, Manchester square—718
Aiken, W. Edinburgh—141
Allen, Miss M. 38, Half-moon street, Piccadilly—705
Allen J. 18, Ludgate hill—90, 92, 231, 274
Allingham, C. 31, Cecil street, Strand—169, 191
Ames, J. Bristol—531
Anderson, W. 48, Bell street, Paddington—111, 418
Andras, Miss C. Modeller in Wax to Her Majesty, 80, Pall-mall—667
Archer, J. S. 10, Wardour street, Oxford street—810
Argles, T. 18, Gower street—744
Arnald, G. 18, Buckingham place, Fitzroy square—39, 45, 59, 63, 73, 79, 145
Artaud, W. 4, Henrietta street, Covent garden—264, 548
Athow, T. 8, Arlington street, Camden town—70
Atkinson, J. A. 8, Conway street, Fitzroy square—258, 277

B

BEECHEY, Sir WILLIAM, R. A. Portrait Painter to Her Majesty, Harley street, Cavendish square—18, 61, 71, 82, 93, 116, 147, 387

BIGG, WILLIAM REDMORE, A. 13, Great Russell street, Bedford square—95, 120
BONE, HENRY, A. Enamel Painter to His R. H. the Prince of Wales, 15, Berners street—101, 301, 6, 8
Baker, J. Knightsbridge—131, 730, 747, 735
Bacon, J. 17, Newman street—772, 882
Bacon, W. 11, Great Earl street, Seven Dials—11
Bailey, J. Lambeth—741
Barenger, J. Kentish town—221, 830, 513
Barney, J. 16, College street, Westminster—268
Barrett, J. Park street, Westminster—292, 526
Barry, J. 16, Edgeware road—655
Barth, J. S. at Mr. Cribb's, 288, Holborn—337
Bartlet, W. 15, Wardour street, Oxford street—811
Bate, T. 36, Brownlow street, Long acre—35
Bate, C. Brownlow street, Long acre—110
Benwell, S. 6, Bath place, New road—873
Bestland, C. West End, Hampstead—488, 705
Biedermann, C. 31, Queen Anne street East, Portland chapel—157
Binstead, J. at Mr. Sintzenich's, Spring place, Kentish town—464
Bird, E. Bristol, or at Mr. Cromek's, 64, Newman street, London—124
Bond, J. L. 87, Newman street—746
Bononi, J. 51, Great Titchfield street—748
Bott, C. 6, Delancey place, Camden town—750
Bourne, J. 10, Princes street, Cavendish square—334, 556
Bowring, J. R. jun. Dove court, Pavement, Moorfields—835
Boyne, J. 43, Penton place, Pentonville—455
Brighty, G. M. 45, Red Lion street, Holborn—110
Brastow, E. Windsor, and at 40, Oxford street—228

295

This first page (above), listing exhibitors in 1809, records that Beechey had 8 paintings accepted. Of these, exhibit number 62 is the double portrait. Interestingly, it is this exhibit in the Royal Academy's own catalogue copy for which the entry has been correctly amended with the sitters' names being noted as Cockerel (itself a misspelling of Cockerell) rather than Wetherell.

The 1907 Beechey biography provides clarification on this amendment. On page vii, Roberts comments,

> *"The Earl of Altamont … has settled several points … notably in connection with the group exhibited at the Royal Academy in 1809, No. 62. Some of the papers of*

the period described this picture as representing Mrs. and Miss Wetherell, and others as of Mrs. and Miss Cockerell. Lord Altamont tells me that it represents Mrs S. P. Cockerell, and Miss Cockerell, afterwards Mrs. Hungerford Pollen. This picture, with the portrait of Samuel Pepys Cockerell … now belongs to Miss Cockerell of Mandeville Place".

The Mandeville Place location in 1907 tallies neatly with that expected from the sequence of Pepys's heirs tracked in our narrative (and as summarised shortly in Chapter 11).

Returning to the catalogue listing on that same page, there are some other entries with links to the Cockerells. Number 54 is a portrait of Sir G Beaumont by John Hoppner RA. This image appeared earlier, in Chapter 7, describing the family relationships between the Cockerells and Beaumonts. John Hoppner was also a speculative name on one of the labels on the reverse of the double portrait frame. Also fascinating, although maybe only a coincidence, is that Exhibit number 61, immediately before the double portrait (number 62) of Samuel Pepys Cockerell's wife and daughter, is a painting with an Indian subject by Thomas Daniell

RA. It was Thomas Daniell who collaborated with Samuel Pepys Cockerell on the Indian design of the Cockerell's Sezincote House in the same decade as this 1809 exhibition. One of Thomas Daniell's paintings of Sezincote features on the rear book cover. Even more notable is that the previous Exhibit, number 60, is a portrait of Sir W W Pepys, Bart. by H Thomson, RA, a further link with the wider Pepys and Pepys Cockerell family network. This is Sir William Weller Pepys, master in chancery, 1741-1825. It seems likely that, because of the Pepys and Cockerell connections, Exhibit numbers 60, 61, and 62 were deliberately hung next to each other.

Sir William Weller Pepys, Bart.
Mezzotint by Henry Meyer (from the portrait by Henry Thomson RA in the 1809 exhibition)

The Painting's Significance and its Journey from 1809 to 2019

While a continuous forensic trace of the double portrait's ownership and location is not possible, the evidence points strongly to the most likely scenario. Three crucial fixed points in its history are known, each approximately a century apart. Firstly, there is firm evidence about its origins in 1809. Secondly, evidence exists for its precise ownership and location in 1907, and thirdly, definitive ownership and location details in 2016 are well recorded.

The two individuals in the portrait each play a central role in the lively history of the wider Cockerell and Pepys Cockerell family. As already set out, Samuel Pepys Cockerell's wife Anne, the elder female in the painting, had 11 children, several of whom and their offspring contributed both to the perpetuation of Pepys's legacy and to the nation's cultural story. Her daughter Anne, the younger figure in the portrait, married Richard Pollen and had two sons who, together with their own subsequent offspring, made impacts at a national level in fields as diverse as the pre-Raphaelite arts and naval gunnery.

These two Annes, mother and daughter, also had close relatives who achieved high social status and significant responsibilities, as we have seen, including a Governor of the Bank of England, a Countess of Shrewsbury and an Archbishop of Canterbury.

From its completion in or shortly before 1809, the painting appears from the evidence to have passed through successive Pepys Cockerell family generations alongside numerous artefacts and documents originating from the 17th century diarist Samuel Pepys. As already outlined, these documents, largely comprised of Pepys's private correspondence (1662-1703), together with later Cockerell family heirlooms including the double portrait, became known as the Pepys Cockerell Collection. The Collection's journey through the family generations is now mapped out in the final chapter.

CHAPTER ELEVEN

The Pepys Cockerell Collection

The Pepys Cockerell Collection as it came to be known in the 19th and 20th centuries comprised items accumulated by the Pepys Cockerell family, dating as far back as the original private correspondence of 17th century Samuel Pepys.

The website extract below emphasises the importance of this private correspondence within the Pepys Cockerell Collection, passed down through the sequence of Pepys's heirs as outlined in the main text above. This extract evidences the crucial role the Pepys Cockerell family generations played in guarding these original letters and papers through to the 20th century.

The most important collection of [Samuel Pepys] *letters which, until recently, remained in private hands is the so-called Pepys Cockerell Collection. Five volumes of Pepys's letters not incorporated in the Pepys Library came into the possession of his nephew John Jackson and descended through his family until 1931. The collection was arranged and bound by Lord Braybrooke, first editor of the Diary, early in the 19th century. Four volumes were classified as 'Private Correspondence' for the period 1679-1703, and the fifth as official papers, although the distinction is often arbitrary. The four volumes of private correspondence, comprising nearly 600 letters, including 155 by Pepys (36 of them autograph), have appeared twice at auction: at Sotheby's, 1 April 1931 (John Pepys Cockerell sale), lot 18, and at Christie's, 11 June 1980 (Arthur A. Houghton, Jr sale, Part II), lot 363, to Davids. These four volumes have since been acquired by J. P. Getty, Jr. Most of the documents have been described and edited in Private Correspondence, ed. J. R. Tanner, 2 vols (London, 1926). Among the pages illustrated in the Christie sale catalogue is one (Plate 11) of a three-page autograph memorandum of 'Home-Notes for my selfe to attend, when able' (c.1700), in Volume IV, f. 151r, a memorandum edited in Tanner (1926), I, 165-70. The volumes also include Pepys's corrected list of 'Works of Publick Utility and Charity Least Subject to Corruption or Abuse in their Execution' c.1702 (Volume IV, f. 145r; edited in Tanner (1926), II, 294), as well as 'Notes touching ye Navall Strength of England employ'd in the Spanish Invasion 1588' (Volume IV, ff. 155r-6v; Tanner (1926), II, 244-7) and 'On the conditions of a Private Library' (Volume IV, f. 153r; Tanner (1926), II, 247-8). The fifth volume of the collection, comprising three gatherings of largely official letters for the periods 1662-5, 1665, and 1665-79, about 450 leaves containing texts of some 940 letters and documents in all, was separately offered in the Pepys Cockerell sale in 1931 as lot 19 and is now in the National Maritime Museum (LBK/8). Its contents have been largely edited in Further Correspondence, ed. Tanner (1929), and in Shorthand Letters, ed. Chappell (1933). Several pages of these divided collections are illustrated in the respective sale catalogues.*

https://celm.folger.edu/introductions/PepysSamuel.html

Alongside these important original letters, and other of Pepys's documents within the Collection, were artworks, principally portraits of various Pepys, Jackson, Cockerell, and Pepys Cockerell family members. Gradually, however, a large part of the Collection passed out of the family's possession, much of it sold when demand for anything connected with Samuel Pepys increased significantly in open-market monetary value. As noted in the extract above, John Paul Getty (junior) was a high-profile purchaser of a large number of the private letters. When the remaining elements still in the possession of Elizabeth Pepys Cockerell were sold at auction, the items almost exclusively originated from the 18th to 20th century generations of Samuel Pepys's heirs rather than directly from Samuel Pepys.

In tracking the Collection, a good starting point of reference is the evidence from the early part of the 20th century. It was certainly owned in the 1920s by John Pepys Cockerell, the latest in a line of Pepys descendants inheriting responsibility for its curation. We know this because in 1926 a substantial body of these documents was published by G Bell and Sons Ltd with the title '*Private Correspondence and Miscellaneous Papers of Samuel Pepys 1679-1703*' and '*edited by J. R. Tanner, Litt.D. Fellow of St John's College Cambridge*' is explicitly noted as being '*in the possession of J. Pepys Cockerell*'. This was followed up in 1929 with a supplementary publication covering the period 1662-1679. We also know from the biography of Sir William Beechey that a few years earlier in 1907 the double portrait, together with another Pepys portrait, had been in the possession of Mary Theresa Cockerell at 11 Mandeville Place, London.

The fate of the Collection during the rest of the 20th century can be traced with a degree of confidence from the knowledge that the double portrait (which the Courtauld Gallery's record explicitly evidences as being part of the Pepys Cockerell Collection in the middle of the 20th century) together with a large collection of family paintings and other memorabilia were in the possession of Elizabeth Pepys Cockerell at the time of her death in 2016. As already outlined, she inherited this collection from her husband John Lawrence Pepys Cockerell (1924-1985), who had inherited it from his father Frederick William Pepys Cockerell (1876-1932). The evidence suggests that the collection had been passed to Frederick from John Pepys Cockerell (1866-1930) because John had no male heir in England to whom he could entrust it.

Having traced the collection's more recent passage through the 20th century and into the 21st, the other obvious approach is to work through the successive heirs of Samuel Pepys himself, from his death in 1703, and follow this through to 1900, linking it with the known journey thereafter.

After Samuel Pepys's death in 1703, the heirlooms first passed to his chosen heir, his nephew John Jackson. Clearly there were many financial legacies, but we are concerned here simply with physical heirlooms. After the marriage of John Cockerell and Frances Jackson, these inherited items were joined by that part of the Jackson family memorabilia which Frances Jackson brought with her. Frances was not the senior member of the Jackson family and some of the Jackson heirlooms stayed with other Jackson family members. She did, however, retain Pepys's private correspondence, numerous family paintings, and the oral memory of much of Samuel Pepys's life and career. Her husband John Cockerell was the senior member of the Cockerell family and had retained most of the Cockerell family heirlooms. Their joint holdings were therefore a hybrid from several different closely related families. After their marriage, John and Frances, in pooling their respective inheritances, held a very rich and diverse collection of historic Pepys/Jackson/Cockerell memorabilia.

In the process of passing down the generations, parts of the inheritance were almost certainly dispersed among relatives other than the sequence of heirs. However, many core items had remained held by the Pepys sequential heirs until the mid-20th century, despite original memorabilia attracting increasing interest and financial value, with numerous items sold on the open market. Most of what Elizabeth held at her death in 2016 dated only from the early 18th century, with original 17th century Pepys material having been sold during the 20th century. The following sequence summarises the successive Pepys heirs responsible for the overall accumulation and care of family inheritances from Samuel Pepys's death in 1703 onwards. These heirs are indicated as such in the various family trees interspersed in the text.

Samuel Pepys (1633-1703)
Inheritance passed to his nephew John Jackson after his death.

John Jackson (Samuel's nephew) (1673-1723) and Anne Jackson (nee Edgeley) (1690-1756)
When John died in 1723, his wife Anne inherited. When she died in 1756, the Pepys/Jackson inheritance passed to her daughter Frances Jackson.

John Cockerell (1714-1767) and Frances Cockerell (nee Jackson) (1722-1769)
When Frances married John in 1740, the inheritance was joined by Cockerell family memorabilia, and after the deaths of John and Frances it all passed to their second son Samuel Pepys Cockerell

in London. Their other two sons were John and Charles, destined to be employed by the East India Company and based in Bengal.

Samuel Pepys Cockerell (1754-1827) and Anne Cockerell (nee Whetham) (1757-1843)

From Samuel and Anne, the collection passed to their eldest son John. However, it is not clear if it moved very strictly down the male line in terms of timing, i.e. went to John when Samuel died in 1827, or only later when Anne died in 1843, or sometime in between.

John Cockerell (1785-1869) and Joanna Cockerell (nee Crawford) (1801-1873)

On John's death the collection passed to their eldest son Andrew Pepys Cockerell. Andrew never married and nor is there any record of him having any children.

Andrew Pepys Cockerell (1830-1886)

When Andrew died in 1886, he had no children to inherit the collection, but he had two surviving siblings, Horace Abel Cockerell (1832-1908) and Mary Theresa Cockerell (1836-1914). Given that the collection had passed down from eldest male to eldest male with only one exception explained above, after Andrew's death it would logically have passed to his brother Horace Abel Cockerell.

Horace Abel Cockerell (1832-1908) and Julia Mary Cockerell (nee Drummond) (1843-1891)

From Horace it would, by tradition, on his death have been passed to his eldest son, but none of Horace and Julia's six children was male, and so the next most senior person in the succession was Andrew's sister Mary Theresa Cockerell (1836-1914). Not only was she the next logical heir, but she and Horace were at the same address. In 1881 the unmarried Horace was living at 11, Mandeville Place, and his sister Mary is later recorded as living at this address in the 1891 census, five years after Andrew's death, and was still there in 1907 with the collection also at that address.

Mary Theresa Cockerell (1836-1914)

This is the point at which the succession dovetails with, and is corroborated by, recorded evidence of the whereabouts of at least some (and probably all) of the collection in 1907. Not only is it known from the history of the Sir William Beechey double portrait that it was in Mary's possession at that time, but her address is also known. When she died in July 1914 her address was still given as 11, Mandeville Place.

John Pepys Cockerell (1866-1930)

The documents were certainly in the possession of John Pepys Cockerell (1866-1930) in the 1920s, and they had probably passed to him at, or shortly after, Mary's death in 1914. As already noted, he was subsequently instrumental in the publication in 1926 and 1929 of Samuel Pepys's private correspondence. The two volumes published in 1926 each contain the image of an object. In Volume 1 the object is a painting of Samuel Pepys by Sir Godfrey Kneller and for Volume 2 it is a medallion by Cavalier, 1688, featuring an image of Samuel Pepys. These items are both recorded as being '*in the possession of J Pepys Cockerell Esq*'. Taken together with John's ownership of Pepys's Private Correspondence itself, and given that some portraits are recorded as being in the Pepys Cockerell Collection in this early part of the 20th century, there clearly remained a substantial volume of artefacts passed down through the generations to at least this point.

However, after John Pepys Cockerell died in 1930, reliable sources report that at least some of the documents were then, over time, partially split up and sold. After John's death, with one son killed in the First World War and the other seemingly in South Africa, there were no obvious family members to take responsibility for what remained of the Collection. The evidence suggests that they passed to a Cockerell cousin, Frederick W Pepys Cockerell, from the same generation. Although several portraits remained within the family, and in this case held by Frederick, there is reliable recorded evidence that the documents had been split up, some perhaps distributed among other family members, but many simply publicly sold.

Frederick W Pepys Cockerell (1876-1932)

Frederick would only hold the remains of the Collection for a short period, as he died only two years after his cousin John. After Frederick's death, the remaining Collection passed in the normal way to his son John. By this time the Collection appears no longer to hold significant original Pepys letters or documents, and was then comprised mainly of physical artefacts, notably paintings and some items of furniture.

John Lawrence Pepys Cockerell (1924-1985)

John certainly owned many family portraits and other artefacts, but again there is no evidence of him holding many, or any, of the historic family documents. When he died, his second wife Elizabeth inherited.

Elizabeth Charteris Pepys Cockerell (1925/8-2016)

Elizabeth then held the remaining portraits and artefacts John had possessed at his death, but after her death these were auctioned as part of the settlement of her estate. There were no documents in the auction.

EPILOGUE

Having traced Samuel Pepys's heirs, and those relatives who were most closely associated with perpetuating his name and legacy, some summarising comments are appropriate, not least because the lengthy narrative above ended abruptly with the succession of heirs having finally run out. Although increasingly remote from Pepys with the passage of over 300 years since his death in 1703, the fact that this succession of his heirs ended so recently provided a motivation for this book. The publication in 2025 of this account of his heirs and their roles in safeguarding his legacy is also timely and appropriate as it coincides with the 200th anniversary of the first publication of his Diary, the source of his enduring fame.

The research and resulting narrative have highlighted notable family initiatives, achievements, adventures, and public profiles which have their own substantial merit alongside their Pepys connections. In providing a counterbalance to the many family achievements and successes, various mysteries, failures, embarrassments, and several violent deaths have been recorded, reflecting the reality of human challenges and frailties faced even by these privileged individuals. In attempting a modest addition to the Samuel Pepys story, it is hoped the book may also trigger further research on the Pepys, Cockerell, Jackson, and Pepys Cockerell family histories.

In summary, Samuel Pepys, the 17th century diarist and naval administrator, was extremely eager to secure his legacy and gave great thought to the practical measures for ensuring the preservation of its physical evidence. He focused on two main aspects – his Library, primarily, and then all the other material evidence of his life. His Library was the legacy he cherished most acutely. Accumulating it throughout his life, and continually improving its content, breadth, and categorisation, he was absolutely determined to ensure that it was protected, and its importance, quality, and significance acknowledged in the public domain. It was a source of enormous pride. Given his modest origins, I believe he saw it as the manifestation of his success in fulfilling aspirational social, financial, and cultural ambitions. In his early years, even with his considerable self-belief, these ambitions must have seemed frankly fanciful. Indeed, his recorded comments betray degrees of surprise as he gradually rose to prominence.

He probably realised that the legacy and reputation of his career successes – massively impressive, but not entirely unblemished – would be subject to the whims, political distortions, and revisions of those coming after him. The legacy record of his career was therefore something he was powerless to guard and control. In contrast, his Library was something he could attempt to preserve and protect in perpetuity on his own terms, and he went to great lengths to secure its long-term future. The Pepys Library remains to this day gloriously housed at the University of Cambridge. Even if there were no other Samuel Pepys legacy, this will forever survive, as much as anything can. Within the Library was Pepys's coded Diary. After eventually being deciphered, this personal journal has taken centre stage, even though it covers only a small period of his life. It has largely eclipsed the rest of any public awareness and perception of his life and legacy, probably not what he would have expected or wanted.

After some specific Pepys bequests to individuals had been arranged and dispersed, much other tangible evidence of his life, including letters, documents, and physical possessions were entrusted to his nephew, and adopted heir, John Jackson. The bulk of this subsequently passed down through generations of John Jackson's family. After the 18th century marriage of Frances Jackson to John Cockerell, much of what remained of his material, and particularly the documents, later became known as the Pepys Cockerell Collection and was referred to as such well into the 20th century.

Unlike his Library, which remained sacrosanct, the various Pepys documents and artefacts found a variety of homes and ownerships over time, some remaining distributed within the wider family but others attracting more public interest both as academic and souvenir material. In parallel with other national cultural figures such as Jane Austen, there is a dedicated Samuel

Pepys Society, a further dimension of his legacy therefore established and perpetuated. One consequence of all this is an ongoing demand for original Pepys material, which continues to change hands from time to time.

Given Samuel Pepys's high profile in the national psyche, it is easy to forget that at the time of his death he had no natural heir. Had he not been so determined to secure his legacy, and lavish time and money on grooming his nephew John Jackson to be his 'legacy guardian', much of the physical evidence, and particularly personal correspondence, could easily, and probably would, have been lost in the years immediately after his death. So, even in this act of self-interest, Pepys lived up to 'the unequalled self' epithet chosen by his biographer Claire Tomalin.

While John Jackson assiduously fulfilled his responsibilities as Pepys's direct heir, without similar commitments from the succession of heirs who followed, John's efforts could easily have been undermined, with the Pepys's legacy and memorabilia undervalued, and its care neglected. The fact that so much survived is testament to the family pride in the Samuel Pepys name and associations. For the next three centuries his successive heirs not only kept the Pepys reputation and legacies alive but enhanced their profile through their own achievements and their almost compulsive resurrection of his names by incorporating them into their own. This book records the bare bones of their impressive lives.

Selected Bibliography

Brendon, V., *Children of the Raj*, London, Phoenix, 2006

Cockerell, S.P. (Ed), *Travels in Southern Europe and the Levant, 1810-1817. The Journal of C. R. Cockerell, R.A.*, London, Longmans, Green, and Co., 1903

Coote, S., *Samuel Pepys – A Life*, London, Hodder & Stoughton, 2000

Frater, A., *Chasing the Monsoon*, London, Penguin, 1991

Gregory Smith, G., (Ed.), *The Diary of Samuel Pepys*, London, Macmillan, 1906

Hague, W., *William Pitt The Younger*, BCA, 2004

Musgrave, C., *Royal Pavilion*, *A Study in the Romantic*, Brighton, Bredon & Heginbothom, 1951

Pearce, S. & Ormrod, T., *Charles Robert Cockerell in the Mediterranean – Letters and Travels, 1810-1817*, Woodbridge, The Boydell Press, 2017

Pollen, A., *The Navy in Battle*, London, Chatto & Windus, 1919

Roberts, W., *Sir William Beechey, R.A.*, London, Duckworth, 1907

Sumida, J. T. (Ed.), *The Pollen Papers – The Privately Circulated Printed Works of Arthur Hungerford Pollen, 1901-1916*, London, George Allen & Unwin, 1984

Tanner, J. R. (Ed.), *Private Correspondence and Miscellaneous Papers of Samuel Pepys 1679-1703 in the Possession of J. Pepys Cockerell (Vols I & II)*, London, G. Bell and Sons, 1926

Tanner, J. R. (Ed.), *Further Correspondence of Samuel Pepys 1662-1679 from the Family Papers in the Possession of J. Pepys Cockerell*, London, G. Bell and Sons, 1929

Tomalin, C., *Samuel Pepys – The Unequalled Self*, London, Penguin Books, 2003

Waller, M., *1700 – Scenes from London Life*, London, Hodder & Stoughton, 2001

Selected Index

www.ingramcontent.com/pod-product-compliance
Lightning Source LLC
Chambersburg PA
CBHW020642030726
47498CB00002B/327